AN
ADOPTED
WOMAN

Also by Katrina Maxtone-Graham
Pregnant By Mistake: The Stories of Seventeen Women

FOR MY CHILDREN

Sarah, Ian, Emily, Guy

KATRINA MAXTONE-GRAHAM

AN ADOPTED WOMAN

Rémi Books
New York

Grateful acknowledgment is made for permission to reprint portions of lyrics from the following:

ET MAINTENANT by P. Delanoe and G. Becaud
    ©1962 EDITIONS LE RIDEAU ROUGE
      All Rights Reserved
      Used By Permission of WARNER BROS. MUSIC

THE MOUNTED MESSENGER by B. Brecht and K. Weill
    ©1928 UNIVERSAL EDITION
      Copyright Renewed and Assigned to WEILL-BRECHT-
        HARMS CO., INC.
      All Rights Reserved
      Used By Permission of WARNER BROS. MUSIC

WHEN I'M GONE Lyrics and Music by Phil Ochs
    ©1966 Barricade Music, Inc. (ASCAP)
      All Rights Administered by Almo Music Corp.
      All Rights Reserved—International Copyright Secured

Library of Congress Cataloging in Publication Data

Maxtone-Graham, Katrina.
    An adopted woman.

    1.   Maxtone-Graham, Katrina.   2.   Adoptees—
United States—Biography.   I. Title.
HV881.M34 1983   362.7'34'0924 [B]   82-71563
ISBN 0-943362-00-8

Rémi Books, Inc.
205 East 78th Street
New York, N.Y. 10021

Distributed in the United States by
Kampmann & Company, Inc.
9 East 40th Street
New York, N.Y. 10016

Manufactured in the United States of America

ACKNOWLEDGMENTS

First of all, I want to thank the other people in this story—I am referring, of course, to the helpful ones—the friends, family, professionals, and strangers, who were kind. They made a difference to my life, and I am grateful.

Next, my thanks to editor Nancy Brooks, whose talent and diligence made a difference to my book. Again I am grateful.

My thanks as well to Alison Bond for early editorial guidance, to Bob Markel for believing in the manuscript, to Diana Tummons for preparing the manuscript for computer scan, to Kay Diggins for seven years of photocopying care; and—for their help throughout the project—to Fred Kleeberg and to Susan Devaney.

I am indebted also to Dominick Anfuso, Marsha Cohen, Mokus De Barcza, Sandy Dorfman, Mike Gladstone, Carol Hardman, Bertram Hirsch, Andrew Jason, Eric Kampmann, Leslie Krakower, Linda Mason, Natalie Parnass, Carolyn Parqueth.

To the many friends who listened and gave encouragement along the way, I offer my thanks; and for both personal support and practical aid, my special thanks to Martus Granirer.

The events described in this book are true. Most names, however, are changed, as are addresses, telephone numbers, and occasional identifying details.

CONTENTS

AN
ADOPTED
WOMAN

chapter one

RETURN TO THE AGENCY

On the 26th of April, 1973, I returned to the agency from which I was adopted.

I always knew that I was adopted. I always knew that I was adopted at the age of three and a half. I also always knew that I would never find out who my natural relatives were, nor where I had been during the first three and a half years of my life.

I had thought of my loss at all times, and since as long ago as I can remember. Every moment, every breath, I was consumed with wondering and longing and searching. Each stranger on the street, each house along the road, posed the same questions: Where? Why? Who? There were no answers; and so my yearnings were without resolution, a confirmation of my inadequacy.

My return to the agency held the prospect not of release but of making the shrouded passage of existence more comfortable. I had not been aware that there might be any more information about me. I thought of my origins as a vacuum. I possessed a birthdate: March 9, 1935; a birthplace: Borough of Manhattan, New York City; and a beginning: July 1938. In my mid-twenties I had gained the additional fact that at some other time my name had been Judith Virginia Williams.

I held, as well, two images. They were not memories but scenes in my mind's eye. In one, I was "playing" a piano, a small upright, in the far corner of a narrow room; then I was sitting on a toilet, with a woman leaning over me, yelling at me to pee. I kept trying to tell her that I had no pee left to give her, but the woman would not listen. The other scene was of a field. There were tall grasses, the edge of a house.

During my childhood I had regarded these scenes as dreams of no significance. But when I was about eighteen, my adoptive mother had told me, "I remember the day we went to pick you up at the agency. You were banging away at the piano, and I couldn't stand the noise. So I took you down the corridor to the bathroom." With this validation of the first scene, I suspected that the second image might be of a real place, too.

Now I was thirty-eight years old and the mother of four children. My adoptive parents had been dead for a number of years. I had grown up in Michigan and had settled in New York City. I had cared for my family, done some writing while the children napped or were in school, and performed as best I could my duties for the surrounding world. My children— Sarah, Ian, Emily, Guy—spanned the ages from thirteen to six; and, at the time of this story, I was still married. These were facts by which the outside world could define me; for my own definition, there was no resource.

Then, by chance, I learned that some adoption agencies keep secret files on some adoptees. In April, 1973, I discovered that the Children's Aid Society in New York was holding a secret file on me. Something was recorded of that wasteland between my conception and the age of three and a half! Workers at my own adoption agency could be instructed to enter a storage room, remove an aged folder, and deliver it, like a frozen corpse for thawing, to an upstairs office to be read. My lost experience could come to life in the eyes of a reader.

The chosen reader of my file was a representative of the Children's Aid Society, the successor agency to the State Charities Aid Association, which had originally handled my case. Her name was Mrs. Meinhauser, her profession social worker. I was to be allowed to meet this stranger whose private reading confirmed my being, and to hear what she had to say about what she had read. Adoptions, I knew, were sur-

2

rounded by total secrecy, and I had no expectation that I would be told my parents' names. But I would learn something about that blank in my life and would thereby learn something of myself. It was the opportunity for which I had passed through thirty-eight years.

On the morning of April 26, 1973, I walked along East 45th Street to the impressively unweathered canopy that announced "The Children's Aid Society." When I had been three, the old State Charities Aid Association had been housed on East 22nd Street. I would not be able to look in this place for forgotten memories.

Timidly, I crossed the small, carpeted lobby. The white-haired ladies at the reception desk acknowledged my appointment and pointed to a pair of elevators. No, I explained, if there was a staircase I would rather walk, as I had a fear of elevators. Again matter-of-factly, almost as though the phobia was commonplace here, one of the women offered to ride in the elevator with me.

Upstairs on the fifth floor, seated on a plastic sofa facing the doorway, I waited with the banal placidity that comes at times of crisis. This was the moment of a lifetime for me, the unthinkable dream, yet I was sitting there as though it were an ordinary event. Casually I reached into the shopping bag at my feet and withdrew a blue 3 x 5 index card. On one side I had neatly printed Mrs. Meinhauser's name and address. On the back, in pencil, scrunched up and overcrowded, was last night's listing of potential questions.

> Williams a real name? Who named me?
> rape
> genetics—diabetes? retarded?
> Also, scar, eyes (were they tall?)
> *Why* the Kanzlers?
> Room I was picked up in—piano, etc.
> The house with the field.
> How many homes? What sort? Why did they not keep
>   me?

Any clothes? Any messages? Did anyone ever ask about
    me?
Is she still alive? Are foster homes still alive?
Was I outgoing then? What was I like?
Any report?

I was aware that the cost of this visit was finality. After
today there would never again be something left to hear. The
closed door, cracked open for me so briefly, would shut forever. So be it; the fate of adoption, eternal and irreversible,
was nothing I could fight. I was glad to pay the price of finality if, in exchange, I could become a more nearly whole person. The total of my lost past I would never know; but with
whatever I could acquire today, I might be able to put to rest
some of my life's aching mysteriousness.

It was frighteningly clear that all was up to me at this
meeting. The possibility of an improved existence lay in my
ability to obtain information from the all-knowing Mrs.
Meinhauser. From this single reader-informant I had to acquire the most, however much that might be; before my sole
judge and benefactor I had to do my best, however that was
done. Free to learn whatever Mrs. Meinhauser chose to tell
me, I had to make her be kind.

I wished that the person in whose power lay my relief
were not Mrs. Meinhauser. I would have rather it were, instead, the sweet Miss O'Malley who had answered the telephone the day I had first called the Children's Aid Society.
Miss O'Malley had responded with warmth and welcome. After I had announced that I was adopted and, shakily, had
asked if anything was known of me there, Miss O'Malley had
seemed as curious as I. She had made a note of my address
and phone number and my several names, Judith Virginia
Williams, Katrina Kanzler, and my current identity as Mrs.
John Maxtone-Graham. She had explained apologetically that
it would take her a day or two before she would have anything
to tell me. When I had mentioned to her that I was thirty-

eight years old, Miss O'Malley had said, with the ease of someone who is instinctively thoughtful, "I hope it was a good thirty-eight years."

"No, actually, it wasn't." I had made my voice light.

"I'm sorry," Miss O'Malley had replied gently. To my surprise some of the pain of those years had mellowed right then, from Miss O'Malley's tone of genuine concern and from this unusual acceptance of my viewpoint. I had implied something negative about adoption, and I had not been criticized in return! Immediately I had found myself considering happier thoughts. "I'm sure the next thirty-eight will be better," I had told her. Better for all of us, I had said, citing improved contraception and the recent abortion reform. Fewer children need be born unwanted.

"Oh, we work very closely with Planned Parenthood," Miss O'Malley had replied with enthusiasm, "hand in hand!"

As promised, Miss O'Malley had called back within a few days. Yes, they did have a file on me. If I could come into the office, someone would talk with me.

"How soon can I come in to see you?" I asked her.

"No, not me. You'll be meeting with a social worker."

"I don't understand."

"It always is a social worker who talks to the people."

She had had to repeat it several times before I had grasped her meaning.

"But couldn't I see *you* anyway?"

"The social worker has had special training. You see," she gave a quiet laugh, "I'm only the—"

"But that doesn't matter! Please?"

Miss O'Malley had gently insisted.

Several days later, the social worker, Mrs. Meinhauser, had called to set up an appointment. She had suggested a date about six weeks away. Expecting the warmth of another Miss O'Malley, I had spoken openly: I could not imagine waiting so long, it meant so much, I was dying to come in immediately, now, tomorrow, at least next week?

Cold and clear had come Mrs. Meinhauser's reply, each word isolated, chiseled to a razor-edge of mockery: "After—all—these—years?"

I was devastated, my courage slashed. Gasping for air, I had been unable to utter a defense: It wasn't my fault, I hadn't known people could come back to the agency at twenty-one. Had I known, God, I would have been there! The guilt of having taken too long, the terror that I was now too late.

But Mrs. Meinhauser had kept on talking. She only came in on Tuesdays and Thursdays . . . next Tuesday, an important meeting . . . she had a very busy schedule . . .

I had kept my horror quiet. When it had been necessary to speak, I had been careful not to say anything that might again incite Mrs. Meinhauser's sudden ridicule. The remainder of the conversation had been superficially pleasant and Mrs. Meinhauser arranged a meeting in less than six weeks' time.

But I was left terrified of this person's power to attack my frailty, and in the days that followed I wondered how there could be any communication between us. I considered contacting Miss O'Malley and begging her to see me after all. But I had feared that if my plea failed and news of it got back to Mrs. Meinhauser, Mrs. Meinhauser might be even more hostile. I could not take the risk.

Then I had tried convincing myself that Mrs. Meinhauser's lack of understanding did not really matter. What was important was that she not be hateful. She could not know that I would have liked to have come in the first instant I was allowed. Maybe she was really a very sweet person.

Now the long days of waiting were over. I slipped the blue index card back into my shopping bag. It was nearly eleven o'clock. Mrs. Meinhauser would soon appear. I had to like her, so that she would like me, so that she would tell me whatever it was that she might know. I drew in a deep breath, trying to make myself feel grown-up and strong, not foolish for yearning for a childhood when I had children of my own.

6

My children were big now, but I remembered how I used to look at them, long ago when they were fleshy pink babies giggling and kicking, and how I used to wonder: Did anyone ever look at me this loving way? Did anyone ever hold me? Somehow, I must have been fed, I used to reassure myself. But then images of feeding machines, suspended on cranes from ceiling tracks, would erase my momentary confidence. Metal cribs in rows, racks of bottles. Still, machines were operated by people, and a real person could have walked past my crib . . . It was not impossible, I would tell myself. Did anyone look at me, and I smile, and that person think, "Look, the baby is smiling"?

In the doorway stood a woman, very short, with very dark hair. So utterly unlike me in her shortness and her darkness, she was someone who could not possibly be my mother.

Now, hand outstretched, a direct and friendly look on her face, the woman was saying my name. I realized that she was the social worker, Mrs. Meinhauser. We exchanged greetings and walked down the hall. She did not seem as unsympathetic today, I thought. She had smiled; it was possible that she was going to offer me help.

Right away, Mrs. Meinhauser informed me she had "such good news" and remarked that I "must be worried about bad things" about my mother. I did not dare correct her as she was smiling so broadly. She had a large amount of information, she told me.

Contrary to my expectations, there was no file visible in her office; but Mrs. Meinhauser had a pad on her desk written on in longhand. Lowering myself into a chair, I noticed that the writing was so faint that even if I leaned forward I would not be able to make out any words. I asked Mrs. Meinhauser if she would be giving me a written report when we finished.

"No, we never give anything in writing," Mrs. Meinhauser asserted with glowing definiteness. "But you may take notes if you like." She opened a drawer of her desk and offered me one of her own pads. Embarrassed to be inconveniencing her, I fumbled in my shopping bag to provide my own pencil.

7

"What do you want to know?" she asked.

"Everything. Everything," I answered, liking her generosity.

She glanced at me quizzically, as though adoptees usually wished less.

Mrs. Meinhauser began. My mother was not married; she was eighteen years old when I was born. She came from a "good, but ordinary" family.

I realized that I had never thought of my mother as having been part of any family.

My mother was very close to her own mother, Mrs. Meinhauser continued. She met my father at a party and went out with him for several months.

"You mean she knew him?"

Mrs. Meinhauser smiled, indicating that she found my question slightly silly. The question was not silly to me, but still I glanced down, wanting to hide my pleasure at learning that my mother had known who my father was. How lucky I am, I thought.

I asked about the commonness of Williams. Had I been named by the alphabet? "W is next. We've done Walker and Watson and Weston. How about Williams?"

No, responded Mrs. Meinhauser with such firmness that my years of conviction to the contrary were obliterated, Williams was not an institutional invention.

"Then who named me?" I was impressed with Mrs. Meinhauser's wealth of knowledge. "Do you know that?"

"Yes." Mrs. Meinhauser was peering at me contentedly, but she said nothing. It was several moments before I realized that she was waiting for me to put the question.

"Did my mother name me Williams?"

"Yes."

"Did my mother give me the name Judith?"

"Yes."

"And Virginia?"

"Yes."

Wow, if my mother had picked my names, that meant my mother had known me!

8

"Was her name Williams?"

Pause. "Yes."

"Was I named after her? Was her name Judith, like mine?"

"No."

"Then why . . . was her, or her mother's, name Judith or Virginia?"

Mrs. Meinhauser did not answer. I looked at her, waiting. Raising her hand slightly, she moved her head to avoid my eyes. Suddenly I realized I was not supposed to have asked that. I had been inept.

To cover, I quickly asked, "Williams is Welsh, isn't it? Was my mother Welsh?"

"I don't know," Mrs. Meinhauser answered blandly. "She was American-born."

Mrs. Meinhauser went on, referring to her pad; and I made notes: "Mother—18 yrs. old; American-born; high school graduate; Protestant." She was "tall, slim . . . "

" . . . And willowy," concluded Mrs. Meinhauser.

"Willowy!" I burst out. "Does it really say 'willowy'?"

"Tall, slim, and willowy," Mrs. Meinhauser repeated matter-of-factly.

Only once in my life had I heard anyone described as "willowy." Nineteen years before, in the local newspaper write-up of my wedding, the bride had been "the willowy Katrina." How John and I had laughed at the pretentious choice of words, and through the years we had made a joke of the phrase. Now, suddenly, another young woman—my mother—is described as "willowy"!

I shared this with Mrs. Meinhauser. She listened good-naturedly, but with a lack of interest, due, I suspected, to my inability to make the family joke vivid.

Mrs. Meinhauser had more to tell. My mother "had a happy home life." Her mother "was an understanding person." Her father died in the 1920's. There were three siblings, two sisters and a brother. She was number three of the four. The brother lived elsewhere; the married sister lived at home, too; the other sister was seven years younger. All were

"American-born, Protestant." My mother was "steady, reliable, friendly—a bit highstrung."

Again I interrupted: "A bit highstrung" could be a way of describing me! Surely being eighteen, pregnant, and unmarried was cause for anyone to appear highstrung; still the word had been said specifically of my own mother, as separate from all other unwed mothers. For an instant I was considering that my own highstrungness might be inherited! This was certainly an unfamiliar idea. Genes and heredity had never been for me, they were for regular people. Even more exciting was the thought that a perfectly ordinary word was being used to describe this mythical creature, my mother—and so other perfectly ordinary traits and emotions of real people might have been hers as well.

Mrs. Meinhauser continued. It is a remarkable experience to sit across from a person who knows who your parents are when you do not; to hear, at the age of thirty-eight, someone tell you simple facts about your own private spectres. "Your father was six foot one, brown hair, blue eyes, a college graduate."

Just like that, you *know* something. Not six foot two, not six foot even. Six foot one. "Brown hair." Your own hair is brown, too—what a glorious coincidence! You try to imagine what a man with brown hair and blue eyes and six foot one *looks* like. You had not even expected to hear anything about your father; you had not thought his identity was even known. And now, "six foot one." I could go home, mark a spot on the wall six feet and one inch from the floor and proclaim in victory, "There, there is my *father!*"

"He came from a substantial middle-class family," Mrs. Meinhauser stated with finality.

I giggled at the phrase. "What on earth does that mean?"

Mrs. Meinhauser checked her pad and repeated the statement. That was all she knew about it, she said; my mother never saw him again.

Perhaps it was then—it was certainly very early in the meeting—that Mrs. Meinhauser announced, seemingly out of the blue, "Your mother married a man with an unusual name. I've looked for the name in the phone directories of all five boroughs of New York." She paused. "But it's not there."

This was an astounding revelation. My mother—*my mother*—was a real person with an address. For an instant she had been almost tangible enough to light upon the pages of a telephone book. But even as I was mentally hugging the five huge New York phone books on Mrs. Meinhauser's shelf, she had flown off their pages, as hopelessly untouchable as ever.

I was impressed, though. Mrs. Meinhauser was more understanding than I had suspected. She had known what it could have meant to me to learn that my mother was named in one of those five books. I felt badly now for having thought ill of her.

This kind woman was allowing me to feel comfortable, and I began to talk about myself a little. Mrs. Meinhauser must surely want to know as accurately as possible the feelings of an adopted child. I told her how I always stared at every woman I saw. I described how I would study each one in an attempt to decide if she were "too short," "too fat," and so forth, to be my mother. It was easy to pour myself out to Mrs. Meinhauser's smiling, attentive face.

I went on, telling how as a young child I had longed for both my natural parents. I had imagined they were poor and could not afford to keep me. I had imagined they must be teachers, because teachers, where I grew up, were poor. I told Mrs. Meinhauser how I had thought of myself as having been bought by the Kanzlers. I described the store window as I could still see it: A big red ball, a white doggie, and a yellow-haired girl of three. "We'll choose that one," my adoptive parents had said when I was not looking.

I also told Mrs. Meinhauser about my having "realized," when I was about seven years old, that babies were not made, as I had previously supposed, by a mother and a father. Mothers made babies all by themselves, mothers gave away babies all by themselves. Since that time, I had ceased thinking

11

about my father, as obviously none had been involved in my creation.

I confided to Mrs. Meinhauser that I had had thirteen and a half years of psychiatric treatment, and that I was hoping today's information would lead to some progress. Adoption created emotional problems, I said to Mrs. Meinhauser. She did not agree, but I persisted. To support my point, I mentioned the disproportionate number of adoptees in psychiatric care. To my surprise, Mrs. Meinhauser did not deny my statistics. She attributed them, however, not to the state of being adopted, but to the adoptive parents' being more alert than other parents to their children's emotional difficulties.

I did not argue, feeling reaffirmed by Mrs. Meinhauser's lack of a denial. Indeed, Mrs. Meinhauser's acceptance of the statistics gave them a new validity that almost frightened me.

I explained how my own adoption had been a failure. It was not her fault, I assured Mrs. Meinhauser; it was an error of judgment for which she had no responsibility. Of course, I knew that adoptions were so much better done nowadays; one was always hearing wonderful stories. But I begged Mrs. Meinhauser not to be fooled by material circumstances when placing a child today. My case was proof that a comfortable home did not guarantee a happy one. I would gladly have traded all my "advantages" for a sense of belonging, I told her. I was pleased to have this opportunity to be listened to. If other children could benefit from my experience, my life would have had some value. It had always been my prayer that accomplishing something wanted could justify the existence of someone unwanted.

Mrs. Meinhauser listened, nodding and smiling. She returned to her notes to tell me that my father left town for "job reasons" before my mother had realized she was pregnant. My mother never told him about me; he never knew anything.

Surely my mother might have written him, I suggested.

No, the relationship was not that deep; my mother "had not wanted to marry the man."

For an eighteen-year-old in trouble, she must have had quite some strength of mind not to get married. Underneath, I was wishing that my mother would have at least informed my father of the pregnancy; it would have been more fair to him. Still, this was surely evidence of courage and independence on my mother's part, and I wanted to understand and to think generously of my mother. I confided to Mrs. Meinhauser that my mother struck me as being rather spunky.

No, Mrs. Meinhauser corrected me, it was more a question of geography.

She went on. My mother had been "available, cooperative about information." For two months after I was born, she had stayed with me. For two whole months! I was amazed. In "the shelter," where she had spent the latter part of her pregnancy, she had been "cheerful, not depressed." As I wrote out the words I struggled to visualize a pregnant young woman, cheerfully skipping along a maternity hospital's corridor.

I knew something about shelters, I told Mrs. Meinhauser happily; I had recently met a woman who, before giving up her baby, had spent three months in a Salvation Army home. The woman's voice had been soft and loving when she spoke of the Salvation Army's Booth Memorial Hospital. It occurred to me to ask Mrs. Meinhauser the name of my own mother's "shelter." To my surprise, there was no answer. Instead, there was the same floating hand motion and sideward look that meant, "Discontinue this line of questioning." I was surprised that the name of the shelter would not be allowed, but I felt it was best to drop the subject.

I asked if my mother had considered abortion. No, Mrs. Meinhauser replied understandingly, in those days abortion, being illegal, was very dangerous. My mother did not come from a background that could have been able to afford a safe one. I wondered, too, whether my father, as a college graduate, and older, might perhaps have been a married man. No,

Mrs. Meinhauser did not think so. I was skeptical, but Mrs. Meinhauser insisted; it was simply the change of jobs. He had been moved by his company.

My mother had been working when she met my father. My mother's employment was, of course, quite ordinary. "Clerical," said Mrs. Meinhauser in a tone of disdain.

"Clerical," I repeated, nodding my head with enthusiasm, so that Mrs. Meinhauser would know I was not so stupid as to expect my mother to have done something special.

Later on, Mrs. Meinhauser continued, my mother had worked in a publishing firm. In publishing! Again I blurted out a coincidence: I'd just had my first book accepted for publication. It was this sign of personal accomplishment that had given me the courage to call the agency, I confessed to Mrs. Meinhauser. The very day I had received the contract was the day I had telephoned Miss O'Malley.

"What was her publishing house?" I wondered, sensing the possibility of mutual experience.

"Why would you want to know?"

I felt foolish. "My publisher is Liveright. Everyone is so nice."

Mrs. Meinhauser stated directly that my mother had not worked for Liveright. I had the feeling that my mother's had been a less prestigious house. No matter. Besides, Mrs. Meinhauser was interested in hearing about my book.

It was a study of unwanted pregnancies, I told her, a plea for improved education and contraception. Remembering Miss O'Malley's "We work very closely with Planned Parenthood," I radiated camaraderie. I was proud of my book; my mother, if she knew of it, could think well of me. Mrs. Meinhauser listened attentively. Then she asked for Liveright's address! My heart pounded with hope. If my mother came into the agency, maybe Mrs. Meinhauser would tell her the publisher, and then my mother could find me! Instinctively I knew not to articulate that hope to the woman across the desk. But I could think of no other reason why Mrs. Meinhauser would actually write it down, *except* to tell my mother.

I explained to Mrs. Meinhauser that it was during the work for the book that I had first learned adoptees could sometimes get personal information. Belatedly I was able to defend myself against her piercing reprimand. Mrs. Meinhauser was listening. "After all these years" was a phrase I would never have to hear again.

I told her that when I was about twenty-six, my adoptive father had, at my pleading, given me some papers; that was how I had learned about "Judith Virginia Williams" and the State Charities Aid Association. The agency was defunct, my father had said. But when, during an interview for my book, I learned of another adoption agency's secret file on an adoptee, I determined to find out for myself.

Now I was here and I smiled at Mrs. Meinhauser in gratitude. I was glad to be able to express myself openly to her, for she was the conduit to my mother. I wanted Mrs. Meinhauser to know me—the good, the bad, everything; I wanted to portray myself as truthfully as possible so that, should my mother come in the following day, or month, or year, Mrs. Meinhauser could describe me as a person. I wanted my mother to know me, and this was my one chance.

We had covered only the first months; there were still over three years to know. Where did I go then? What happened next? Mrs. Meinhauser was at first reluctant to move on, seeming to prefer to talk about my mother, repeating that she had been "available, cooperative about information." Finally, the information started rolling forward. My hurried notes summarized the story:

1) Shelter—2 months.
2) First Boarding Home, 1 year. Good physical care. Visited by trained nurse: "Foster mother—tended to foster dependency."
3) 2nd Boarding Home—Large motherly person. Until the end of 1937. Age 2¾. Trained person: "an independent child with a strong will."
4) Placed in a private home with the possibility of adoption—for 5 months. Dec. '37-May '38. The mother was

15

          sophisticated, conscientious, mechanical. Couldn't han-
          dle my tantrums. Returned.
5) Another Boarding Home. Foster mother "did not see
          me as a difficult child, but I needed structure"—
          stayed one month.
6) The Kanzlers—kept.

It was fantastic; years of guesses were turning out to be true. Yes, there *were* foster homes, there *were* multiple changes, there *were* repeated separations. My forgotten childhood experience and my present adult reactions were indeed related. The information came out fast, with a stunning reality, although not as simply as my notes imply; I interrupted, asked questions, went back. Why was I moved from the first foster home? Because I needed more stimulation. Why was I moved from the second foster home? To be placed for adoption. Why had not these places kept me? They were only foster homes. Might they possibly have wanted to keep me? They were only foster homes.

Mrs. Meinhauser was trying to move on, noting that foster home visits in those days were made by trained nurses, not social workers, and hence were poorly done. What about the "large motherly person"? Here was someone special, I told Mrs. Meinhauser, *the* someone special of my early life. I had long sensed that there had been someone once who had cared for me as a mother. Someone I could not remember, yet still missed, someone whose maternalness had enabled me to be a mother myself. I begged to hear more about her. I had been in her home for nearly two years. Who was she?

No. The wave of the hand.

"Please!"

No.

"I'm sure, I'm sure she was the one." Even if I could not have her name, I wanted to linger over the miraculous existence of this special person. I rambled on joyously, barely noticing that Mrs. Meinhauser was talking about my next home, the family that had intended to adopt me.

Mrs. Meinhauser seemed eager to discuss this one at length; and the more I heard, the greater my interest became. I had been two years and nine months old when I had arrived there.

"The adoptive mother couldn't handle your tantrums," Mrs. Meinhauser was saying. "She did all the right things, but it didn't work."

"I was probably acting up because of having been taken from that large motherly person!"

Mrs. Meinhauser had no opinion. "The adoptive mother was college-educated," she went on, "but she was too busy trying to do things by the book—"

"Then it really is true that I was given back?" I interrupted.

"The placement did not work out," Mrs. Meinhauser corrected me.

I explained my interest: "The summer I was eighteen, one night very late, my mother—my adoptive mother—told me I had been adopted before. 'You've always been a difficult child,' she said. 'The first family that adopted you gave you back!' For years I believed her, but my friends, and doctors and such, finally convinced me it was an invention. Now you say it's true after all."

"It is not your fault that the placement—"

"Was the father there a policeman?"

"Why do you ask?"

"My adoptive mother said he was a policeman. For years I stared at—"

"No, not a policeman," Mrs. Meinhauser stated abruptly.

She continued to insist that the mother, not I, had "failed," but she was foggy in her narration of what had actually taken place. It was difficult for me to draw out of her whether the agency had taken me back or the family had returned me. After much discussion, Mrs. Meinhauser did acknowledge that yes, the family returned me. "But if they hadn't," her face was suddenly cold as stone, "the agency would have taken you back themselves."

"Really?"

Mrs. Meinhauser's voice was filled with venom. "We saw to it that they never got another child!"

I was startled at the intensity of Mrs. Meinhauser's remark. The family ought not to be blamed, after all. I must have been so upset at leaving the good foster home. There was something very disquieting about Mrs. Meinhauser's vengeance toward that family. Then, fortunately, the ugly moment retreated.

There had been a brother, too, in that potential adoptive home, she informed me. "He was their natural child, and older. You got along well with the brother and the father."

"How old was the brother?" I asked.

"About ten."

"How awful! One day he had a sister, and then that sister was gone."

Mrs. Meinhauser shrugged.

"It must have been terrifying!"

"I don't think it was very important."

"He lost his own sister, Mrs. Meinhauser!"

The family had not been competent; Mrs. Meinhauser's tone was insistent. Poor brother, I thought. I wondered what the grown-ups could possibly have told him in explanation.

"I'd like to let him know that I'm all right. That Judith is alive and well." There could be relief for him, too, in the unraveling of a mystery. "What's his name and address?"

Mrs. Meinhauser looked confused.

My pencil poised on the pad, I began to explain. "I'd like his name, please, so I can write him and tell—"

"Surely, you know better."

"But he's not a real relative. I'm not—"

"Mrs. Maxtone-Graham!" Mrs. Meinhauser glared.

I waited; her expression did not soften.

"Do you even have his address?"

"I have the address, in the file. Not here." Mrs. Meinhauser straightened her pad. She had regained her composure and was preparing to introduce her next topic.

"Then, please," I asked, "would you write and tell him for me?"

"We have had no further contact with that family since then. And we never wished to," Mrs. Meinhauser pronounced with finality. "You must realize," she added, regarding me sympathetically, "that he has forgotten the whole episode."

I made a last desperate try, "Surely he wondered. What happened to my sister? Why?"

No. For Mrs. Meinhauser the possibility did not exist. It simply did not exist. "The mother did everything by the book," she said again. "The agency tried unsuccessfully to teach her to be more natural. She had the good sense, however, to send you to a nursery school for—"

"I remember a nursery school!" I exclaimed. "I always thought it was the one at the Kanzlers'. Did it have a large tricycle?"

Mrs. Meinhauser chuckled, so I realized I had been humorous.

I was careful to word my next question very lightly. "I have a memory of a field, with tall grasses. I know it's from before. Of course, I'm aware that a field is no use," I acknowledged, "but it's funny. I see the field, the edge of a house; I think I almost see a man and a boy. But I'm not sure. Maybe not." The grass was very tall.

Mrs. Meinhauser said nothing.

I asked if the family had changed my name. No, they had not. That was nice of them, I thought. My feeling toward them was warm, grateful. I asked if I had been called Judith or Judy. Mrs. Meinhauser did not know. I hoped it was Judith.

I was interested in my tantrums in that home, I went on, for they provided some link with my earliest days as Katrina. My first two weeks of belonging to the Kanzlers were spent not in Michigan with them but in a New York hotel room with a psychologist. I have no recollections of the changing of my name, nor of Dr. Sadie Robinson, nor of the I.Q. tests she administered. But Dr. Robinson's report to my parents was

19

among the papers my father gave me years later. After eight pages of "regular temper tantrums"—"She throws things, tears her clothing, pulls out her hair. She jumps up and down, and cries or screams . . . "—Dr. Sadie Robinson heartily concluded: "I wish to congratulate you on your find. I do not know when I have felt so safe in recommending a child for adoption. You have THE child."

The tantrums were put to an end at the Kanzlers' and, like everything else, retreated to the other side of memory's blockade. The too-hard-to-handle, spunky terror was replaced by the quiet, timid, ever-so-well-behaved child of my recollections. Judith and her fiery independent spirit were gone; in her place was Katrina, the silent observer. But now, through the tantrums, I as Katrina was linked to the departed Judith. Not exactly the "dream child," but she had had something, this Judith. Judith had dared; Katrina did not.

Mrs. Meinhauser made the point that, after returning from that first adoptive family, I had not been seen as difficult. "Needs structure," the next mother had said, "but is not a difficult child." Mrs. Meinhauser repeated this comment as though it negated the connection between Katrina and Judith.

"Was that foster home, the last one, one of the ones I'd been at before?"

No.

"Why not?"

The wave again. It was not my business to know.

"It would have made more sense," I suggested, "to have sent me back to the home where I was just before, the good home . . . "

Mrs. Meinhauser shrugged.

"Were there any siblings, there, at that good foster home?"

She glanced at her pad. "There was a foster brother, older."

"It seems everywhere I went there was always an older brother."

20

Mrs. Meinhauser scowled. Then she brightened. "What would you like to know?" she inquired cheerily.

"Everything," I answered as before, confused she had not understood. "Whatever there is to know."

What facts remained in her possession? I was wondering too, whether I would be lucky enough to frame the right questions. Often a good guess would produce a stream of information. If only I knew what I was meant to ask; what not to ask was so much easier to define. By now I was avoiding Mrs. Meinhauser's forbiddens not out of self-protection but as a matter of tact. It was only common decency not to make her uncomfortable with prying questions like, "What is my mother's name?"

Sometimes topics I thought would not offend her evoked the disconcerted gaze; and then others I had almost not hazarded would turn out not to be upsetting. I was never totally sure.

Cautiously, I asked where I had lived. Immediately, the cold foggy glaze came into her eyes. I had guessed wrong. I chatted on, pretending I hadn't asked.

"Why does it matter to you?" interrupted Mrs. Meinhauser.

She still didn't understand that it all mattered to me. "I mean, I was born in Manhattan, and I grew up in Michigan, and all those years in between . . . I was just wondering."

"The Greater New York area," Mrs. Meinhauser answered with pointed ambiguity, her strong smile indicating that this was all she would say.

I nodded appreciatively and wrote, "The Greater New York area," realizing that I didn't know to whom this referred: The adoptive family? The foster home? Me? My mother?

I asked about a phrase I had remembered from the papers my adoptive father had given me: "Dependent on private and public charity since birth."

Mrs. Meinhauser nodded.

"Was State Charities Aid Association a private charity?"

21

"Oh, yes."

"Then what was the public charity?"

I saw that Mrs. Meinhauser was reluctant to answer. "Something like welfare?" I suggested lightly.

"Something like that." Mrs. Meinhauser smiled.

And why had my mother waited so long? Why was I already two and three-quarter years old when my adoption was first discussed?

Bureaucracy, Mrs. Meinhauser explained, that's how things were done in those days.

I'd known quite a few adoptees when I was growing up, including my own two adoptive brothers; yet I was the only one adopted that "late."

It was bureaucracy, Mrs. Meinhauser repeated; she knew about these things, I did not.

Still I wondered if my late adoption could not have indicated some interest on my mother's part in keeping me?

No, my mother very definitely had not wanted to keep me. That was absolute.

Although I pursued the issue, I could not glean from Mrs. Meinhauser's responses a precise reason for my mother's choice. Her own mother had been "retiring" and "sensitive," but "understanding." This was no help. Pressing further, I learned that my grandmother was "not in terribly good health." Yet this still did not seem to be the real reason. The obvious explanations—the family too poor, too sick, too proper—were not produced. My mother was sort of poor, her mother was sort of sick, there was a hint of lack of family enthusiasm over an illegitimacy; but as actual reasons these did not hold up. The only "explanation" offered by Mrs. Meinhauser was that my mother had "made this decision after careful consideration." Mrs. Meinhauser was quite insistent now. My mother had not kept me because she had "made a decision" not to keep me.

"It was *not* because you were not pretty," Mrs. Meinhauser said very firmly. She was looking at me intently, the cliché unfinished. I helped her out, nodding in agreement, speaking the rest of the words aloud: "Or that I wasn't good or that I wasn't nice."

Not until I'd completed the sentence for her did I realize that Mrs. Meinhauser had not been meaning to add the extra phrases. She had only thought of "pretty." Even I knew better, I thought, feeling sorry for Mrs. Meinhauser.

It was at this juncture that Mrs. Meinhauser came out with another of her statements of overwhelming emotional significance. Mrs. Meinhauser's tidal waves were always as concise as they were unforgettable: "Your father had an Irish-sounding name."

My father? A sound? A name? Irish, I'd never even *thought* of Irish. Because of my looks I had thought maybe English, Scottish, Norwegian; especially Norwegian. I'd yearned to be Russian; Russian, Eastern, Jewish. I loved the music, Russian novels, gypsies, guitars. But Irish! I thought I'd thought of everything. And right here, in New York, St. Patrick's Day Parade! Then it suddenly struck me—an Irish *Catholic?* What would my father think of me? Me, the advocate of improved contraception? Me, in an adoption that crossed religious lines? "My God, not an Irish Catholic, I hope!"

Mrs. Meinhauser raised her eyebrows.

"Oh, I'm not anti-Catholic!" I assured her. "It's just Pope Paul's stand against contraception. I'm not anti-anybody. Only rigidity."

I was glad to see Mrs. Meinhauser smile as I explained my outburst. I would not have wanted her to think of me as an intolerant person. As for my father, if he was Catholic, it made no difference, I thought to myself. I'm me after all. I believe in what I believe. "Reading my book, he would surely understand why—"

"He died twenty years ago," said Mrs. Meinhauser.

"Oh."

It was over. I had only had him for a part of the morning. "What did he die of?"

"I don't know," answered Mrs. Meinhauser calmly.

"He died young, though." I couldn't imagine what else to say. I felt sad, but not deeply.

I was a little frightened. My grandfather dying young, my father dying young. Early death seemed to run in my family. I worried for myself, and then, because the dead were males, on behalf of my sons.

My mother had returned to the agency, Mrs. Meinhauser was now telling me. She "came in once, recently married— visiting New York, early 1940's, seven years later." She "did not want to marry early, did not want to have children right away." There was "one thing she had forgotten to say": She had "an insufficiency of absorption of calcium through normal channels."

It would have been helpful, I told Mrs. Meinhauser, had I known about the calcium problem sooner, when my children were still babies, when the information might have been critical to their health.

My adoptive parents should have told me, Mrs. Meinhauser stated firmly.

Or the agency, I thought, but I said nothing. If there was something worse in my medical background, I did not want to frighten Mrs. Meinhauser into withholding it, and so I concealed my anger. The thought that I might have unwittingly hurt my own children was almost unbearable.

My mother had also "left a picture of herself." At first I understood Mrs. Meinhauser to say that she had left the picture "to the agency for my benefit when I returned." Excited, I asked her to tell me about it, but suddenly Mrs. Meinhauser became strangely unsure. She replied to all my questions, but each answer contradicted the previous one. I thought she was being evasive, but after a while I became convinced that she was as unknowing as I. One moment, Mrs. Meinhauser was making a definite declaration, the next she seemed genuinely confused. This went on for about twenty minutes. I was becoming increasingly frustrated: Did she know anything about a picture or did she not?

"It was sent on loan to the adoptive parents and never

returned," Mrs. Meinhauser proclaimed abruptly.

At last. I wondered why Mrs. Meinhauser had not said this in the first place.

"I'll bet they burned it."

Mrs. Meinhauser glared disapprovingly.

"It would be like them." I tried to explain, but Mrs. Meinhauser did not want to hear.

"I can't understand why it was sent," she admitted, sounding annoyed. "It certainly should not have been." Now Mrs. Meinhauser was warm and companionable again. She seemed almost as disappointed about the photograph's disappearance as I was. "Perhaps Mrs. Kanzler compared unfavorably with the woman in the photograph," she suggested suddenly.

I was surprised by the unmistakable bitchiness. Did social workers really say such things about adoptive parents, I wondered. Yet how extraordinary and delicious an idea, that my own mother could be attractive in someone's eyes.

Had my mother come back again? No. There were no further visits, no letters, no communications of any sort. Nothing since then. Not from my mother, not from anyone. I posed the questions very specifically, and Mrs. Meinhauser was as direct in her responses. The finality made me sad inside, but I welcomed Mrs. Meinhauser's definiteness. She left no room for uncertainty, and I was thankful. Rather the truth, however harsh, than deceptive vagueness.

And if my mother had not been to the agency since the early 1940's, then my failure to have returned the day I became twenty-one had not done irreparable hurt. The terror that my mother had come in when I was, say, twenty-three, to learn that "I didn't care" was passed. My relief was immense.

I asked, "If my mother did come again, would you tell her I had been here?"

Mrs. Meinhauser caught me off guard by pausing for a very long time, then replying with a question. "Would you want us to?" she asked.

I started to speak, but I could not; my voice would not work. I was startled. I had not expected to cry. Earlier in the meeting I had told myself that I had done well in not crying; now, when I had thought the danger was over, it was happening.

I nodded my head in reply. And then the tears gushed. I shook and sobbed, without sound. Mrs. Meinhauser sat and waited for me. How well Mrs. Meinhauser is handling this, I thought. Watching patiently, she did not try to change the subject.

Finally, I was able to whisper hoarsely, "Sorry." I felt embarrassed to have exposed my weakness in front of her maturity. But Mrs. Meinhauser did not treat me as though I had in any way changed in her eyes.

She began talking about a legal document called an "order of adoption." It was "a bad thing" for an adoptee ever to get hold of one, Mrs. Meinhauser told me. And although I could not, myself, envision how seeing a document might hurt me, I was certain Mrs. Meinhauser knew best. Nonetheless, if there was one for me floating out there somewhere, I knew I wanted it. But it was abundantly clear that Mrs. Meinhauser would not help me here.

Obviously the meeting could not go on forever, and yet I was not prepared for it to end. There was so much to ask about, so much to learn. I was grateful that Mrs. Meinhauser had never rushed me; and I felt guilty when she pointed to her watch and told me, in an unhurried way, that she had missed a portion of her lunch hour already.

Thrusting my pencil and notes away, I made small talk. Mrs. Meinhauser suggested that she ride down with me in the elevator, insisting it was no trouble at all. Because she shared my curiosity over the reasons for my mother's return visit to the agency, Mrs. Meinhauser also offered to reread my file after lunch, and then, if it was convenient, she would telephone around 2:30.

We were about to leave when Mrs. Meinhauser made a

pronouncement: "Your mother has made a new life for
lf. The episode is forgotten."
was standing, facing her, my coat on, as she continued
ng with smiling clarity. "It is all over with for your
r. It's over, and done with, and finished."
hether I blinked, or reacted in any way, I didn't know.
elt myself staring at Mrs. Meinhauser, stunned, with a
nner core of incredulity. True, my mother might not
r me. She might even hate me. But however ill her
toward me might be, the fact of her motherhood could
e "done with."
s. Meinhauser was gazing at me, strong, knowing, her
ile telling me there was no argument. Quite unex-
, from far inside my frailty, came a sudden sense that
certain creature did not know what on earth she was
bout.
etime afterwards—perhaps as we stood waiting for
tor, perhaps during the pleasant strong handshake
hank-you's in the lobby, or perhaps as I walked daz-
e Third Avenue bus stop—I realized that, were my
walk into Mrs. Meinhauser's office tomorrow, she
told, "Your daughter is married, the mother of four
ldren. She has made a new life, and it's forgotten,
's all over and done with for your daughter, it's over
finished."

chapter two

INITIAL REVELATIONS

At home, I wrote out four questions in preparation for Mrs. Meinhauser's 2:30 telephone call: When my mother returned to the agency did she want to have me back? Did she visit me in my foster homes? What did she think about the unsuccessful adoption? Was my father married?

Mrs. Meinhauser called punctually, sounding very cheerful. "You asked about your father's religion."

"I did? No; I asked if he was married."

"You asked his religion," Mrs. Meinhauser insisted, voice suddenly brittle. "He was Protestant."

"Protestant," I wrote after the last question on my list.

"He was not married," Mrs. Meinhauser offered, harshly now. "I have the file in front of me. It says 'unmarried.' "

Gaining courage, I asked my first question.

Mrs. Meinhauser's answer was firm: No, wanting me back "was not the intent of that visit. It was because she brought a picture to the agency." Mrs. Meinhauser, now uncertain about my mother's motive for returning, apparently clarified the issue of the photograph.

I asked her how my mother had responded to the adoption that failed. There was no answer.

"When she came to the agency and someone talked to her—" Then I made a guess. "Was she told about it?"

Pause. "No. She was not told anything."

I did not doubt that news of a failed adoption might

been upsetting, yet it struck me that my mother had not been dealt with fairly.

But I did not pursue this. Changing the subject, I asked Mrs. Meinhauser about my mother's visiting me in the foster homes. Mrs. Meinhauser seemed delighted to answer. My mother had "visited frequently at the beginning," but as time went on had "lost interest" and "finally stopped visiting altogether." The actual surrender was "not until 1937." I made notes beside question two.

Mrs. Meinhauser kept talking, her manner unhurried. I listened gratefully, linked by the telephone and her voice to the papers now actually on her desk. Mostly she was repeating what she had told me in the office, but suddenly she was saying something new: She was now talking of my mother's "dilemma" about keeping me! I interrupted to be sure I understood. Oh, yes, Mrs. Meinhauser insisted. Amazed, I wrote on the bottom of my page, "She did consider it!" That was not what I had understood from our office discussion. How fortunate I was to have this extra dividend of Mrs. Meinhauser's time!

Then, because I was feeling more relaxed now, I came out with a question I had little expectation of her being able to answer. Laughing to acknowledge my silliness, I asked Mrs. Meinhauser, "Was I breast-fed?"

"Yes," came the quick reply.

"Really?"

"For two months. In the shelter."

It was good luck that I had chanced to ask—and how odd that Mrs. Meinhauser had not mentioned it before. It seemed the sort of personal, tender detail that one would go out of one's way to include. I wondered what else waited to be given to me, provided I specifically asked for it.

"Do you want to know your birth weight?"

"My birth weight! Do you have it?"

"Yes. You weighed eight pounds, four ounces."

"That's huge!" The thought raced through my mind that therefore I was not retarded.

29

"Three months, twelve and a half pounds; six months, fifteen and a half pounds; one year, eighteen and a half—"

"What time of day was I born?" My ignorance of this piece of trivia was the wedge that had most conspicuously separated me from other children when I was growing up.

Mrs. Meinhauser told me she did not have that information.

At the end of the conversation, Mrs. Meinhauser announced that she had found a picture of me from the summer of 1937. Did I want it?

Summer 1937 was over a year earlier than the first photographs of me I had seen, which the Kanzlers had taken. I had never imagined there could be a picture of me from the forbidden "before." Mrs. Meinhauser and I arranged to meet on her next working day, when she would give the photograph to me.

It was not until fairly late that evening, alone, in a steamy warm bath, that finally I had my private cry. I sat in the tub crying, then resting, then crying some more. It was not an unhappy crying; it was just a mixing of hot tears with moist air, with soapy water, with sweat. It was the crying of completion. "I've done it, I've done it, I've done it." I spoke the words aloud. I was me, here, and this day had actually happened.

In this one day I had learned of living in a total of six different homes by the time I was three and a half. Six homes, I counted over and over, to be sure I had the number right. I thought back on my notes, repeating to myself "American-born . . . the shelter . . . party . . . " I had always imagined my mother to be, like me, a floater. Instead, she had had a childhood, relatives . . .

I tried to build an image of my mother. I knew I should be creating a matronly woman nearing sixty, but what I saw was an eighteen-year-old girl, running, hiding herself from me. Shadowy, faceless, still she had the height and slimness to look as I had looked at eighteen, her hair long, as mine was now. The mother I was looking for was a girl of eighteen just like me. Only I was not eighteen, I was thirty-eight. This mother-child whom I was pursuing—if she was not me, then she must be someone *else*. She must be a real person.

To have someone who has never existed suddenly take on substance is to turn the world upside down. It is to set grass in the sky, to gaze down on air.

The others, too, must have been real. The "large motherly person," the brother who lost his sister. Places, departures, new people. I repeated each word, to try to make the experience mine. Me, a real foster child such as children one reads about in the newspapers. My obsessions with separation and disaster and disappointment had an origin. As of today, I knew I was not a lunatic who had invented fears and anxieties.

I cried with gratitude for the freedom of this knowledge. I cried with thanks to the woman I had interviewed for my book whose chance words had brought me to this day. And I cried because I felt proud of myself, that I had managed even as well as I had.

Then an abrupt anger arose at my adoptive parents, anger that they had knowingly deprived me of my history. Damn it, I had not been born at the age of three and a half! By rejecting my background, my adoptive parents had denied me a portion of myself. Their prejudices had stolen my chance for self-respect.

The next morning, I trotted off to my psychiatrist with my precious notes. It would take months, I was realizing, to describe all the changes, the new wonder. Exuberantly, I rushed to spill out those first emotions, the excitement, the searching, the mystery, the gratitude to know anything, the fired yearning to learn more.

"I wonder," said Dr. Thomas, "what your constitutional rights are."

I hardly heard him. There was so much more to tell.

At home, I concentrated on my recollections of yesterday's story, attempting to mold each tiny cloud of innuendo, trying to guess the gaps. I certainly did not focus on the doctor's remark, but throughout the day it echoed, meaningless yet persistent. What *was* my relationship to my own facts? Was it possible that this one meeting with Mrs. Meinhauser was not, after all, the ultimate day of my life? I had never thought of an adoptee having any choices, any rights. The connections were not explicit—me, the law, the Constitution—yet I was realizing that the doctor's query was not an irrelevancy. Somehow, I might have a place in this world of other people's institutions.

Mystery and denial had been the givens of my life; only now—at four o'clock in the afternoon of April 27, 1973—did it occur to me that I might have the right to dispel them.

Picking up the telephone, I dialed Charlie Perkins, a long-time friend and personal lawyer. "As an adopted person—what are my constitutional rights?"

"Well, gee, Katrina, I don't think you should do this. Think of what you might find . . . "

The reference to my unknown facts became, as it always did, a discussion of my natural mother. I tried to explain that this was not about my mother but about me, my childhood, my lost years. Finally, his advice: "You and John have a good marriage, you're happy, I mean, why rock the boat? I've got to say, as a friend, I would be wrong if I didn't say—"

"And as a lawyer?"

"Well, I could do some preliminary research but, you know, your kids, John . . . "

While I understood Charlie's equating my interest in my personal history with finding my mother—of course I wanted to find her, it was she who held most of the answers, after all—I was impatient with his arguments. I had heard them all, over the years: "You'd have nothing in common with . . . " "You're you; it doesn't matter what . . . " "Think of your children, if you found a . . . " The same half-finished sentences, the same unspoken horrors. My protests were always silenced as my friends, too polite to complete their images, changed the subject. They had accepted me in their world, they had forgiven me my darker one. It was a portion of their largesse, their liberalness, that my origins did not matter. With love and tolerance, they denied my interest in my unknown evil. And always before, I had been routed by their tact.

This time, however, I did not retreat. "I want to know everything there is to know," I told Charlie firmly. "And including," I added pointedly, "my mother's married name."

Charlie was reluctant but, finally, he agreed to look into the legal status of grown-up adopted children.

In the days that followed, the thoughts of a lifetime flowed freshly through my mind. It was the same dark river, but I was no longer a drowning victim; I was clinging to a rock of fact. The Children's Aid Society had given me an inadequate, but real, vantage point from which to look anew at the raging waters of my mind.

By about the age of eight I had settled upon an explanation of my position: Because whatever I was as a person was not reflected in the world around me, I figured that this world did not make sense. I am right, they are wrong, I had explained to myself, but, they *think* they are right—so they also must be crazy.

So I had determined at eight. But I had further had to acknowledge that the world, however crazy, was reality—and I, being not of that world, was therefore not of reality. Thus it was I, after all, who was wrong, I concluded. And it must be I, not they, who was crazy. It had been the devastation of absolute isolation.

As a child, I knew the story of Cassandra, who prophesied the truth but whom no one believed. I felt I was like Cassandra, sensing a truth no one listened to. Yet Cassandra knew she was right. I did not. Not till my teens did I find some consolation, in the words of Spinoza: The truth of one's existence, he said, is undeniable in the mosaic of history.

I remembered, as though it were only a second ago, the sensation of childhood's wondering: Why me? Why am I chosen for this punishment? Who am I, that I am so worthless that I must be given away? What is it about me that makes me unkeepable? Now, from my place in midstream, I lived again my childhood response: Fate, greater than I, had known me. Fate knew why. Fate knew best. And I had no weapons against this Fate that made me different, separate, unwanted. I could offer no challenge. Accepting Fate's dictum, I nonetheless hoped that Fate had had a reason, that there would be a purpose I could serve, a means to justify in some positive way my having been placed on this planet. And while I longed to find Fate's reasons, I always feared Fate's power to hurt me yet more.

To me life was the passage between a death and a death. I imagined that death's afterworld might contain my own beforeworld. Being alive was the prayer that the same doom which had made me separate at birth might bring my answers in death, that my first foe might be my final friend.

As I waited for death's resolution, Fate was ever my guardian angel. I had been given away; therefore, was anything of mine safe? Fate was always there, around the next corner, in the dark, under the bed. Any moment, Fate might speak: The knock on the door, the ambulance siren, the midmorning phone ring. When, how, will you address me, Fate? Whom will you take from me? My child? My husband? My sight? My brain?

So I learned to hide, staying in the house, putting warm leggings on the children, avoiding strange places. I have been working so hard to keep you at your distance, Fate, but is there something I have forgotten? Will the children wait until the traffic light is green? I have put mufflers on my ears and folded close the shutters. I shall keep everyone and everything outside, and then you shall not touch me. Not yet. Please. Katrina dares nothing. She will not, in any way, ever tempt Fate.

On Monday Charlie did not call with a report, so I had to contact him. He had done no research at all. Again, I had to plead with him to believe that I meant what I was saying.

The next day I met Mrs. Meinhauser in the lobby of the Children's Aid Society. Proudly she held out a snapshot of a grinning little girl in a checked sunsuit standing in a garden. The sunsuit was unfamiliar, as were the slightly overgrown yard, the bricks around the flower bed, the high wall behind. The child, however, was unmistakably the round-faced blonde girl whom the Kanzlers had photographed a year and a half later. I had not expected to recognize myself. A total stranger with thick black curls would have been less surprising than this child I already knew.

"Oh, I don't look any different than in all the other pictures I already have!"

"You don't want it then?" Mrs. Meinhauser quickly pulled back the picture and was about to slip it into her folder.

"Oh, please, yes, I *do* want it. It's just that I was startled, that's all. I'm sorry, I didn't mean to seem unappreciative."

The photo in my hand again, I turned it over. On the back, in neat black ink, was handwritten, "Judith Williams, Summer 1937." My God, I thought, it's true: I really *was* Judith Williams.

"Did my mother take the picture?"

"No."

"My foster mother?"

Mrs. Meinhauser laughed. "I shouldn't think so."

"Then why did someone take my picture?"

"They *always* did."

"I don't understand."

"For the files."

"Really?" I was so naive, so unknowledgeable.

"You look very cute." And Mrs. Meinhauser concluded our meeting.

"Judith Williams, Summer 1937." The handwritten words were proof of my existence even when I was two and a half. But what of the child who had carried that name? I wondered more and more what she would have been like had she stayed in the strange garden. Or at the place before. Or at the place after. I could not grasp hold of the connections between this departed Judith Williams and that physically similar Katrina Kanzler who had crawled from her ashes when they both were three and a half. What might have become of the girl in the sunsuit if she had lived? Would she have liked books? Music? I supposed she would have looked somewhat like me. But would she have had a funny accent and rude manners and no consideration for others? Would she have been "my sort of person"? Or would she have derided me for my inadequacy?

May was here already, and Charlie still had not come up with a quick legal way to obtain my file from the agency. This issue, which I had hoped to place behind me within a week or so, was not yet even set in motion. I hated the waiting, and I was becoming increasingly busy, readying the family to accompany John on a research trip over the summer to New Guinea. While the focus of my external life was arranging cholera and typhoid shots, yellow-fever vaccine, malaria pills, and clothes, luggage, and Woolite for seventy-five days, my internal life was arguing on the telephone with Charlie. Although he continued to oppose me, he was at least a person with whom I could discuss adoption for more than two or three exchanges. Trapped by the responsibility of the client-lawyer relationship, he could not escape into tact. And I was curiously unintimidated by my single captive listener. I found myself arguing increasingly forcefully against Charlie's protective warnings. My words sounded good to me.

It took hours and hours of hearing my entreaties, but at last Charlie began to study the law. He could find nothing about adopted adults, he told me, only adopted children. He was hoping to know more in a few days.

The weeks passed. Finally, Charlie had information. All adoption records in New York were sealed by state law. There was only one way in which they could be unsealed. One could petition the court by "showing good cause," and then the judge could order the adoption records opened.

This was what I had been wanting to hear. I would show my good cause, see the record, get my mother's name, and be done with this mystery. Then I could leave with my family for New Guinea without being afraid as usual of never returning home. My book was going into galleys, the summer lay ahead, my life was about to begin.

Charlie pointed out that first we had to decide what constituted my good cause. A severe medical condition would be best. Maybe an inherited illness? My health appeared excellent, and of course I had no way of knowing if I carried in me any latent inherited disease. We talked and talked. A lifetime spent wondering, "Who is my mother? Why was I given away? What happened during those three years?" was not enough. From the law's point of view, declared Charlie, these questions were "idle curiosity."

Maybe there was something usable among the facts which the agency had told me, and I went over them with Charlie. What about my mother's return to the agency? Her missing photograph? There was also the agency's inexplicable knowledge of my father's death twenty years ago, when I'd been told no communications had been received in thirty years. My mind, too cluttered in Mrs. Meinhauser's office, now busied itself inventing wild explanations. If I knew the reason, would I have my good cause?

"They shouldn't have leaked all this stuff," Charlie exclaimed. "It's cruel."

But I was grateful they had. Because now there was a chance that I might be able to find my mother and be done with not knowing.

I was aware that by "finding" I meant more than "locating." If my mother was still alive I would pursue, I knew, some sort of a meeting. Yes. But I never thought about that meeting. It was too distant and too important to imagine. So, too, were meetings with the others—the good foster mother, the one-time brother—beyond safe thinking. I dreamed instead of acquiring facts, of holding agency papers, of seeing solid words on pages. Both consciously and unconsciously, I

37

limited myself to one name—my mother's—and to one act— "I will find her."

Quietly I plotted. Already in my forthcoming book, I had discreetly sprinkled the names Williams and Judith and Virginia into the text; now, as the manuscript was readied for the typesetter, I rearranged the names into more forthright clues. I renamed an adoption agency the Judith Williams Agency. I changed the birth weight of a baby to my own eight pounds, four ounces. If my mother read the book, she would know the author was her daughter. I felt a little frightened, exposing myself thus; I wondered if I were setting myself up to be murdered.

Charlie began talking of "making new law." I did not know what the phrase meant, but I sensed that it would be expensive. Moreover, "making new law" smacked of selfishness. Since the rest of the adopted population was presumably content, they must not be hurt because I—a single, isolated oddball—chose to pursue the question of my origins.

Another of Charlie's suggestions was to leave my mother some money. There was the money my adoptive parents had left me. Was I willing? Well, would it work?

All these strategies were weak. I was not discouraged, though, for there was still a whole month left before our departure for New Guinea, and Charlie was at last treating my case seriously. Even now he was embarking on a study of the good causes used by previous petitioners.

At home, however, the subject was avoided. John was vehemently opposed to my efforts. After the first arguments, we tacitly agreed to keep the peace by saying nothing. John knew, however, that he had not convinced me and grew increasingly upset. Finally he sought the opinion of a psychiatrist.

The psychiatrist was as fervently opposed to my ideas as was John: Finding my mother would be a terrible experience for me. This was an old rejoinder, but it carried the new sting of medical disapproval. And, continued John's psychiatrist, there was a second reason: I would be a terrible experience for my mother! Here was a suggestion with which I had never before been confronted. Because it came from a psychiatrist, I presumed its accuracy. I could not, myself, imagine how I was so bad, but I accepted the implied guilt. Frightened and ashamed, I acknowledged that I would continue just the same.

Charlie's research into what other people had used for good cause disclosed that there were no cases parallel to mine and that the few related attempts had all failed. Even in the instance of a man who, with the opening of adoption records, might have been excused from a ten-year prison sentence, there had been no unsealing of the records. Unless I could prove "dire necessity," Charlie saw no possibility that the surrogate judge would award me my information.

The only heartening fact that Charlie uncovered was that the judge had the authority not only to open the court records, but also to order the agency to disclose its files. That would mean definite access to my mother's married name. Charlie noted that, of course, the agency could oppose us. However, this was all academic: A "Petition for Good Cause Shown" seemed impossible to develop.

Finally, my departure date approaching, Charlie and I recognized that there was but one good-cause option left: If my psychiatrist would testify to my "need to know," we might be able to make a case.

"No, no," the doctor told me. "I can't."

I was stunned.

"I can't," he repeated.

I did not dare ask why he was refusing his testimony, and I changed the subject. I was determined not to hear from him that the wish to find my mother was destructive. Instead I spoke of the coming airplane trips and my terror of flying.

The bleakness of my situation was not apparent to me. I was soon to be out of the country for two and a half months; Charlie would have ample opportunity to uncover a legal solution. I was now ready to accept a delay until fall. If I did not die in faraway lands, I would find my mother on my return.

Only four days remained before we were to leave on the first of a series of twelve flights, and there were still two more dental appointments, Emily's birthday and her school commencement, galleys due from Liveright, and last suitcases to be packed. In the midst of this family chaos Charlie telephoned, excitement in his voice.

"There's a woman, and she says what you say." The words were tumbling out. "On television this morning she kept saying the same thing. She's written a book. She was adopted, and she found her parents—"

"She found her parents?"

"—And I'm reading the book now, and I . . . "

I leaped into a taxi and sped the thirty blocks downtown to McKinley and Hart, Charlie's law firm. On his huge brown desk lay a copy of *The Search for Anna Fisher* by Florence Fisher.

"She found her mother, but the reunion wasn't a success; it was just for three hours."

"Three hours! That's a success to me!"

"But with her father it worked out wonderfully . . . "

I was touching the words under the title: "The dramatic story of an adoptee who was determined to find her natural parents—and, after twenty heartbreaking years, did." Somebody had done the impossible.

"I was looking through it for the law, but it seems Fisher found pretty much what we found. You can only open the records by a good-cause petition. Of course, I've only read about halfway . . . "

The inside flap said that Florence Fisher had started an organization called the Adoptees Liberty Movement Association—ALMA. There were real people in this world who felt as I did!

I left Charlie's office with *The Search for Anna Fisher* under my arm. I was no longer alone.

Over the summer, my lawyer would find out about ALMA and prepare a case. When I returned in September the two of us together would march into court. The light of our scrubbed faces, innocent and honest, would shine our way to victory.

I read *The Search for Anna Fisher* on the plane from New York to San Francisco, and I knew I was not crazy or wicked, ungrateful or dangerous. I was, like Florence Fisher, seeking no more than what other people already possessed. For the first time I was struck by the inequity of being bound against my will by a contract others had signed in my infancy. Gone was the guilt for being interested in my own life. Florence Fisher had articulated the truth within me that I had been unable to define. I felt exhilarated. My God, if someone *like* me can vanquish the mystery, *I* can, too.

John read the book that night, and at last he understood. Reading the words of Florence Fisher, he was convinced, he was completely with me. All was well. When the summer ended, I would tackle the impossible. Now, with my husband and our four children, I would concentrate on the experience at hand. I departed for the South Pacific, terrified but triumphant.

chapter three

SEARCH AND LAW

My return to the agency had given me a belief in my birth and early childhood as real events. Florence Fisher's book had made success a genuine possibility. By September, 1973, my lifelong yearning for answers had evolved from an embarrassing fantasy to a program for hope. My lawyer, however, was not ready with a plan. Over the summer Charlie had not settled upon any "good cause" for my case, nor had he contacted the Adoptees Liberty Movement Association.

The next landmark came therefore not through the law, but through the acquisition of tools for search—the receipt of membership information, upon my own request, from ALMA. Reading ALMA's covering letter, I was sure that the organization could help me. Its primary objective was to "raise the consciousness of the country to the injustice of the 'sealed records.' " For ALMA the requirement to "give good cause" to see our own birth records was "an affront to human dignity." Within a few days of my application, two ALMA members, one an adoptee and the other a mother who had given a child up for adoption nine years ago, called to offer practical advice. D'Arcy, the natural mother, was a most vivid confirmation of my suspicion that mothers could continue to care for their relinquished offspring. They told me how to begin a search, gave encouragement and ideas; they suggested I contact a genealogist who was helping other ALMA members. Genealogists and their fascination with blood relationship and ancestry had always seemed particular enemies; I was surprised that they could be allies.

On the evening of September 17, I made yet another beginning. I looked in the Manhattan telephone directory to see if there were any Judith Williamses. There was one. It was silly, and yet there was a chance. If my mother was looking for me, she might have called the Judith Williams in the book.

I had to start somewhere. I would ask this Judith if anyone had inquired after a different Judith Williams.

"Hello, may I please speak to Judith Williams?"

"This is she."

"Hello. My name is . . . actually, my name is Judith Williams, too." I laughed, hoping to set her at ease, and made up a story about being recently married and just moved back to town. The other Judith Williams was pleasant and receptive, and I asked her if she had received any mistaken phone calls. Yes, she told me, once a few years ago someone had asked for an actress named Judith Williams. Again a coincidence: I had been an actress myself for several years. The other Judith Williams wrote down my name and my number; if anyone did call, she would be sure to put us in touch.

A ridiculous beginning, yet I recognized it as a statement of commitment.

It was then that I took a looseleaf notebook from my desk and began a diary of my search. Already I realized that I could not risk inadvertently contacting the same individual twice or confusing my invented stories. I would have to note all information and record all action taken lest I forget the one detail that might mean the difference between success and failure. As I started writing, I felt a sudden strength, a seed of confidence that what I was doing made sense.

A few days later, I spoke with the genealogist for the first time. It is hard now to imagine a time of not knowing Melia Portoverdi.

Melia, I had been told, had flaming red hair, was in her late forties, was attractive. There was a hint that she might

43

be frail, as she never came into New York from her home in New Jersey, not even for ALMA's monthly meetings. I saw a mad, scrawny redhead, all imagination and heart. I never met her; I heard her. For Melia was a voice, and a voice of unfailing encouragement.

"No one disappears without a trace," Melia told me in that first conversation. "Each person goes through life touching other lives." This was a new concept for me, that the natural mother lives, moves, has addresses, votes, has jobs, joins clubs, participates, continues—and leaves memories and records behind.

Melia enlarged on the value of documents—birth certificates that provide addresses and can lead to people who remember, death certificates naming informants and nearest of kin, cemetery registers of visitors. By researching grandparents and great-grandparents one could trace forward to a parent. Half the time calling me Katrina and half the time Judith, Melia gave me what seemed endless suggestions.

Search Diary, Thursday, 20 Sept. 1973
   Melia talked about checking school records, high school yearbooks, typing schools, etc., etc. Told me to go to library and photostat all the Williamses in 1935 phone directories of all 5 boroughs for later reference(!). Said to find out whether adopted in New York or Michigan. Advised to routinely avoid reference to being adopted—as will be given automatic turn-downs. Said not to believe any names given out by adoption agencies. Told me to write to N.Y.C. Bureau of Vital Records, 125 Worth Street, ask for a Certificate of Birth, Amended, in full.

I told Melia I already had applied for a birth certificate, years ago, when my adoptive father gave me the papers he held. I had signed my request Judith Virginia Williams. I had been shocked to receive, weeks later, a simple slip of white paper: "This is to certify that Katrina Kanzler was born on

March 9, 1935, in the Borough of Manhattan." I had been caught out; somebody up there *knew* that Judith Virginia Williams was a blank, and that the sender of the letter was in fact Katrina Kanzler!

Melia explained that the real birth certificate of an adoptee was sealed at the time of adoption and replaced with an altered—"amended"—certificate. An adopted person had access only to this substitute, the "Certificate of Birth by Adoption." The document I had received was the shortened version of that certificate; it was what was always sent to adoptees, she told me. But there was a longer version of the amended certificate also, to which adoptees were actually entitled, if they only knew to ask.

This was the first time I had had it explained why my own certificate was a flimsy slip of white paper with the facts written in longhand, whereas my children have something bigger, a formal black photostat with neat white print.

That afternoon I sent away to Worth Street for my certificate of birth by adoption, long form.

Following Melia's instructions, the next day I telephoned the man who had been my father's executive secretary to ask if he knew of any documents about my adoption or any unfamiliar photographs. Dick Whittaker quickly found two sets of papers with unfamiliar names. "But," he drawled, "those are boys' names, aren't they? So I guess they're your brothers'. No, nothing here with a girl's name."

Just like that—no lecture, no criticism, and answers were given! Dick commented that each of the papers with the boys' names was called "Order of Adoption," so there would have to be one for me, too; probably in New York. I realized immediately that the papers my father had given me must be my own order of adoption! Mrs. Meinhauser's dangerous document was that same bland series of pages my father had handed me so long ago.

The papers were in my desk. Right on the outside were the words, "Petition and Order of Adoption." Mrs. Meinhauser must surely have realized from my description that I already possessed my adoption order; I was furious, now, at her silence.

I read through the document with new eyes. Ten years earlier what had struck me had been my name, which I learned then for the first time: "Judith Virginia Williams." Damn, I had thought. I had been a Kanzler, a Maxtone-Graham; a one-of-a-kind birth name could have been my salvation, and I got a Williams.

The only paragraph that held anything personal was the last paragraph of the last page:

> That both the mother and said child were abandoned by the father; that the said child was cared for by public and private charity from the time of her birth; that on December 7, 1937, said child came under the care of the State Charities Aid Association for placement in a family home; and that on June 30, 1938, said child was finally surrendered to the State Charities Aid Association by her mother for adoption.

"Abandoned by the father." This phrase I had previously imagined to be a delicate allusion to rape. I realized now it was merely a crass means of stating that my father had not been told of my mother's pregnancy. "Abandoned" indeed!

I did not know what Mrs. Meinhauser had been afraid of: The document revealed no new names nor obvious clues. I could only hope that Melia's trained eye would spot a subtle detail.

Search Diary, Monday, 24 Sept. 1973
   Received copy of short Birth Certificate from Dick. Birth Record Number—6742. Extra, unexplained, number in longhand—top righthand corner—289786.
   Wrote out notes from meeting with Mrs. Meinhauser for Melia.

Search Diary, Wednesday, 26 Sept. 1973
    Mailed above (having made copies)—i.e., notes
of meeting at agency, plus Xerox of Order of Adop-
tion, also Xerox of Certificate of Birth, and brief let-
ter—to Melia.

Having received my papers, Melia told me to go to the
genealogy department of the 42nd Street library to study the
birth records for 1935. I was to look under Williams, Judith
V., and see if the file number was given as 6742. Melia explained that if my file number did not match the one on my
certificate, then I was not Judith Williams either. I resented
the possibility of being yet someone else—although, if it had
to happen, I hoped I would be something easier to research
than Williams!

Search Diary, Friday, 28 Sept. 1973
    Went to N.Y. Public Library, Genealogy Dept.
(with John, who, wisely, suggested that I look up
Florence Fisher's "Acknowledgments" to some staff
members in library). I made note of a Jim Hen-
drickson.
    First, man gave me the book for 1935, and, yes,
I was able to verify: Williams, Judith V., March 9,
1935, 6742. When I returned book to man, he asked,
"Did you find what you were looking for?" I replied,
"It was the right book but, no, I didn't find what I
wanted." Man: "May I help you?" K: "Yes, but I
don't know what to look for. I really wanted my birth
record." Man (to my utter horror and dismay): "Are
you an adopted person making a search for your
natural parents?" K (aghast at being caught): "No, I
want to do a genealogy . . . an astrological chart."
Man: "You need . . . birth certificate . . . blah blah
. . . " and 3 minutes of instructions re Bureau of
Vital Records at 125 Worth Street. K (suddenly, with
one last prayer): "Are you by any chance Jim Hen-

*drickson?" Man: "Yes, I am." K: "Oh . . . then my
answer to your first question is yes."*

*He is very nice; got me a book listing "Homes
and Asylums"; told me the urgency of finding hospital of birth, of hoping to get a record via someone's
"slip." Re the hospital record, I asked, "Legally or
illegally?" He replied, very matter-of-fact, "Either";
then laughed and added, "Mostly: Imagination!"*

I photocopied the Williams listings in the telephone directories for 1934-35. As John fed the quarters into the machine, I marked the still-wet prints with identifications,
"Brooklyn—page five," and on and on. There were fifteen
New York City pages of Williamses. Among those thousands
of Williamses might be my grandmother or my uncle. We
made two full sets, one for Melia and one for me.

We also copied the page of "Homes and Asylums." I was
struck by some of the names which, though irrelevant to me,
would be other people's painful realities: Colored Orphan
Asylum, Franciscan Sisters Reception House for Committed
Children, Home for Incurables, Howard Mission for Little
Wanderers, Society for the Relief of the Destitute Blind,
Washington Square Home for Friendless Girls.

A few days later I received the first section of Melia's
"Search Plan." Written in longhand on six pages of legal paper
it was a series of suggestions, questions, observations. I was
both heartened and overwhelmed by the variety of Melia's
imagination. Among the inclusions:

Number in upper righthand corner of certificate of birth,
short form—289786. This must mean something, but
don't know what. First certificate I've come across showing additional number. We'll find out!

How does agency know natural father died? Did he
perhaps inquire after you?

Research: Death Register—Public Library
1) Male Williams—1920's (grandfather)

2) Male Williams—1952, 53, 54, 55 (father—just in case)

You said "it seemed as though" your mother had been out of high school for a year when she met your father. Try to pin down agency. Would like to know whether graduated 1933 or 1934. If 1933, this would make her only 16 at time of completing high school. Might she have been gifted student?

NOTE: Mother signed surrender 6-30-1938, same day as given care of adoptive parents! She must have been still resident of N.Y. City and in contact with agency!

Please note Item 15 of Petition for Adoption: "Request that no notification of this adoption be transmitted to the Commissioner of Health of the City of New York!" Why?!! Ask agency about this. Question: Is it possible your mother was employed in that department?

There was a long and mysterious paragraph about researching basketball players; I finally realized that, in writing up my agency notes, I had described my father as 6'11" rather than 6'1"!

That afternoon, I had to check in for a three-day hospital stay for the surgical removal of a tumor. Before, when asked procedural questions like "place of birth," "mother's name," "father's name," I had stoically disregarded the lash of the questions and had dutifully proferred the substitute information. This time, in the cold lifelessness of the hospital admissions procedure, I suddenly determined to speak out for life. "I don't know," I answered. It was like diving off a mountain to discover if I could fly. The earth did not yank me back to crash. Instead, the kindly woman admitting me said, "Gee, that must be a terrible thing to worry about, not knowing your origins."

The tumor was benign and I was soon wondering whether the woman in admissions might have access to information from the Bureau of Vital Records that would be refused to me. Without any fuss at all, she took my list of "information to request" and promised to call me if she had any success.

AN ADOPTED WOMAN

Home again, I began studying the fifteen pages of 1934-35 Williams telephone listings. There were no Judiths at all, and only one Virginia, in Manhattan. I looked in the current Manhattan phone book; there were now several Virginias, but none near the address of the 1935 one. Making random calls to all the current Virginias would take more strength than I had; I would have to reserve my energies for efforts that held at least a remote possibility of hope. I studied the 1935 addresses as well as the names, looking for two Williamses on the same street, hoping to match a "Mrs." (my widowed grandmother) with a "Jr." or a different "Mr." (my uncle). It was not very scientific, I realized, but maybe a giant inspiration would leap out from the tiny print.

I was doing nothing else anymore. Any further writing projects would have to wait. I called Melia almost daily, reporting my efforts, receiving instructions, discussing possibilities: Maybe Virginia was my grandmother's name; maybe Judith was chosen because my grandfather's name had begun with a J. We wondered, too, whether my mother, having lost her father at an early age, might have married an older man.

I continued to telephone Charlie as well, but he was still talking in circles about what constituted good cause, and never making arrangements for us to go to court.

Tentatively at first and then wholeheartedly, I was telling my psychiatrist what I was doing. I did not mention his refusal of help last June. Perhaps he had forgotten it, I told myself. It certainly appeared that he had. In any event, he now seemed to share my conviction that I had the right to know the contents of my file.

I began calling hospitals to ask for my birth record. I started with New York Hospital, where my own children had been born. All went well. Even when the records clerk asked, "What's your mother's first name, please?", I was calm. "Virginia," I replied. There was no birth record for either a Judith or a Virginia in 1935. But, the clerk told me reassuringly, if the patient did not return within ten years, the birth record would have been destroyed.

I called an acquaintance who worked at a major New York adoption agency. I wanted to find my mother, I told her, and I wanted her advice on how to get what information my agency held. Janet stated firmly that she disapproved of searching; then, remarkably, she proceeded to discuss it. Approaching any agency from the inside would be impossible, she told me. The records were closely guarded, and even the social workers did not generally have access to their agency's files. I would do better to find the names of 1935 maternity homes, she suggested, and try to get help from them. She mentioned three and named several sources for complete listings. If she had any more ideas, she would call me. About her own interviews with adoptees, Janet said, "I never give the names, but what I do give, I judge individually."

"What *do* you give?"

"It's different in every case. I don't decide what I'm going to say until I'm there, in the room with the client. For instance, I once had a natural mother who had given up a child nine years before. Now, what she did not know, but I did know, was that her child had died three years earlier from pneumonia. Before I went into the room, I didn't know whether I would tell the mother or not."

"Did you?"

"No, in that case—"

"You didn't tell her?"

"But I might have, that's my point, I never know for sure. In her case, she was too upset already."

"But why not tell the truth?"

"She couldn't have taken it. She was very upset, she was crying . . . "

"Maybe the truth would be better."

"Well, if the child had died of something genetic, then certainly I would have told her. It's not the same as, say, a heart defect. It's something that had to do with where the child was placed. The agency could be accused of . . . you see, it happened in the adoptive home, it wasn't the mother's genetics. Maybe it could be said that the agency was at fault."

51

My first thoughts were of that natural mother, going on year after year staring at nine-year-olds, then ten-year-olds, then eleven-year-olds; at eighty-nine worrying about a seventy-year-old—who had died over sixty years ago, at the age of six. Then my thoughts turned to the adoptive parents, who might have been comforted by the sharing of their grief. But the agency was separating the mourners, perpetuating their guilt and withholding the possibility of consolation. Agencies could play God, I realized with horror, even to the extent of raising the dead.

I called D'Arcy and casually asked her what agency had taken her nine-year-old. It was not the one where Janet worked.

On October 12, the mail brought a familiar envelope, addressed in my own hand, returned from the Bureau of Vital Records. Bracing myself for the ignominy of a further useless slip of white paper, I tore open the envelope.

The document was black, with tiny white print. I saw the address first, brightest: "315 E. 15th Street." Above it was typed "Manhattan," below it "Katrina Kanzler." Then, to the right, under *Character of Premises: Hospital, Home, Other*, was typed, "Booth Memorial Hospital."

I was jumping up and down, shouting. Born in Booth Memorial! A Salvation Army baby! I skittered around the living room, waving the paper, calling out my facts, attempting to read the rest of the document but, like a dog with a fresh bone, too excited to make myself still.

Then I saw the familiar signatures of the Kanzlers, their home address, their occupations. I looked to see if my hour of birth was there. It was not. Absent, too, were the lines for *Weight at Birth* and *Attending Physician*. The document had been filed in May, 1939, when I was four years old: "Certificate of Birth by Adoption." No further new information, except that there was a number—P #39679—in the upper left corner; the mysterious handwritten 289786 was nowhere.

I felt proud to be from the Salvation Army. And I was furious with Mrs. Meinhauser, who had sat in her office referring smugly to "the shelter" while I had raved about my friend's experience with Booth Memorial Hospital in Massachusetts. Even under the existing laws, I was allowed to possess the name of the hospital in which I was born. To think that Mrs. Meinhauser had *withheld* this information, knowing the joy it would have given me.

I called Booth Memorial Medical Center to request my birth record and was told that all records had been destroyed in 1959 when the hospital had moved from Manhattan to Queens.

I looked in the current telephone book for maternity homes near Booth's 1935 location on 15th Street; there were two possibilities. Then from the directory pages for 1934-35 which I had photocopied I made a list of about twenty different Williamses who had lived in that neighborhood. Comparing that list with the current listings of Williamses, I found three who might be the same people. Two were possible grandmothers, the other a possible uncle. I was getting somewhere!

I telephoned Melia to report, and she was as ecstatic as I. We had a long discussion about where my mother might have lived, if not in the immediate area of Booth. Brooklyn was our next best guess, or, possibly, Staten Island; both these boroughs had fairly comfortable access to the 15th Street area.

Search Diary, Saturday, 13 Oct. 1973
ALMA meeting (my first). Fifth Avenue Presbyterian Church, 7 West 55th Street. Present: D'Arcy; Nanny, a social worker from Philadelphia, whose natural mother was a forty-year-old schoolteacher. Barry, who has seen his mother, and his siblings, from a distance. Has written his mother a letter and is now waiting for her reply. Betty, a writer, very articulate; she has met her mother but the mother did not want a continuing relationship. An older man, looking for his daughter now in her thirties. A highly neurotic woman from Conn., who has

*located two potential mothers and is soon to make
approaches, but sounds as though she's predeter-
mined to blow them. Luther, has 4 children, had a
foster mother until 2, knows his mother's name. His
adoptive parents accept what he is doing, "They have
a philosophy of helping others." April, whose own
baby was mysteriously ill after birth. She had a nervous breakdown, 3 months in mental hospital. Child
over 2 now, illness still unexplained, but April terrified to have another baby. Various others, didn't get
names, including several natural mothers.*

*It seems the total membership is not very much.
This is real grassroots stuff—no proper indexing, a
half-completed card file, and $800 in the treasury. I
am appalled at how fledgling it all is; and, also, at
the different awareness levels of some adoptees.
ALMA really has a long way to go.*

The meeting opened with business reports and a reiteration of ALMA policy: Adoptees who were minors could not be
members; natural parents of under-age children were welcome but could not search until their children reached eighteen; adoptive parents were also welcome, and were encour-
aged to realize that the adoptee's desire to know was a
natural need and not a rejection of them. ALMA's long-range
goal was to bring a test case before the United States Supreme Court, arguing that the laws that bound adoptees
were unconstitutional.

I found that the other adoptees, like me, were newly
awakened to the concept of having rights equal to the rights
of their fellow citizens. Having been children who were
"second-best" to our parents, we had similarly accepted secondary status from our country. Now our attitudes were
changing. We too had the right to possess our real certificates
of birth; we too had the right to knowledge of our heritage,
ancestry, and genes. The present laws, in essence the same
from state to state, were to us obviously unconstitutional.

Our natural parents and our adoptive parents had made agreements while we were still children for the benefit of our childhoods. Must we, adults now, abide by their contracts? Did the Constitution of the United States of America really allow for two parties to sign away the identity of a third?

The remainder of the meeting was devoted to search advice. April had brought a document given to her by her agency—a birth certificate with all the crucial information whited out! She had sought the help of her adoptive parents, but each time she raised the subject her adoptive mother became hysterical with weeping and her adoptive father furious. The ALMA old-timers, convinced that one day her parents would relent, recommended that April keep on begging for their help.

After the meeting, some of us went to a cafeteria. It was a remarkable experience for me to be with adopted people who talked openly about "my mother" and "my father" and were not meaning—for once—our adoptive ones. Here we were, all together, able to speak naturally of the forbidden halves of ourselves. I no longer felt the absolute possession of my adoptive parents.

Search Diary, Monday, 15 Oct. 1973

Built up a story—and finally the courage—to call Mrs. W. David Williams on E. 71st Street. But she's not at home.

Went to the Salvation Army—120 W. 14th. Wow! They just want to help me. Too long—and great—to write out. Anyway, met by coincidence what turned out to be a Brigadier, in the lobby. She said to see Capt. Iris Haskins, to whose office on the 7th floor she took me in the elevator. Used the name Judith Williams Maxtone-Graham. Captain Haskins said that if I was "over 18, it was my legal right." (She's wrong, but who am I to tell her?) She thinks the Salvation Army has old records some place, and that I should call back on Wednesday.

Met a Major and received about 25 pamphlets, and got escorted down in elevator. It seems, by the way, that Booth did have an aftercare program. Which pretty much confirms, to me, that my mother was in residence at Booth.

Got a call from Melia to try Strang-N.Y. Infirmary, presently at 321 E. 15th, to see if it was around in 1935. Maybe I'd been an out-patient there with my mother.

Search Diary, Tuesday, 16 Oct. 1973

Went to Public Library. Copied out all female Williamses, name, birthdate, record number, born in the 5 boroughs in 1916 and 1917. Over ninety for each year. No Judiths. 3 Virginias: April 26, '16; Dec. 22, '16; Aug. 20, '16. (Last one in Staten Island.)

Search Diary, Wednesday, 17 Oct. 1973

Called Capt. Haskins at Salvation Army. She said all she could get was a confirmation that yes, I was born at Booth. But, she said, there were files out in Flushing on microfilm, and she would try to find out more. She reiterated her belief that the Salvation Army "has no legal right to deny me this information." Then she referred me to a group who might help me—which turned out to be ALMA! She will call again in a few days or so. She also said that the Salvation Army had a children's home near Suffern, and might I have been placed there? Told her I didn't think so, but then, realized I had no way of knowing any of my "facts" as certain.

Search Diary, Friday, 19 Oct. 1973

Got the call from Capt. Haskins. She's still exceedingly nice but, alas, the files have been destroyed. Gave me the name and number of person

she spoke to, "if I wanted confirmation." (Wow!)
She also had checked into foster care files of
Salvation Army, and there was no record of J.V.W.
1935-1938, so I must have been under a different
charitable jurisdiction. (Which?) She further said
that should I ever find my mother's first name, the
Salvation Army had a Bureau of Missing Persons
in her same building. So, end of "Judith Williams
M.G." w. Capt. Haskins.

Of all the institutions I was to deal with, the Salvation Army was the only one whose emphasis was outward-concerned, not inward-concerned. All the other institutional voices proclaimed, "We cannot divulge what is ours"; only the Salvation Army told me, "We cannot withhold what is yours."

Meanwhile, I had been studying the list of Williams females born in New York City, 95 in 1916, 92 in 1917. If my mother had been born in New York, she would be one of the 187 women on this list. I read the names over and over, staring in particular at those beginning with a J or a V. I studied the birthdates, repeating them aloud, as though hoping that one might scream out, "Here, it's me!" I puzzled over the record numbers for possible clues; I compared each birth record number first with my own birth record number, 6742, and then with the unexplained 289786 on my abbreviated certificate. Hour after hour, I would manipulate these birth record numbers, subtracting, adding, dropping digits, inverting digits, seeking a connection between any of my numbers and the number of one of these former babies. If there was a relationship between my birth and my mother's, I would decipher the numerical code and link myself genetically to another female Williams.

Lists, libraries, letters with stamped return envelopes were becoming a total preoccupation. I devoted most of my day to juggling names and numbers, and in the evenings when the children went to their homework, I returned to my desk for more of the same.

Confronted with the realization that everywhere, in every possible source book, there were hundreds of Williamses, I knew that my job was impossible. I needed more facts. Only through seeing my adoption records could I obtain the additional information I needed to pursue a search. It was clear that I had no alternative but to bring a case into court.

My understanding of legal language was better than it had been five months earlier. The "making new law" that had sounded so alien last spring was actually the constitutional case of which all of us at ALMA dreamed, and it was the case I now, on principle, preferred. In such an action, I would be declaring that the present laws requiring me to show good cause were unconstitutional, that I had a right as an adult citizen to the same information about myself as other Americans had. I would be making new law in the sense that if my case were successful, my victory would establish a legal precedent applicable to all other adoptees as well. Such a case, however, would be long, costly, and complicated, whereas a successful good-cause case, which would rescue only the petitioner, was quick and easy. Obviously the individual case was the wiser choice for now. Much as I would rather bring the constitutional suit to save us all, for the sake of my family I had to select the route which drained me least. I had been actively searching for over a month, and I knew I could not bear the strain too long. A few more weeks, then this misery must be over. Once I had resolved my own problem, I could work with my ALMA peers to help bring about a class action.

I pressured Charlie yet more heartily. I had heard at ALMA that only the records of the court were sealed and not, in fact, the records of the adoption agencies. This meant the social workers were legally free to give us our information. Charlie neither refuted the claim nor was impressed by its implications. Mostly he kept repeating the rather offensive observation that it was "such a big help" that my adoptive parents were dead. I was becoming annoyed with both his words and his inaction. I wanted to go to court, and soon.

Search Diary, Wednesday, 24 Oct. 1973
Got a call from Melia, who (like Charlie) has
received papers from me. But she (unlike Charlie) is
full of action, and has already drawn up a state-
ment—in draft form—for a petition to open my
files! (It's a combination *of civil rights and of medi-*
cal grounds—so the Judge can pick his preference.)

Her instructions: Obtain 2 copies each of death
certificate for both adoptive parents. Define self, in
request, as "legally adopted child." Say "needed for
legal purpose."

Obtain statement from Dr. Thomas confirming
that I have been in psychiatric treatment for four-
teen years.

She will send me the petition, which I can type
out, and I am to sign as KMG/a.k.a. KK/a.k.a.
JVW. Then put full address under signature.

Should send it Registered—Return Receipt Re-
quested. Should make photocopies of final docu-
ment, one for self, one for Charlie (in case I'm called
for a hearing).

Mail all this to the Presiding Judge (by name),
Surrogate Court of N.Y. County, and street address.

Also: Call agency, and ask for new appt. One of
my reasons will be "any medical or biological info
I've not been given." (Must think out what else I
could claim for reasons.)

Further: Melia says that, if I was not under
agency's jurisdiction until Dec. 1937, the previous
agency may still have records.

I started to put her plan into action. First I placed a call
to the Children's Aid Society, where I got the sweet Miss
O'Malley again. She promised that Mrs. Meinhauser would
return the call.

Search Diary, Thursday, 25 Oct. 1973
Received a call from Mrs. Meinhauser. Very
pleasant (which made me feel guilty, and also made
me feel intimidated). She said she felt that she had
told me all the medical info, and perhaps there was
no more. I referred to some of the loose ends, "sickly
grandmother," "natural father died 20 years ago,"
etc. and tried to sound strong.

Face change: Yes, she was happy to see me
again. Quite profusely apologized that it might be
two weeks before the files were removed from under
lock and key—which secrecy she described with ap-
palling fullness, as though she "knew."

Called Surrogate Court to ask the name of the
presiding judge. It changes apparently. Now it's
Vernon someone. November, it will be Anthony Car-
pentieri.

When I received my adoptive parents' death certificates
from Dick Whittaker I realized that I had never before given
thought to the years of their births, 1891 and 1892. My adoptive parents had been almost the age of my own grandparents. My mother could have been my adoptive parents' child!

Melia's petition arrived the following day. It was glorious: "The petitioner further avers her original name, her
identity and all heritage relating thereto, is her sole property,
with right of tenure as a citizen of the United States, and
should not be subject to any condition or contingency after
her full age of majority, and against her express will and consent. The petitioner feels that the silence, mystery, and secrecy attached to the truth of her heritage, birth, and early
years have constituted unintended cruel and inhuman treatment, the pains of which can be assuaged by the present removal of silence, mystery, and secrecy, and the present acknowledgment of reality and truth." The statement hardly
seemed like a legal document at all. It was assertive, passionate, vital—all the things I wished I could be.

I look back on the next several days as having been a sort of bewildering dance in which I tried to make partners of human need and legal reality. The resulting confusion and frustration were overwhelming. I was devising plans, absorbing rumors, hearing unexplained terms and following dead-end leads. I was not understanding what was going on, yet I believed the whole must be making sense. I conscientously reported each new event in my diary, but my entries were no more than an ordered narration of chaos.

Search Diary, Tuesday, 30 Oct. 1973
So ghastly a day, I don't even want to write it up. In brief: I was all set to mail Melia's petition, but showed it today to Dr. Thomas. He warned re Court's potential prejudice against psychiatrists. He also suggested I take it to a lawyer, any lawyer, to "clean it up," grammar and presentation-wise.

Communications with Charlie and Melia—too painful to notate—the upshot being Charlie negates everything Melia says. Charlie wants to present an A-1 case, full of references to Civil Rights Acts of 1800-something-or-other; plus he wants to wait and talk to some other lawyers.

I'm accepting Charlie's viewpoint, but this has so depressed me that I'm vacillating, with ideas of trying to present Melia's petition, slightly improved, and maybe backed up with more enclosures.

Am also considering trying to get myself unadopted. (Then get my brothers to adopt me back!)

The problem is: THE ESTABLISHMENT HAS NO IMAGINATION! I want to out-wit them, to out-imagine them (Lord knows, I've had enough practice!), to bash my head against their wall and by God to break it open! I want to be right—for once in my life. But I don't want to do it through them, through their way. I want to be within the Law, but, oh God, not through the Law.

Search Diary, Wednesday, 31 Oct. 1973
Called D'Arcy. Told her my predicament. She
told me re an adoptee now in court upstate and
about to get her papers opened—13 years of psychia-
try. No agency, so no opposition. Lawyer: Grace
Bauman.
D'Arcy gave me Florence Fisher's home phone
and address.
Called Florence Fisher, an event as encourag-
ing as yesterday's were discouraging; and, once
again, too much to write about. Suffice to say, we
are meeting next Tuesday, the 6th, for lunch, and
then proceeding to office of lawyer Grace Bauman,
who will I hope be my lawyer for this case.
Got a call from Mrs. Meinhauser (believe it or
not!) and we've made an appointment for Thurs.,
Nov. 8. She's found a sort of medical summary,
which she has had Xeroxed.
Called Charlie and severed our professional re-
lationship, explaining that I wanted to go with my
peers as I would benefit from their emotional sup-
port. He took it very graciously.

Talking with the doctor, I established that yes, he was
after all willing to help me. He was appalled by the agency's
behavior toward me. Yes, he believed that I both needed and
had a right to all information about myself. And he was indeed in support of my petitioning the court. I asked him outright if he would provide the affidavit that would be my good
cause. Outright, he said yes.

I quit while I was ahead. Not until 1976 did I finally ask
Dr. Thomas why he had refused my first request. He answered simply: He had refused in June, 1973, because he believed that the doctor must not interfere in the patient's everyday life. I must do this on my own, he had thought. But as
the months had gone on, he had realized that I had no means

of doing it on my own, and that his original refusal had been the greater interference.

Much to my surprise, beginning the following day I received a series of telephone calls from Charlie. In the first conversation he said that he had been thinking that maybe I still had a chance legally some other way. What he meant was not exactly clear, but I ended up with a full page of notes. The next time Charlie called he had a second lawyer from his firm, Ron Tucker, on the line with him. Both men seemed to think I would be able to obtain the information I wanted *without* petitioning, and also get it faster. Charlie called again. This time he wanted me to come in for a talk with yet another, a third—and very important—lawyer. When I asked why, Charlie simply said, "Just to talk."

It was all so mysterious, the sudden attention, the veiled optimism, the suggestions of immediate results, the hints at subterfuge. It seemed very deceitful. And very exciting. I called Florence Fisher to tell her I had decided to stay with McKinley and Hart after all.

The next day, I met Florence in person. When we sat down to lunch, we talked as though we had known each other for years. I forgot about lawyers and court cases. I was back on search and agency information. With my next visit to the agency just two days away, I needed Florence's suggestions.

What perturbed me most, I confided, was the dichotomy I felt between Mrs. Meinhauser's warm friendliness and pleasantness—how nice she was to me—and the utter frustration I felt when in her presence. It was so confusing, and I was afraid my discomfort would limit my pursuit of information.

"Will you stop worrying about Mrs. Meinhauser being so *nice?*" Florence exploded. "If she were *really* nice, she'd tell you your mother's name!"

The penny dropped. It was like growing up in fifteen seconds. I suddenly stopped thinking about how lucky I was to receive anything.

"They can't hurt you any more, Katrina," Florence said. "They can't give you up for adoption a second time."

Search Diary, Wednesday, 7 Nov. 1973
    Lawyers: Charlie, Ron Tucker, and Mr. Big (who, I find out later, is a hot-shot trial lawyer). Anyway, for 1¹/₄ hours, I sat with these three fellows in their padded office. I did all the talking, and it was very boring. There was no mention of hanky-panky, and Mr. Big's talking about a good-cause petition, using Dr. Thomas's affidavit. Next step, one of them goes to Thomas's office. They asked whether I had ever been "investigated"; they think that if I'd ever tried to join some highfalutin club there might be a detective's record somewhere. Far out. And this, I guess, was the hanky-panky intimated.

I still did not know what the meeting in Mr. Big's office was all about. But at least the plan was settled. I could petition the court after all, and my psychiatrist's statement could be my good cause.

The taxi home stopped at a traffic light; the sun was shining on the stream of pedestrians filing in front of me. Bright yellows, and reds and greens and blues, shone off the women's jackets and coats as they crossed the street. I felt a surge of affection for these people in their cheery sun-reflecting colors. Not *all* of them had given me away, I thought. I did not have to be afraid of all of them. Only one person had given me away. And all these people who were left over, glistening in the afternoon sunlight, had not.

chapter four

SECOND VISIT
TO THE AGENCY

Mrs. Meinhauser was waiting for me in the lobby of the Children's Aid Society building. She handed me the Xeroxed medical summary even before we reached her office, her face beaming as though to say, "See, see how helpful I am."

Emphasizing medical curiosity had worked, I thought. The way was paved for me to pose some crucial questions about my grandfather. His death certificate was the most valuable document for speedily concluding phase one of my search, finding my mother. To obtain it, I would have to learn both his age at death and the year of his death. The former would be the easier to couch in terms of medical necessity.

I skimmed the full-page, single-spaced report of a child's medical check-up: "Neck—no scars or masses . . . tonsils medium size . . . breathing normal . . . liver and spleen not felt . . . " The information was certainly boring, yet its printed existence made me believe that there *was* a file on me. If this was "the medical page," there surely must be four or five pages more.

"You may keep it," Mrs. Meinhauser announced, "I made that copy for you."

My first question was the detail that had caused me the greatest personal uneasiness since my meeting with Mrs. Meinhauser in April: How had the agency learned of my father's death?

The answer came quickly. When my mother returned to visit the agency, she had replied to a question by saying,

"He's dead now." Perhaps she had learned of his death from friends, suggested Mrs. Meinhauser.

The mysterious report from an unknown source of my father's death in the early 1950's was replaced by a direct statement made by my mother in the early 1940's. Although now his death was even more premature than I had thought, the discomfort of that implication was outweighed by the relief of resolution. At least his death was now less ghostly, in that the news of it had come in a rational fashion. The picture of my mother, "cooperative" in giving information to the agency, was of an accurate person; if she said my father was dead, he was.

By this simple exchange, six months of senseless guessings were ended. We talked a bit more about my father, his relationship with my mother, the job transfer, his never having known about me. Mrs. Meinhauser was repeating information she had given me in April, but I was taking notes anyway, so that when I heard a detail that would help me search, I could write it down without attracting attention.

I plunged into the subject of my grandfather, decorating my curiosity with impressive-sounding worries: "Cancer? Stroke? Diabetes? Heart?"

"He died of acute indigestion," pronounced Mrs. Meinhauser pleasantly.

I thought of my own stomach cramps when I am nervous. "He must have been very young. My poor mother, only a child . . . how old was he?"

"He was forty-two when he died," stated Mrs. Meinhauser. She paused, then added pointedly, "He died without a death certificate."

This was the worst of all possibilities but, sensing that Mrs. Meinhauser was watching me for a reaction, I did not blink an eyelash. She must have read *The Search for Anna Fisher*, I thought. I would have to be extra careful.

"He worked on a ship, as an engineer," Mrs. Meinhauser continued. "He might have died at sea. Maybe that's why there was no certificate. He was an intelligent man, and always provided well for his family."

This was not the moment to ask for the year of his death, and the conversation turned to safer areas. I asked about my grandmother's "sickliness." Mrs. Meinhauser said she knew no more about it than my own mother's comment, "My mother is not very well."

As Mrs. Meinhauser talked, I recognized many of her phrases from our first meeting. I was reassured. I was eager for accuracy and confirmation even of details that might not directly aid in search. Then, confronted by my specific questions, Mrs. Meinhauser began to change her original story. Subtly, and yet unmistakably, a new picture of my mother emerged. The hazy figure who had given up her child because she had "made a decision" became instead a plausible individual beset by the realities of "simply no way to manage a child financially." Now, the "house was crowded"; "all who could work, had to." My mother, her married sister, even my sickly grandmother, worked. And then—this took intense questioning—Mrs. Meinhauser finally brought out that my grandmother "couldn't face her daughter's bringing home a baby without being married." The confident "decision-maker" of April was replaced by a young woman without money, without a home for her child, and without familial sympathy—a woman without a choice.

Like her family situation, my mother's job also had undergone a change since Mrs. Meinhauser's first telling. Whereas on April 26 my mother's work had been "clerical," on November 8 she was a "secretarial plus." Moreover, she was now acknowledged to have had "better jobs, promotions."

Trying to pinpoint Mrs. Meinhauser's facts was often difficult; surprisingly, she accepted my challenges agreeably. I was able to repeat and refine questions until her reply was finally concise. Then I would proceed to a new set of questions.

Melia had told me that school yearbooks were search tools, so I attempted to gain certain dates. My mother was still a definite eighteen at the time of my birth, but the year of her graduation from high school remained unclear. She still had been "working for some time" before meeting my father;

and yet she had not "graduated young." I could not make the facts jibe. I decided to myself that my mother probably had not been a "young eighteen" at the time of my birth; more likely she had been an "almost nineteen." I had the hunch that her birthday came shortly after mine. On my list of female Williamses there was a Virginia who would have turned nineteen the April after my birth. Of the three Virginias, the one with this early spring birthdate seemed the most promising.

Had my mother lived in Manhattan?

"No," said Mrs. Meinhauser.

I had moved to New York from Michigan because I knew I had been born here and had felt drawn to return. Was Mrs. Meinhauser *sure* my mother did not come from Manhattan?

"No, she lived in one of the five boroughs of New York, but it was not Manhattan," Mrs. Meinhauser stated.

So I would have to research those four other boroughs of New York which were not Manhattan. Plus Manhattan, of course—I was no longer so accepting of everything Mrs. Meinhauser told me.

There was a vague conversation, then, of women's education and work conditions in the mid-1930's, which interested me because Mrs. Meinhauser told me that she had grown up in New York in the same years as my mother. Knowing about her experience would help me get closer to my mother.

I asked Mrs. Meinhauser if, in those days, my mother would have used contraception.

"No! None of them does!" she exclaimed, her voice harsh and her face crackling with distaste for every unmarried pregnant woman. My suggestion that just as contraception can fail married people, it can also fail single people, was anathema to her.

"No, they never use contraception!" Mrs. Meinhauser clung to her certainties.

It was useless to argue further. Besides, I had to try for my grandfather's death year.

Did my mother's husband know about me? This question created another long and confused pursuit of fact. With Mrs. Meinhauser again my apparent ally, it finally came out that although my mother did not tell her husband about having had a child, she may have told him she had been married before.

"She may have told him she had been married before," I read aloud from my notes. Mrs. Meinhauser concurred.

But upon further questioning Mrs. Meinhauser's story wavered. I scratched out "may have" and replaced it with "definitely."

"She *definitely* told him she had been married before?"

Yes.

For sure?

Yes.

Definitely?

Definitely.

I asked, beautifully casually it seemed, what sort of work my mother's husband had done.

"No. I can't tell you that."

"Really?"

"I cannot tell you anything that would assist you in a search."

"Really?" Oh shit, I was thinking. Mrs. Meinhauser was on to me.

Mrs. Meinhauser changed the subject.

I put a great deal of effort, once again, into trying to understand the occasion for my mother's return to the agency in the 1940's. *Why* did she come back? To bring the photograph. But *why?* So she could tell the agency about the calcium deficiency. Was there not some further motive? I was stronger than I had been last spring, more alert to contradictions and less deceived by doubletalk. Mrs. Meinhauser was vague and confused and uncomfortable. She talked round and round in circles. The more I asked about this visit, the less I learned. Through ALMA I had become aware how seldom a natural parent returned to an agency; natural parents were even more afraid of being ridiculed and rejected by their agencies than were adoptees. There had to be some explanation for my mother's visit. I was getting to know Mrs. Meinhauser's methods well enough to suspect that if I posed the precise question, I might, even after a long period of evasion, evoke a direct answer.

Not this time. After about half an hour of non sequiturs, the "answer" Mrs. Meinhauser finally offered was the abrupt statement that the caseworker's report of that visit had not been written up until a year later. Mrs. Meinhauser could not understand how a social worker could have waited a whole year. I nodded. Mrs. Meinhauser went on to assert that she did *her* reports by the following week.

It was then that it first struck me that Mrs. Meinhauser possibly wrote up reports about meetings with people like me! I wondered what I might have done differently had I suspected I would be reported upon.

I moved on. I asked under whose auspices I had been until my connection with the State Charities Aid Association. Mrs. Meinhauser gazed at me implacably, yet ever smiling. She did not speak.

We were in indisputable confrontation: I was directly requesting the name of the agency that had handled me for two and three-quarter years; she was directly refusing to give me that name. I held my eyes to hers. Still she refused.

Finally Mrs. Meinhauser looked away. It did not matter, she said, since the case had become that of State Charities Aid. I had the feeling that Mrs. Meinhauser was telling me that all my records had been transferred with me.

I tried once more. "Still, the place must have had a name."

Little darts of "no" sprang from Mrs. Meinhauser's eyes. Another subject closed.

Mrs. Meinhauser asked if I was still seeing a psychiatrist. I said yes. She smiled ambiguously, and the conversation moved on.

We had been talking for an hour and a half when Mrs. Meinhauser asked me if I had read a book that she called *The Story of Anna Fisher*.

"The story of what?" I asked, carefully not correcting her.

"Story of Anna Fisher."

"No, I don't think so," I replied, making my voice seem questioning.

"Hmm."

Mrs. Meinhauser was believing me, I felt.

"Should I have? What's it about?"

Mrs. Meinhauser explained.

"Oh? That sounds interesting." I tried to imagine what I would have said had this really been the first time I was hearing of Florence's book.

"Yes, I knew you'd think so."

Wait till Florence hears this one, I thought.

"How do you spell Fisher?" I asked. "S-c-h or s-h?"

"I don't know." Mrs. Meinhauser scowled.

"Is the book good?"

"It's very shallow!" Mrs. Meinhauser declared with conviction. "And I have not read it."

Afraid I might giggle, I stared earnestly at my notes. Fortunately no response was required; Mrs. Meinhauser had proceeded to a new subject, my father.

"How old was my father exactly?" I asked.

"Mid to late twenties, I believe."

"But that's such an age difference, between them. What was a girl of seventeen doing going out with a man of twenty-seven?"

Mrs. Meinhauser offered to find out his exact age. She did not have the information with her, she declared, as the file was in another room. If I would not mind going down the hall and waiting, she would be glad to go look at the file for me.

Oh, yes, that would be nice, I agreed.

This was my chance. Nearly two hours had passed since I had asked the age of my grandfather at his death. It was now or never.

"In what year did my grandfather die?" I asked. "And isn't there something about Beethoven?" I added, to throw in a red herring.

"Father's age, grandfather's death, Beethoven," Mrs.

Meinhauser repeated as she wrote on her pad.

Mrs. Meinhauser pointed me toward the central area, while she turned down the corridor in the opposite direction. Glancing behind me, I saw her small dark figure disappear into an office beyond hers. I kept on walking, making loud steady paces of departure so that she would not be worried about my sneaking up and grabbing my own file away. What mattered now was not the vision of a glorious flight out of this building with my life's papers in hand but rather the real possibility of learning the year of my grandfather's death. I sat on a chair near the elevator, my back to the wall and the corridor behind me. This way, I could not see anything; Mrs. Meinhauser could feel secure. It was really a ridiculous charade.

After a few minutes, Mrs. Meinhauser came to escort me back. We greeted each other like friends who had unintentionally gotten separated during a cocktail party. Mrs. Meinhauser apologized for the delay; "Oh, no, not at all," I said; and, smiling cordially, the two of us marched back into her office.

"Your father was twenty-nine years old," said Mrs. Meinhauser. "He was six foot one, had brown hair, blue eyes; was employed. There is no reference to Beethoven. But your father had an interest in music and books."

"He did?" Why had she not mentioned this before?

"The records do state that your parents went to concerts together," Mrs. Meinhauser went on. "Your grandfather died in 1923. He had retired from the sea and had an office job. He always provided well for his family."

"How sad for my poor mother," I said.

Age forty-two in 1923—I had done it! In two hours of mumbo jumbo, I had pulled out the most crucial details. It was not very much really, but it was a start. I wanted to scream for joy, but instead I sat there with cautious blandness.

I knew that the meeting was about to end and that a third appointment with Mrs. Meinhauser would be impossible to extract. Now that my grandfather's facts were safely mine, I could dare a more open query in this last precious minute.

"I was wondering . . . I'm interested in . . . what sign was my mother born under?" I smiled demurely. "I'm Pisces, myself."

"I'm not sure I could tell you that."

"Well, could you find out?"

"I can't go back to the file now. Furthermore, I don't know if I could answer that or not."

"But you do know her birthdate, don't you?" My voice dripped with artificial sweetener.

"Oh, yes!" asserted Mrs. Meinhauser proudly. "It's late now. I'll call you after my lunch."

"That would be most kind."

On the bus ride home, I repeated to myself, over and over, "Age forty-two in 1923, age forty-two in 1923, I got it, I got it." I stared at the other people on the bus. All were under fifty or over seventy. None was my mother. I gazed at them almost victoriously: *Their* grandfathers had not died in 1923 at age forty-two!

At home, I spent an hour studying the horoscope in the newspaper, afraid that I would expose myself to Mrs. Meinhauser by not having the signs of the zodiac on the tip of my tongue.

The phone rang. Mrs. Meinhauser.

"No, I cannot tell you what sign your mother was born under." Her refusal was definite.

"Would you please tell me what season, then?"

"No."

I got stronger. "All I am asking is a mere season."

"We cannot give identifying information."

"Spring, summer, fall, winter—that's hardly very identifying!"

"No!"

"Summer or winter, Mrs. Meinhauser?"

No answer.

"Come on, can't you tell me summer or winter?"

There was a heavy, agitated silence, as though Mrs. Meinhauser were preparing to rev all her engines at once. Finally she spoke, enunciating with excessive clarity: "There are *certain things*, Mrs. Maxtone-Graham, which you will *never* know."

It was as though a battalion of tanks had flattened me. I had no words to push away the claustrophobic terror of her prediction. The future that Mrs. Meinhauser articulated so brutally was the same hopeless future that had already oppressed me for thirty-eight years.

Mrs. Meinhauser drove on. "Do you talk about these things with your psychiatrist?"

"Yes," I replied, my strength returning with the recollection of our more recent talks.

"Well, I suggest," declared Mrs. Meinhauser, "that you discuss them *fully* with your doctor."

With the fortitude of knowing that our "discussions" were soon to materialize as an affidavit and a petition, I replied, "I *most certainly* will!"

Since that last hearty suggestion of Mrs. Meinhauser on November 8, 1973, there has been no further word addressed to me by any employee of the Children's Aid Society.

I mulled over Mrs. Meinhauser's story, juggling what I knew. She had all the records; I had nothing. The social worker was free to invent whatever she wanted while the adoptee listened, begging for clues, struggling to pick up some detail that would help, knowing that all the clues and details could be invention on the social worker's part. To me it was the epitome of indignity to grovel for truth from someone I could not trust.

Worse still, I had pursued my end by deception. I had been in Mrs. Meinhauser's office under false pretenses. I had disguised, I had omitted, I had performed. I had *social-worked* the date of my grandfather's death out of the agency.

chapter five

FORWARD MOTION

In case Mrs. Meinhauser had lied about my grandfather's having no death certificate, I went to the library to make a list of forty-two-year-old male Williamses who had died in 1923. There were two, George E. and Lazarus; both had died in Manhattan.

Because my ALMA friends had advised me always to give a little leeway with dates, I made note of the ten additional males who, though not precisely forty-two, were close to it. Of these, two lived in Queens, three in Brooklyn, one in the Bronx, and four in Manhattan.

If, on the other hand, there was indeed no death certificate in 1923 for my grandfather, it was possible that he had not died then but instead had run off from his family. People who disappear, Melia had told me, are recorded as dead seven years later. I looked in the book for 1930 and made note of one male exactly the right age and five others who were near it.

Simply because I had the time, I decided to check a further year. In 1924 there were no male Williams deaths in Richmond or Queens. There was one in the Bronx whose age was a year off, and three more who were forty-two-year-olds. In Brooklyn there were two more forty-two-year-olds. Furthermore, the two in Brooklyn—which I was considering now as the most likely borough—both had names beginning with J.

In all, I had twenty-five more or less possible grandfathers—that is, of course, if Mrs. Meinhauser was wrong about my grandfather's dying without a death certificate. Eight of these were the right age exactly; two of them—the Manhattanites, Lazarus and George E.—fitted Mrs. Meinhauser's specifications both in age and year.

Next I investigated the City Directory, a Manhattan business directory in which people from all boroughs could have themselves listed, and which was used more frequently during the 1920's and 1930's than telephone books. Among the several hundred Williamses in the 1922 edition I found the name and address of one Lazarus, two George E.'s, and one George. The last, plain George, was further identified as an engineer! Excited, I then looked up the remainder of my eight starred "possibles"—James, Joseph P., Abraham, Edward, James J., Samuel—but I discovered nothing further worth noting.

At home, I mailed an application to Worth Street for George E.'s death certificate. If it came back giving "acute indigestion" for cause of death, I would have found my grandfather. This same document would give me George E.'s address, the name and address of the funeral home, the cemetery, and the informant of the death. The informant would most likely be his widow—my grandmother—and her name might be listed in the 1935 phone book. From one death certificate, I could trace. I would have liked to send in for Lazarus's death certificate as well, but I was afraid that if I applied for more than one certificate at a time, a clerk might spot my name and refuse the requests.

Then I began to research shipping in the early 1920's for an engineer named Williams. Among our family acquaintances was a steamship historian who gave me the names of ten men who had been ship's engineers in the early 1920's.

My conversations with these people were delightful. But it was no fun dialing the phones of very old men whom I did not know and disturbing them with queries about "an engineer who died fifty years ago called Williams, whose first name might have been George." Only their kindness made it bearable at all.

I called the Marine Inspection Office, the Marine Engineers Beneficial Association, the Steamboat Inspection Service, and the U.S. Coast Guard. Nothing.

At my next psychiatric appointment, Dr. Thomas composed his affidavit. For the first time in fourteen years, the meeting went on twenty extra minutes as we polished each phrase. The letter was forceful and stated my situation clearly. His conclusion read:

> It is my professional opinion that if this information about the first four years of her life was made available to her in its entirety, her symptoms, fears and anxieties would be seen in their full distortion, viz. that they relate to the concern surrounding the multiple separations (rejections) and that progress towards recovery would therefore be immeasurably facilitated. Without this information I believe that no significant change can be reasonably anticipated.

The last sentence was a little frightening, and Dr. Thomas's first draft had not even included the word "reasonably." It was my guess that it was not comfortable for this man to realize that, after fourteen years of his and my efforts, the prospect of my improvement was dependent upon persuading outsiders to cooperate. The "reasonably" was a straw against absolute despair.

Search Diary, Thursday, 15 Nov. 1973
Call from Charlie. We'll definitely go for a Good Cause Petition and probably include the Children's Aid Society. He'd rather file it this month so as to get it before the more sympathetic judge, Carpentieri, who won't be coming up again until February. I'm to come in on Wednesday to sign the petition. Dr. Thomas will have signed it Monday, and it will be filed probably on Monday or Tuesday, the 26th or 27th.

It seemed we were *always* deciding on a good-cause petition. True, this time it was going to happen. But it had been
"going to happen" so many times.

At least I now knew better than to take a rest from my
research. Just because my petition was about to be filed did
not mean the work I was doing would not be useful.

That work took me to the library to study microfilmed
editions of the *New York Times* for 1923. Reel after reel, I
read the obituary columns and death notices, seeking a Williams who was "beloved husband of . . . dear father of . . . "
three girls' names, one boy's. No relevant Williams's death
notice appeared. Instead, a tiny "Public Notice" on July 6,
1923, jumped to my eyes:

> Information Wanted of Florrie Deener, adopted 25 years
> ago by a Mrs. Mott, living at Kings Highway, Coney Is-
> land; by her uncle Johann Hunter, care Jacob Stamper, 335
> East 86.

I worked out the time span: Florrie Deener would have
been adopted in 1898, so now she would be at least seventy-
five years old.

Suddenly I was remembering a picture I had seen fourteen years before. There had been a photograph on the cover
of *Life* magazine—the weekend before I had first sought psychiatric help—of an elderly man who had enjoyed a full, rich
life. I had not understood then why the photograph upset me
so deeply. Today, the same feelings were emerging, but this
time I could articulate them: Would I ever be like that elderly
gentleman? Would I ever be able to look back on a life in
which I had participated? Or must I grow into an old woman,
and still be a child? I could not bear to be Florrie Deener,
seventy-five years old, at the end of a life that had not yet
begun.

I began reading the death notices in the daily papers,
too. I looked for Williamses. I looked for people with unusual

last names. I looked for any dying that touched a family with one brother and three sisters.

> *Search Diary, Saturday, 17 Nov. 1973*
> *ALMA meeting—my second—larger group. Excellent rundown by Florence. Some new people, just starting searches. Talks by a natural mother, to be united with a twenty-five-year-old son next month, has talked with him on phone—a tear-jerker for those of us who long to find a mother like her. Followed by adoptee Jessie Weinstein, who found her mother dead, but has had reunions with her three older siblings (poverty—so as the last child, she was given away). Irish Catholic family "with a little Jewish sister." Brothers, who hadn't spoken for 20 years, now reconciled, thanks to Jessie, and her (never known before) existence—and appearance.*

One of the new people, Lyn Cobb, a vivacious blonde teacher of twenty-eight, asked me afterwards for advice about searching. Lyn knew the hospital of her birth but felt it would be useless to go there for help. No, she ought at least to try, I insisted, surprised to hear myself sounding confident and knowledgeable.

We stayed on in the meeting hall, perhaps forty or fifty of us, milling around for almost two hours after the formal talks had been concluded, giving and receiving advice, making new friends, catching up on old friends' news. April, I learned, had at last succeeded with her adoptive parents. There had been another scene of raging hysterics, but on her next try April had been handed her adoption papers. Now her parents were their normal selves again, and April possessed a birth name.

Many of the adoptees were completely without family. Usually raised by older couples, adoptees tended to be younger than other people when their parents died. They were younger when they lost their grandparents, aunts, uncles. It seemed, too, that adoptees more often were only children. Furthermore, if any relatives remained after the adoptive parents' death, those family members who had never accepted adoption then felt free to drop their pretenses of relationship. And so frequently the adoptee in mid-life was again alone, and again different.

But here at our meetings, we had become our own family. We were kin, pouring out stories and sharing experiences and caring for each other. Everything we had ever felt about being adopted was spilling out. Pains from the past, never acknowledged even to the self, now screamed their memories out loud. We were related, as well, by the extreme intensity of our searching. For each of us, the search, once begun, became a total commitment and preoccupation. It was as though our searching selves, repressed for so long, now had to make up for all that lost time.

When I went for my appointment with Charlie, the petition was not ready for signing. Charlie, with Ron Tucker "sitting in," reported a new twist: For persons adopted *before* 1947, he informed me, the court held only their orders of adoption. In 1947 the law had changed, and after that date copies of the agency files had been included in the court records. This meant that it was pointless for me to petition for the court's record, as I already possessed its one document, my order of adoption. The records I wanted were held solely by the agency, and thus we would have to include the agency in the proceeding. Depending on the agency's attitude, this might present some difficulty, noted Charlie. But I was delighted to hear his determination. We would be petitioning for the agency's files in their entirety. This was what I had been after all along.

Charlie speculated aloud about who was counsel for the Children's Aid Society, while Ron nodded sympathetically. I had a sense that this was all an old boys' club, and that they were hoping that the agency's counsel would be "one of them." Somebody said something about compromise, but that to me was unthinkable so I dismissed it. More important was the hint that this might all go so smoothly between friendly lawyers that I might see my records first and then not even have to file a formal petition.

In spite of myself, I was impressed that all this wall-to-wall gentility really functioned. I did not like the Establishment, but I was awed by the fact of its existence. It was not a myth in the minds of those of us who opposed it but a genuine functioning machine. The polite phrases, casual references, and confusing remarks were wheels in motion. Although I was disappointed about not signing the petition today and still only discussing its drafting, there was reason for optimism. I could bear another four or five days of waiting.

> *Search Diary, Wednesday, 21 Nov. 1973*
> *A call later from Charlie, just as Emily, Guy, coming home from school on start of Thanksgiving holiday: Children's Aid Society lawyer is Charlie's brother's father-in-law! And his brother's attorney! Partner of ever-so-prestigious firm of Curry, Pell. (Here we go round the mulberry bush.)*
> *Followed by some thinking: 1) I must not agree to any "compromise." 2) I must continue to hound Charlie re the "right to copy"—lest I be rushed when reading my file and make boo-boos. 3) And, as I think of it now, I must see my records by next Thursday, Nov. 29, so that if there is anything missing, I can still file the formal petition on Friday, the last day of November and thereby not miss Judge Carpentieri.*

Thanksgiving weekend brought a long, wild letter from Melia, five pages of search instructions concluding, "P.S. You didn't say, but I bet your lawyer flipped over that petition. At least, he will know now that you are serious." She was right: It was Melia's legally inadequate petition that had given me faith and courage and hope, but it was the formalism of the legal profession that would give me my papers. Homemade petitions, the only kind most of my friends could ever know, would never win. Damn.

How I hated my connections, my entrees, my relationship to the Establishment. It made me angry to be winning not by the truth but by chance membership in this thin-aired upper atmosphere. How despicable that those who were less "fortunate" than I, without access to this gentlemanly world, would not be treated with the same politeness and sense. I was furious and shocked at the unjust ease of my imminent victory.

Charlie's draft of my petition arrived Monday. It was dry, boring, and beautiful. The only inaccuracy was in my name. I called Charlie to ask that I be allowed to use my name as I used it, Katrina Maxtone-Graham. No, said Charlie, it would be better for this proceeding if I were Katrina Kanzler Maxtone-Graham. I did not want to bring the Kanzler name into this, I pleaded; it had nothing to do with them. Besides, I had dropped my adoptive name immediately upon marriage. Charlie insisted, I had to be Katrina Kanzler Maxtone-Graham, because the Kanzlers were mentioned in the 1939 adoption decree. Repressing my resentment that even now I could not choose my own name, I finally acquiesced. Winning my papers was more important; and Charlie was, without question, going into action at last.

Charlie explained that "nothing goes on" in the courts on Fridays; so "to keep it with Carpentieri," the last day for filing would have to be Thursday.

Search Diary, Tuesday, 27 Nov. 1973
      To Charlie's, to sign petition. He'd talked with "Uncle Andy," whose "special baby" (to use his unfortunate phrase) is the Children's Aid Society. Uncle Andy was startled to hear how much information had been given out. ("Gee, what are they doing over there? They shouldn't have told her all that.") He'd instructed them not to say anything. By "leaking,"

*the agency has apparently decreased its ability to
prove "privilege."*

*Uncle Andy is reportedly a great guy, but as it
now stands it sounds as though he is rather low in
consciousness.*

*The next step is: Charlie has to speak to Uncle
Andy, to make sure whether he's calling it the Children's Aid Society, or the State Charities Aid Association, and which is the correct address. Then the
petition is filed, the 28th or 29th. (You can be sure it
will be the 29th.) Then the Clerk of the Court orders
the Children's Aid Society to show cause why my relief should not be granted, and a date is set—minimum 8 days—but more likely to fit into the lawyers'
lunch schedules. At which time Uncle Andy either
appears with a cause, or simply does not show up.
In the former case, we then move on to hearings. In
the latter case, the Court then sends out an Order for
the file to be opened—which Order consumes a week
or two. Then people get on their telephones and arrange a convenient date for me to read my file.*

*Uncle Andy appears to have implied that via
the petition is a better way, rather than an "informal" showing. (And, he's right—if he'd favored me
over others, I'd have blasted him from here to King-
dom Come, so he'd better do it straightforwardly.)*

I had signed my petition. The key points were there:

9. Your petitioner is desirous of obtaining access to
and inspecting the sealed records pertaining to her adoption and believes that she has demonstrated sufficient
good cause to enable this Court to issue an order allowing
such access and inspection.

10. Your petitioner is also desirous of obtaining any
and all information concerning her family background and
her life prior to her adoption which are in the possession

83

of State Charities Aid Association or the Children's Aid Society. . . .

Attached to the petition were the death certificates of my adoptive parents and my "good cause shown"—the letter, typed in affidavit form, which Dr. Thomas and I had worked on together in his office. I was on the runway to freedom.

chapter six

COMPROMISE

Search Diary, Wednesday, 28 Nov. 1973
   Uncle Andy will contest it. He's apparently willing to give me the information I wish ("What does she want to know?"), if the Court so orders; but not to open up the entire file. Charlie is not even upset. In a court case, says Charlie, I may end up with far less than this—plus, of course, a lot of expense—so this "compromise" is being presented to me as not only the better alternative, but also as being "exactly what I want, anyway." I can't buy that.
   And how Dr. Thomas is going to take a compromise, Lord only knows. I told Charlie precisely what it is I do want to know: Cold, hard, specific facts. Names, dates, addresses.
   Meanwhile, the rush is only in my head, as Charlie has out-and-out refused to file the petition. He can't displease Uncle Andy. Natch.

However unbearable it was to accept compromise questions, half-answers to what I really wanted to know, I knew I had to. Still, in my covering letter to Charlie, I stated my position clearly:

What I *really* want to know is *everything;* everything there is to know, every scrap of paper that has been withheld from me for thirty-eight years, every mystery that is controlled by others, and for which I, a sane adult citizen of the United States, must grovel and compromise. Please understand that I am stating but a *fraction* of what I would like to know; and that I am accepting this compromise out of desperation.

My first request was for "a real copy of my own original birth certificate in full." The questions followed. I began by asking for the names, birthdates, and occupations of my grandmother, grandfather, aunts and uncle. Next I wrote the questions about my parents:

My Father: I would like full name, date of birth, place of birth, place of residence in New York area, place of residence other than New York area, place where he grew up (if different), college attended; cause of death, date, place; full occupation details; marital status (in 1934) with full details. If known, I'd like to know, too, if he married after 1934, plus details. Was he in the Armed Services?

My Mother: Her full name and birthdate.
Where was she born?
Where did she grow up?
Where did she go to school?
Where did she live—exactly—when she knew my father (1934)? If different, where did she live during the period of my fostering (1935-1938)?
Where did she work—exactly—in 1938 (1935-1940)?
What were her positions? (She apparently had promotions.)
When did she marry? Was her husband an older man?
What sort of man? What is her married name? Why did she return to the agency in 1943? Where was she living at that time? (You may omit street address, if you have to.)
I would like to have the dates of my mother's, and my, stays at Booth Memorial Hospital. Also, why Booth? Was there a family (or other) interest in the Salvation Army itself?

After leaving Booth, and prior to being brought to State Charities Aid (i.e. approx. June '35 to Dec. '37), was I under the jurisdiction of the Salvation Army? If not, then under what agency or charity?

Foster Homes: I would like exact length of each stay, full names of foster parents, names of other children in homes, precise locations of homes, and any other details re influences. Am interested in frequency of mother's visits and my reactions to same, also her reactions. Also, my activities in later homes. I am especially interested in fullest details regarding the second foster home (about June '36 until Dec. '37) and also the potential adoptive home that followed. If available, please include physical descriptions of house, play yard, etc. of both.

When was the last time I saw my mother?

When was the last time my mother saw me?

The last time I saw her, did I know who she was?

How did I relate to her? Was I hostile at that time? Did I like her?

The last time she saw me, did she know it was the last time? How did she feel? How did she behave?

Did she receive a payment for relinquishment? Did the Kanzlers make a payment to the agency for adoption? Amounts, please.

Post Script: And please, if the facts are other than has been implied to me, if my mother was a resident of a mental institution and my father was an escaped convict on a raping spree—don't be afraid. I can bear the answers, I can bear the facts and the truth. Truth can be borne, but I can't go on with the questions. The terror is the questions.

When I discussed my questions with Charlie, his only objection was to my asking whether my father had been in the military! That query, Charlie said, could tip off the agency that I was searching. I wondered what Charlie believed all the other questions might be indicating.

Search Diary, Thursday, 29 Nov. 1973
   Charlie has talked with Andy. Yes, Andy is willing to give out all this information if the Court orders him to do so. But, because he doesn't know what's in the file, he does not want to have to give up all of it. And—believe this—we are going to file the petition after all!
   The problem appears to be that none of the legal fellows quite knows how to cope with all of this—neither Andy, nor Charlie, nor de Judge. Anyway, everyone is going to try to find a legal way to grant me this info, because my psychiatrist says so.

Search Diary, Friday, 30 Nov. 1973
   Called D'Arcy. Asked her to send in, for me, for death cert. of potential grandfather Lazarus.
   Called Salvation Army, re its address in '35. Captain out, was given the Brigadier. Gave brief personal bit. She confirmed that 314 E. 15 was correct address for Booth. And then she asked me to "come see her sometime." I asked, "What can I do for you?" and she said, "Just have a cup of coffee." I said yes, sometime. It was a very strong invitation. What on earth did she mean by that? Does she have info? Or, the worst, is she going to save my soul? Oh, dear, I have to find out. And yet I have to make like it's all for coffee.

My petition was filed, my questions read, Uncle Andy had said yes. There was nothing to do now but wait. December was here. This was going to be the best Christmas ever.
   I had my first vague fantasy of actually meeting my mother. She was hovering in shadow, in the background. All I could see was that her hair was dark brown. Her clothes were dark brown, too. In the foreground three men were approaching me. They were her sons, three short, squat men with heavy, thick shoulders. Were they really here to greet me?

88

Then it came clear: They were being sent by my mother to stop me before I could get to her. The three of them were going to hurt me, kill me. Broad and stupid, they were pressing closer. It was useless to try to reason with them; all they knew were force and orders. I appealed to the craggy dark-haired figure floating in the shadows behind, but she was not paying any attention. Instead she was shrieking piercing yet inaudible orders of destruction, and her three henchmen were moving in on me so that I saw nothing but their impenetrable, dark square shoulders.

> *Search Diary, Thursday, 6 Dec. 1973*
> *Coffee with Brigadier—a big nothing. Had an (agreeable) argument re "rights of adoptee vs. natural mother." (Not only a waste of time, but an adversary opinion as well!)*
> *Called Dept. of Health to inquire re those mysterious numbers on my birth cert. They don't know either, but maybe if I came in . . .*

At the next ALMA meeting Lyn Cobb, the teacher, rushed to me, bubbling with excitement. She had gone back to the hospital of her birth, the New York Foundling Hospital, and the seventy-year-old nun in the records room had given Lyn her mother's name, Theresa Owen, *and* her mother's address at the time she had signed the surrender! Said the nun to Lyn: "Why, any mother would be *proud* to have a daughter like you!"

Lyn and I sat together for the talks. The first speaker was a social worker who was also an adoptee. Her thesis that "there are some adopted people who should not do a search" was, I noted mildly in my diary, "a condescension not well received."

The second speaker was Audrey, a small, gentle woman in her late forties who had been actively searching for the past ten years. Despite numerous returns to her agency, Audrey had been able to obtain virtually no information. She had neither a birth name nor a birth date; she had no order of adoption. The only document Audrey possessed was a particularly weird birth-by-adoption certificate. Matching this certificate number against the birth certificate numbers of all female infants born in New York City in 1926, Audrey had finally been able to determine that she was born Yvette Klotz. She had located the woman who must be her mother and had placed the critical telephone call. The middle-aged voice on the other end of the wire had been exceedingly unpleasant, had refused to put the elder Klotz on the phone, and had finally identified herself as "her daughter, Yvette Klotz." And so the woman was; additional conversation confirmed it. Audrey was back at zero. The disagreeable daughter had been so nasty, however, that quiet Audrey had at last exploded, "Well, what makes you so *sure* you're the *real* Yvette Klotz?"

The audience cheered. Audrey, who had since got a lead on another birth name, Jennie Abzug, was hoping to place an ad in the "Public Notices" of the *New York Times*. We had all thought about doing that. But did our mothers read the *New York Times?* The *Times*, Audrey went on, was questioning the advertisement's "acceptability" and would let her know early next week. Remembering the Florrie Deener ad, I was optimistic.

Everyone I talked with at the meeting was enthusiastic about my bringing a case to court. Audrey herself was waiting to hear from a lawyer friend who was investigating how she could have her adoption abrogated and thus her records released. Another adoptee, Becky, was considering suing her agency for malpractice; her adoptive parents would join with her.

The consensus among my ALMA friends was that with my psychiatric grounds I might easily win my file. It was well known around ALMA that one member's husband, a prominent psychiatrist, had been given all his wife's information— names, addresses, everything—by a New York agency just for the asking. If a psychiatrist who was simply a husband could be granted information, then one who was actually treating a patient would surely be successful.

There was a lot of discussion that day about the demands made on adoptees for "gratitude." As children, we had readily accepted the world's commands to be thankful for our enforced differentness. I remembered so well proclaiming, "I'm adopted," to anyone in sight; and the invariable responses of, "You're lucky. Just think, you would be in an institution." When we reached adulthood our peers became grown-ups, but we were still seen in terms of obligation to that childhood "rescue." Interest in our births or our ancestry or our genes was forever disallowed for the simple reason that our adoptive parents had once, long ago, decided to become parents. Throughout our lives, friends and strangers alike continued to leap to our parents' imagined defense: "But aren't you grateful to the people who raised you?" Because we had once been adopted, even the mildest expressions of curiosity about ourselves made us "ingrates."

I was learning more and more, not only how little my search had to do with "ingratitude," but how little it had to do with my adoptive parents. My unhappiness as a child had been not their doing, I was beginning to realize, but rather the simple fact of adoption.

Audrey's ad appeared in the next Sunday's issue of the *New York Times:*

Woman born October, 1926, at 57 East 100 Street, N.Y.C., with name Jennie Abzug seeks information on parents or other relatives. X2662 Times.

With my case so near resolution, I was no longer bothering to go to the library. I was trying to concentrate on the coming Christmas season, always a hard time of year for me. I hated shopping, I got anxious about making decisions, I was plagued with spurts of energy and paralyzing panic.

Lyn called to report that she had been back to visit the nun again, and this time had been able to read the records

91

herself. "I'm sitting at this little desk, right? The whole file spread out in front of me, nuns walking by. And all this time there's this sign over my head, 'It is absolutely forbidden, blah blah blah, pursuant to Section 114 of the Domestic Relations Law . . . ' and all this hellfire and brimstone, and I'm taking notes!"

Lyn now had her mother's address as a teenager, her grandparents' names and their origin in Indiana, and the information that her grandfather had died in a bus accident in 1923.

From the records Lyn had also learned that there had been much pain and disruption in her mother's own childhood. The file's description of Theresa's behavior with her child was further disheartening. Theresa had never been to the hospital for prenatal care and had arrived there only in time to give birth; two days later, Theresa had run off, leaving her child. It took the hospital six months to track her down for the surrender signature. The possibility of rejection, which all of us faced, was looming larger for Lyn.

Audrey, too, called with news. Hoping to bring a case to court, she had contacted the Legal Aid Society to ask about financial assistance. But, she had learned, to receive help from the Legal Aid Society one had first to be charged with a crime.

Search Diary, Thursday, 13 Dec. 1973

Received Death Cert. for George E. Williams. It could be he. Address: 146 W. 78. No wife's name. Father: Edward; Mother: Mary Wales. Cemetery: Kensico. Undertaker, Charles Medlar, not listed in contemporary book.

Called Kensico Cemetery. Plot is single. George E. is in Lot B, range 26, grave 25. No names on records.

Called Protestant Welfare Agencies. Spoke to a social worker, asking which agency cared for me from July '35 thru Nov. '37. Seems on my side, but

*tends to psychoanalyze you. Told me to try State
Board of Social Welfare. She also suggested that I
could have asked to talk to Mrs. Meinhauser's "Supervisor" (and sort of accused me of lying, when I
said I didn't even know Mrs. Meinhauser had one).*

*Charlie lunched with Uncle Andy, who (Uncle
Andy) has put the case in the hands of some other
lawyer—still Curry, Pell—called Friedman.*

*146 W. 78 no longer standing. Block is public
school, 1950's architecture.*

For these past few weeks I had been troubled with back
pains. John was urging me to see a doctor, but I refused, sus-
pecting that the problem was emotionally caused. Besides, I
was too busy with Christmas preparations to sit around in a
doctor's office. If I were to sit, I would rather it were at my
desk where the phone might ring with good news.

Search Diary, Friday, 14 Dec. 1973

*Call from D'Arcy: She wants to start a search
workshop. She suggested having it at my place; I
suggested at meeting, to attract largest number of
participants.*

*Talked to Charlie. In sum, it'll probably be Jan-
uary before we get anywhere. But, it does appear
that once we go into our Court meeting—which is
closed, and sounds very informal—then the order is
signed, and away we go. No further long delays. He
also says that Jerry Friedman may not—or may—
require another affidavit saying that yes, this is
what the doctor meant.*

So it seemed I was not to have my answers before Christmas.

Almost every day there was talk on the phone with Melia, and almost every night with Lyn or Audrey or both. It
was a network of shared knowledge and sympathy, and it

filled the hours of darkness before taking on the battle with insomnia and nightmares.

I had a fantasy plan—I called it my "cafeteria theory." If I called my mother and she rejected me over the telephone, I would go to the cafeteria in the place where she worked. I would stand in the cafeteria line behind my mother and, as we balanced our brown plastic trays with tin silverware and white rectangles of folded napkins sliding about, we would speak to one another. A few cheerful words, maybe a joke, a sharing of smiles. Then, as we turned away from the cashier and peered around the room, it would be only natural to carry our trays to the same green-flecked table. The next day, I would go again to the cafeteria, and my mother and I would greet each other like friends. Lunch after lunch we would meet as though by chance in my mother's cafeteria and sit together as we ate. We would talk about things and get to like each other, as people who talk together do. Then one day, when my mother had accepted me as just one more ordinary likeable person—the younger friend who was no different from all her other friends—then I would tell her who I was, and she would not refuse me.

Audrey received only one response to her newspaper ad. It was not even from a possible relative, but from a genealogist who was offering help. Audrey, who always looked for the bright side, did not seem depressed by her results. "It was so nice of someone to answer," she exclaimed, "and he even said he would come to our next ALMA meeting."

I breathed in and out, ticking away the holidays. I tried to concentrate on my family, I tried to enjoy the present of the children's Christmas joy, I tried not to count the seconds until "after Christmas," when I would have my answers.

D'Arcy received the death certificate of my potential grandfather Lazarus. Lazarus Williams was black.

Just before the New Year a large envelope came from McKinley and Hart. It was a proposal for an out-of-court settlement.

NOW, THEREFORE, the parties agree this matter be
settled as follows:

The Children's Aid Society and the State Charities
Aid Association will give the petitioner the following information to the extent contained in their records.

The body of the document was a close paraphrase of my
letter! Charlie was no longer taking the "let's pretend she's
not searching" stance; this was a very specific request for
identifying details about all my relatives and foster homes.
Charlie really had understood. Although I resented receiving
"information" rather than the records themselves, I would
make my voice sound delighted when I spoke to him. Inside,
though, it rankled to compromise principle in order to win, to
lie to obtain truth.

chapter seven

THE AGENCY'S DECISION

It was mid-January when I next made an entry in my diary.

Search Diary, Monday, 14 Jan. 1974
   The legal picture has been primarily one of Charlie's long weekends—Christmas, New Year's, etc.—plus Uncle Andy's Mondays and Tuesdays in Virginia, as well as a post-Christmas cruise! Between Christmas and New Year's I received the document for settling out of court, which was to be— and indeed, was—agreed upon by Charlie, Jerry Friedman, and Uncle Andy (when latter finally returned).
   Then, at the last moment, the hitch: Friedman took it to the agency, and the agency said no.

My initial reaction to the agency's decision was bitterness about the time I had wasted in not pursuing library research. Then I began finding comfort in their opposition. By refusing to divulge the information referred to in the settlement, the agency was confirming its possession of that information. Surely it would not fight to conceal that which it did not have. My nagging fears that the whole story might have been an invention, that the agency did not even know all those names and addresses, that there was no foster care file, were assuaged. Moreover, thanks to the agency's obstinacy, I was not going to be obliged to compromise.

But the decision was definitely a surprise. Everything had been falling so smoothly, albeit slowly, into place with the lawyers that it had never really occurred to me that the agency would not be similarly accommodating. I heeded my lawyers; did not the agency heed theirs? It would have been so easy for the agency to have said yes that I felt hurt by their no.

Immediately, as though in rebuttal of the agency's deafness, I addressed myself to another reputed bastion of impenetrability, the Bureau of Vital Records, to request once again my birth certificate as Judith Virginia Williams. I included this time a personal note, flamboyantly written with a felt-tip pen.

> Please, Please!
> Is there anyone human there?
> I was born Judith Virginia Williams on March 9, 1935, Cert. 6742, in Manhattan.
> I want to know my real mother's name—on my real certificate. If you are unable to send the certificate (copy) itself, then you can just copy out the information. All I am asking for, really, is just the truth.
> Thank you, thank you.
> JUDITH V. WILLIAMS

I enclosed the usual check made out to the Bureau of Vital Records for $2.50.

Charlie's voice was still full of optimism and energy and the legal situation did not yet strike me as threatening. There was action in court; a "big meeting" was scheduled for this week. Next week there would be another. Success was surely around the corner.

I was not invited to attend these "big meetings," but Charlie's reports of them disquieted me. "The agency says you don't really have good cause, that your motives are political." "They guess that you are a member of ALMA, they claim you are trying to change the laws." "They think the story is a fake and that you just want to find your mother."

97

"They say, 'She's waited thirty-eight years, she can wait a bit longer.'"

"Explain to them, Charlie."

"A very high level conference at the Children's Aid Society," said Charlie for the umpteenth time, "and they made the decision: *'We're going to fight this one.'*"

Incredulous, mystified, then ultimately certain, I realized that the vehicle through which "the child's best interest" was meant to be served was my enemy. The agency had chosen to give battle in court.

I threw myself into research. I sent in for a George Williams's 1907 marriage license. The couple were both West Indian. Checking voters' records, I learned that at 146 West 78th Street—George E.'s residence at the time of his death— no one had voted in the 1920 election. No one at that address had possessed a telephone until 1938.

Melia managed to uncover that a George Williams's widow was named Lillie. So from all the Lillies and Lillians who had died between 1935 and the present, I picked out seven whose age most likely could make them my grandmother. Since each request to Worth Street for a death certificate seemed to consume two months, I decided to try instead a mass request. Naming the seven, I requested a death certificate for "only such of the above, who was the widow of a George Williams," and enclosed a check to cover the price of three.

Meanwhile I argued with Charlie. "Protect my mother? That's talking garbage, Charlie."

"That's the agency's position, that they must protect—"

"Protection, privileges, politics—that's all I ever hear. Are they out of their heads?"

Charlie sighed and changed the subject. He asked, again, that I not go to future ALMA meetings.

"I don't see how being discovered in a church hall with sixty adopted people can jeopardize a medical request for help!"

"I just don't want to risk someone seeing you."

"Is belonging to ALMA illegal?" The refrain was familiar. The entire conversation was familiar. "How am I political? A good cause is not precedent—you told me that yourself. Besides, how many adoptees are there with fourteen years of psychiatry and three and a half years in foster homes?"

"I'm not insisting, Katrina. I'm only suggesting that you would do yourself a favor if you were not seen in public with Florence Fisher."

In my head, I argued with the agency. I took on all the old saws: The adoptee will find a prostitute, the adoptee will be upset, the adoptee is going to come upon a Pandora's Box. While the rest of the population coped with life's unpleasantnesses, the adoptee was presumed to be somehow less capable. Why not ask me, Agency—or ask my doctor—whether I am afraid of finding a sixty-year-old prostitute! You know what, Agency? I think she would be an accomplished and intriguing character, my prostitute. And an independent businesswoman, besides. So she sold her body. But it was hers, after all. She was not like an adoption worker who sells the bodies and the souls of little children.

Ah, but our mothers might be, instead, the mayor's wife, and we might be mercenary blackguards. The adoptee, formerly traumatized by finding a prostitute, was suddenly the blackmailer of a mayor's wife. And our mothers, I noted, were never the mayor herself.

For her birthday, Lyn Owen Cobb put an ad in the *Daily News:* "For Theresa. Thinking of you on my 29th birthday. Love, Lyn Owen."

I had been talking to lawyers for nine months now, and I still had never seen a courtroom.

Yes, Your Honor, I *am* a member of ALMA. And of Common Cause. And of the Fortune Society, and the Metropolitan Museum of Art, and the PTAs of three different schools.

Audrey telephoned, very excited. She had located a woman called Ellie whose sister, now dead for many years, might have been Audrey's mother. Ellie had become quite weepy on the telephone, imagining that Audrey could be the

99

daughter of her beloved departed sister. Audrey and Ellie were meeting for lunch on the weekend.

Someone told April that she was "using her adoption as a crutch," which left April feeling hurt and confused. This accusation, a new one, was coming with increasing frequency as the subject of adoption was discussed more openly. Before, when adoption was perfect and unmentionable, no one noticed that we limped. Now, with the unwelcomed hearing of our discomforts, our handicaps were acknowledged—but only as symptoms of some neurosis.

Adoption was not our excuse, but society's way out. The myth was that our mothers did not want us; the truth was that society did not want to face what we represented—illegitimacy, misfortune, poverty. Thus as children we had been silently "placed" beneath the carpet of altruism. But now as adults we were showing our wounds and naming their cause, and the message was unwelcome.

"'No!' Ellie took one look at me and said, 'No!'"
"Oh, Audrey . . ."
"Just, 'No!'" Audrey gave a faint laugh.
"I'm so sorry."
"I guess she was all prepared to see her sister walk in, reincarnated. She was very disappointed." Audrey was silent for a moment. "So was I."

Melia's letters kept pouring in. Occasionally they were brief, just three or four instructions and a cheery sign-off, "Let's mark the first week of February as 'Judith's week.'" But more often these were eight- or ten-page letters, lines and lines of handwriting caressing the spirit. I began to notice that I was only skimming from paragraph to paragraph. There were so many instructions, so many wild goose chases, so much groveling without results. For each formal request— "Would you please aid me in establishing my exact whereabouts in public and private child care agencies between March 9, 1935, and December 7, 1937? Please inform me if I was baptized? What faith? The date?"—there were also hours of careful composition, the neatly printed return envelope, days of vain waiting, unreasonable hoping, and certain rejection. Too much work for too much hurt and too little return.

Only about one in ten of Melia's suggestions had at least a prayer of result. That one I would muster up the strength to try. By skipping the others now, I was leaving a safety valve for some more unbearable future.

I dreamed of rescue. I dreamed that one day the mail would bring a plain, unidentified envelope with an ordinary index card inside. On the index card, typewritten, would be my mother's first name, "Virginia" or "Alice" or "Jane."

Amazingly, an index card did arrive, not in the anonymous envelope of my dreams, but in my own return envelope from the Bureau of Vital Records, enclosing another copy of my certificate of birth. The certificate was, again, the birth-by-adoption one—the useless one, long form. But enclosed with it was an unexpected white card, containing one sentence written in a firm red-penned hand: "Sorry, but this is the only record of your birth which we have."

That single compassionate statement brought hours of comfort. I was grateful, too, for its information; for if the sender of that index card had no access to any other record, I did not have to waste more money and time, trying again, waiting again, failing again.

"So I sign myself Theresa Owen, and I say how I have to review my Social Security status for . . . "

"No, Lyn, you can't—"

"Look, are they going to put me in jail for trying to find my own mother? I can see it now: Channel Five News . . . "

"They'll stick you in the clink, Lyn, then where will you be?"

" 'Schoolteacher goes to jail for looking for her mother!' Listen, that's *great*. She might be watching the program."

Also in January, Audrey's genealogist, Izzie Lerner,

wrote me a letter. Izzie remembered me from the search
workshop at the recent ALMA meeting. Explaining that genealogists had access to certain documents other people were
not allowed to view, Izzie offered to look up various documents on my behalf. His letter concluded, "I'd be interested
to know if permission to research is granted."

How nutty it all was! An unemployed genealogist mod-
estly requesting in writing to aid, without recompense, a bare
acquaintance; while a wealthy private agency, whose charge I
had once been, was refusing its help.

I was more than willing for assistance of any kind. Izzie
began by copying out, by hand, *every* Williams listing in the
1915-16 City Directory; he mailed Xerox copies to Melia, who
highlighted the most likely and forwarded the package to me.

My mother, so the agency claimed, must be "protected."
But from what? What sort of protection could my mother possibly need from me? And if I was so dangerous, what about
protecting my husband and my children and my friends; the
whole city of New York, perhaps.

Why was I given no opportunity to answer their fears, I
asked Charlie. Could I not just meet the judge and the agency's lawyers at one of their secret meetings and let them in-
vestigate for themselves whether I was a hazard?

No.

"Why not?"

"No. You can't be there. They could put you on the
stand."

"But I'd *like* that, Charlie."

"They would ask you questions, like were you a member
of ALMA."

"They told me about ALMA themselves when they told
me about *The Search for Anna Fisher.*"

"We don't want you there, Katrina."

"Did they tell me about ALMA, just so they could now
accuse—"

"Of course, we'll let you know if you're needed."

What about the judge? He, too, had read my petition. He knew that my doctor was not a fly-by-night, twenty-five-dollars-for-a-one-shot "yes, she needs this." How could the judge allow these accusations to be made behind my back and in his presence? What was going on? Remembering Mrs. Meinhauser's "There are *certain things*, Mrs. Maxtone-Graham, which you will *never* know," I tried to imagine what "certain things" could inspire so vehement a fight.

My diary notes changed, became sparse. I noted only the hardest facts, only the most relevant. It was as though I did not want to open that diary at all unless I had something hopeful to add.

One safety valve was my growing assortment of unpursued suggestions from Melia; another was the possibility of "going to Tracers." From the old-timers at ALMA, I had heard that the Tracers Company of America was a New York-based detective agency whose director, Ed Goldfader, was both sympathetic and discreet. Tracers' fees were reputed to be stiff though fair, its methods aboveboard, and its successes fantastic. All of us imagined "going to Tracers" as a potential last resort; now I seriously considered approaching them.

But I sensed the ridiculousness of asking a detective to find "a Miss Williams who was in New York on March 9, 1935." Until I had at least one more certain fact, I felt I ought to wait. Besides, there was to be another meeting with the judge on February 5.

This particular appearance in court was very important, Charlie told me. Again, I would not be welcome. The judge's name, I noticed, was now different. The case had been moved from Judge Carpentieri to Judge Vernon Sylvane. No matter; both judges were really equally fine, said Charlie, and my prospects were as good as ever.

Lyn received a death certificate for her grandfather and had some new addresses and names to work with.

On February 1, I sent to New York State for a birth certificate for Judith Virginia Williams in the one-in-a-million hope that my mother had registered my birth not only in New York City but out of town as well, and that this second certificate had remained unsealed.

With Audrey, I wondered whether I could sue the agency. We thought it a splendid idea. I would sue for "abuse of power" and "obstruction of medical services." Maybe, considering how distraught and depressed I was becoming, throw in "jeopardizing the welfare of my minor children" too.

The more I recognized the determination of the agency's opposition, the more I realized how gratuitous it was. There had been an alternative. Actions of the past could be excused by lack of knowledge or by societal mythology. But now the agency's innocence was gone. The truth about adoption was being spoken aloud by many. The agency had heard the message of the adoption movement; they knew the difference between help and hurt. My case offered them the opportunity to perform a service to one individual, and even without threat to themselves. The effort would have been simple; the legal precedent would have been none or minuscule; the saving of time, money, and struggle would have been great. Here had been the agency's golden chance: They had received my formal petition, had read my doctor's statement, and had been advised in my favor by their own lawyers. In January, 1974, the agency had the information, the education, and the power to have acted differently.

I was not asking them to erase the past. I was asking them in the present to be kind. I could not—and still cannot—imagine an acceptable excuse for the knowing choice of unkindness in the present.

chapter eight

THE JUDGE'S PLAN

February 5—action at last. Today in Surrogate's Court the lawyers and the agency would be conferring about my petition. While they were meeting, I would be taping my first radio interview about my recently published book, *Pregnant by Mistake: The Stories of Seventeen Women;* later in the afternoon I would be starting a course in political philosophy. I was hopeful. The court case would soon be over, and the past could then take its place behind me. Here were stirrings, finally, of a future that would be my own.

> *Search Diary, Tuesday, 5 Feb. 1974*
> *Charlie went to Court—or, rather, a Joe Dono-hue (his fellow lawyer) did. News from Charlie: Donohue says, "Oh, you (agency) can't claim privilege. Only the mother can claim privilege." Judge Sylvane agreed! Sylvane is also reported to have said, re his "inferred" decision to have a court-ordered search for her: "Well, 99 percent of them want to see their children anyway!"*

It felt like a victory. The judge *knew* that mothers cared; the judge was wise, the judge was wonderful.

After the children were in bed, I turned to my philosophy notes on "the role of the individual within the cosmos," and began adding further thoughts. I spilled out five pages of points, queries, and therefores. What did it mean to be hu-

105

man? What were the basic human needs? Finally I scribbled tentatively, "To be believed—to be received—to be free to give love." This was what I really wanted to be working on: A definition of what it meant to be human; from that, a construction of a philosophy; and ultimately the development of a code for action.

I thought back over Charlie's report of the "big meeting" and basked in the judge's positive attitude. Now, however, his terms and their significance were clearer. The judge was, I realized, suggesting that my relief be dependent on my mother's "permission"! And who would look for her? The agency! Charlie had told me, but I had not absorbed it until now. The agency would conduct the search, and the agency would report to the court. Why, the agency could do what they pleased! They could tell my mother anything they wanted, they could tell her nothing at all. They might not even talk with her. After a "suitable" interval they could simply tell the court, "The petitioner's mother says no"—and no one could ever prove otherwise!

This had to be stopped.

Charlie immediately agreed with me: An agency report on my mother's verdict was absolutely unacceptable. Moreover, he was confident that the judge would understand our opposition. No matter how hard the agency might fight for this absurdity, it would never be allowed. Charlie was certain.

I pictured a meeting between Mrs. Meinhauser and my mother. I remembered Mrs. Meinhauser's foggy gaze, her peculiar notions, the smiling unreality of her conclusions. The question of "permission" aside, I knew I did not want my mother to be confronted with the same nonsense. I asked Charlie if it would be possible for the court to forbid the agency to communicate with my mother.

Charlie did not think the court could issue such an order to the agency, but, he added, it was unlikely for the agency to go to the bother of contacting my mother on their own. His assessment sounded reasonable. But 1 was uneasy that unsympathetic strangers at the Children's Aid Society knew her identity and her whereabouts.

There was to be another appearance in court in about ten days, Charlie told me. I asked, again, if these hearings could please take place in open court.

"If you start insisting on its being in open court, Katrina, the agency is only going to say your case is political."

"But it isn't."

"The agency says, 'If it's not political, then she should not mind the closed doors.'"

"But—"

"Look, Katrina, if it makes the agency happy, don't fight it."

It always ended the same way: Let the agency have its way in minor details; winning the papers was what mattered.

At least Charlie had dispelled my concerns. I just had to wait out the ten days until the next court hearing. I could do that.

I wondered if my mother had really said of my father, "He's dead now." Might she not have said, "He's gone now," meaning out of town, or gone out of her life? Was it possible that the social worker, versed in euphemisms, would have interpreted "gone" as "dead"? And what about my mother's "unusual married name"? Was it a truly unusual name? Or was it a name that was unusual to Mrs. Meinhauser? How unusual was unusual?

Lyn Cobb brought her adoptive mother, Natalie, to the February ALMA meeting. Natalie was an immediate hit. Everyone hugged her and kissed her. Natalie accepted, shyly, an invitation to address the group; she did not understand this adulation, she just loved Lyn, and she wanted Lyn's happiness; and if Lyn wanted to search, that was Lyn's business, not hers, and she was happy to help her daughter. Everyone cheered; Lyn beamed proudly.

The scheduled speaker was an adoptee who had found

her mother. No breakthroughs of my own were in sight, and I doubted whether my time could ever come. I glanced at Lyn beside me. Her face told me it was the same for her. It was the same for all of us who had heard the reunion stories: Joy for the narrator, gladness for the hope it gave the new people, and renewed rage at one's own specific roadblocks, which felt less like coincidences of luck and chance than like attacks at one's own person.

I whispered to her, "If I ever find, then it *really* will mean anyone can do it!"

"It's going to be me up there one day," Lyn whispered back, "and you, too! We'll have our day, Katrina, we'll all have our day!"

After the meeting, there was the customary move to the local cafeteria for yet more talk. Finally I went home. I felt depressed and let down. As always I had wanted the day never to end; always, once it had ended, I sat in lonely silence beside my desk telephone. It was the one night each month when none of us would reach out to friends over the telephone. We had already experienced too much emotion for one day, too much earthiness, too much reality.

I was becoming obsessed with reading the newspaper. In particular I studied the Watergate editorials and the Op-Ed essays from the *New York Times*. I felt a kinship between the adoptees' struggle for information from social workers and the citizens' struggle for information from Nixon. I began clipping my favorite pieces; then I started a scrapbook. There was little else for me to be doing. I was waiting while other people performed a play I did not understand in a language that was not mine, a play in which I was the principal, but excluded, actor.

I read obituaries, all the obituaries. As I turned pages the name Judith kept cropping up. A Judith whose flute concert was reviewed, a Judith in politics. Judiths who wrote poems, Judiths who baked pies.

Batches of papers came in the mail from Izzie via Melia. All the Williamses in Manhattan in the 1915 state census, names, ages, names and ages of children, relationships, races, professions, addresses, places of birth. Izzie rejected nothing. Page after page, he copied out in full by hand, and mailed to Melia. Melia boiled them down and starred in red the families that were white and had a male and female child—the composition of my mother's family two years before her birth.

Izzie began on the 1917 military census. Melia starred the engineers, the stokers of engines, the seamen, the people living near Booth Memorial Hospital, the Georges, the Edwards, the J's. My head swam with confusion, but I double-starred the most particularly "likely" ones of Melia's.

Audrey learned from her lawyer friend that because her adoptive parents were deceased, she could not attempt to have her adoption abrogated as a ploy to obtaining her records.

On the theory that I might have been baptized under my birth name, I decided to try to locate a certificate of baptism for a Judith Virginia Williams, Protestant.

Search Diary, Monday, 11 Feb. 1974
Called Protestant Council of the City of N.Y., requesting baptismal certificate. Got a dreadful male snip saying, "What difference could it possibly make?" He suggested I go to the "Hall of Records at City Hall," then added that if I "at least knew" my denomination, "then" he'd have referred me on.

At noon on February 12, Lincoln's Birthday, Lyn Cobb telephoned: "I got her name! I found my mother!" The story came tumbling out. "This old lady, I'm on the long distance phone, and she says to hold on . . . from my grandfather's death certificate, his sister, my mother's aunt . . . an old lady in Nebraska . . . 'No, Theresa's not here, she lives in Manhattan, in New York' . . . and Theresa sent her a Christmas card

. . . 'Now you just wait, dearie, while I get the address . . . ' "

Even as Lyn told me the name I was flipping the pages in the Manhattan directory.

"And after she gives it, she says, 'Now, *what* was it you said you were calling about?' "

"Lyn! She's here!" I read her the listing.

"I've done it!" Lyn gasped. She was crying; and I was crying, too. "Do you understand, Katrina? I've done the impossible!"

Lyn called Theresa. A teenage voice told her that Theresa could be reached at work around 5:30; she would be home after 7:00.

Lyn and I spoke together several more times during the endless afternoon to discuss the best approach.

"That kid could be her kid, Katrina. What do you think? Isn't it better, calling her at work? Even if the boss is there? Don't you agree?"

"Absolutely. Besides, you ask her, 'Is this a good time to talk?' "

"That's *good*. I'll *use* that. But, Katrina, she'll probably think I'm calling to sell light bulbs. She'll be real edgy, 'Yeah, whaddya want?' Katrina, if she says, 'Whaddya want?' *then* what do I say?"

"Well, I guess, then you tell her."

"I suppose I do." Lyn paused. "Oh, Katrina, I'm scared!"

When Lyn called her mother just after 5:30 it was not, in fact, a "good time" for Theresa to talk. Theresa had acknowledged Lyn's identity, then asked her to call back in fifteen minutes.

From 5:45 until 6:00, I held Lyn's hand via telephone wire. She ran through the possibilities: Rejection, acceptance, hatred, Theresa-leaving-town-even-as-we-were-now-waiting. There were still seven minutes to go. We talked on, as though neither of us was peeking at her watch. Two more minutes.

Lyn's voice grew calm. "Okay, this is it. Whatever happens, I'll call you as soon as I finish."

Six o'clock. Dinner. John and the children all knew Lyn Cobb's story. We sat at the table, beaming, all listening for a continuing silence from the telephone.

Three minutes passed. Each minute that went by meant a more positive reception.

6:20. It was almost safe for us to relax, to eat our dinner, to continue with our own lives.

It was nearly eight before Lyn called me. Her mother's reception had been loving and lengthy. Lyn narrated their conversation, moment by moment. Her mother was wonderful, responsive, overjoyed. I scribbled down some of Theresa's responses: "What took you so long?" "Don't you think a mother worries about her child?" "I wondered if you cared enough to look for me." "I'd never make the same mistake again."

Theresa had surmounted the hardships of her life. Yes, she had run off from the hospital when Lyn was two days old—because she had heard that there were papers to sign! Theresa had disappeared to escape signing, to try to arrange her life so that she might be able to keep her child.

Theresa's story was a stunning lesson that these records we all craved so intensely and for which we fought so rigorously were but secondary sources, incomplete and potentially misleading. The primary source was still the human being. The truth was in Theresa, not in a file. Records at best were no more than signposts to the truth.

That night I lay in bed in the dark, very very late, and I cried. I cried to be the same as Lyn, to join her in her completion. I was hurt, not by my friend's success, but by my own failure.

On Friday morning, February 15, just before the start of Presidents' Weekend, I went to a meeting in the McKinley and Hart office of Joe Donohue. A tall, handsome fellow with a shock of sandy hair falling onto his forehead, Donohue was the lawyer who had attended the "big meeting" with Charlie. He looked as though he belonged more on a touch football field than in a courtroom. My disappointment at having to deal with someone other than Charlie was balanced by realizing that having two lawyers working on my case was a far cry from the old days of not being able to interest anyone.

Donohue was preparing an affidavit and wanted more details from me, so again I summarized the information Mrs. Meinhauser had given me about my various foster homes, my mother and her family, her jobs and subsequent marriage. Donohue listened quietly until I told him of Mrs. Meinhauser's declaration that my mother "might have," then, finally, "definitely had," told her husband she had been married before but had not acknowledged having had a child. Suddenly he began contradicting me. At first it seemed we were misunderstanding each other. Then it came clear that Donohue had also been given a story about what my mother had told her husband—and that the two stories did not jibe. In Donohue's version, there was no first marriage, but there was a child who had died. I did not know what to refute, nor what to believe.

Donohue next wanted to discuss Jerry Friedman's comments regarding my "alleged father." I was amused at the term, but Donohue soberly continued. At the hearing Friedman had claimed that my father was—Donohue looked very uncomfortable as he forced himself to utter the phrase—"a putative father."

"A what?"

"A putative father," repeated Donohue, slightly louder.

"What's that?"

"That your alleged father was . . . " He paused. Then he continued, as if displaying quiet courage under fire, "Was a putative father."

"Sorry, I don't know what 'putative' is."

" 'Putative' means unknown, uncertain," Donohue answered miserably. "A putative father is a father whose identity cannot be established, because, uh, because . . . "

"Because the woman can't tell which one he is?"

"That's the general idea." Donohue sighed.

Poor Donohue!

"You mean a sort of gang-bang by a group of twenty-nine-year-old, six-foot-one-inch, brown-haired, blue-eyed concert-goers with Irish-sounding names?"

Donohue appeared stunned by this refutation of Friedman. He asked more questions about what the agency had told me, all the while scribbling notes.

Charlie joined us, and all three of us then discussed the idea, put forward at the February 5 meeting, of the agency's searching for my mother. Donohue was as adamantly opposed to this as Charlie and I had been. We were all agreed, too, that the judge would see our points. But Charlie and Donohue continued to dwell on "the judge's expressed feeling that if the natural mother could be asked to waive her anonymity . . . "

"I thought we had already agreed," I said, "that this search was out."

"Not a search by the agency. By a third party. By someone acceptable to you."

"I don't accept any third parties."

"A search to ascertain if your mother would be willing to waive her rights."

"My mother doesn't *have* any rights over me." I glared at Donohue. "She signed them away, years ago. *No* one has superior rights over me as an adult."

"It is the court's suggestion that if your mother were asked," Donohue continued matter-of-factly, "and agreed to waive her anonymity . . . "

"Someone else would talk to my mother?" Bewildered, I looked at Charlie; he was nodding enthusiastically at Donohue.

" . . . It would obviate the need for a good-cause hearing," finished Charlie.

"No," I said.

"No what?"

"No anything. No search. No permission. No third party. No nothing."

I could be trapped forever if I were made dependent, at the age of thirty-eight, upon an unknown woman's uninformed whim. "It doesn't make sense," I told them. "My grounds are medical; I don't *need* my mother's permission for medical help. When I had a tumor removed last October, I didn't have to have her permission."

Donohue and Charlie glanced toward me, momentarily interested. But neither of them uttered a word.

"How is this any different? Why do I need my mother's permission for what is a medical request? I mean, it's not fair to *her*, either," I raged on, "some stranger bursting in with a briefcase and papers to sign. How can I be a party to that?"

Donohue stated calmly, "It's what the court wants."

"But not me. No way," I responded. "It's wrong. Everything is wrong. For everybody."

"The judge has already made up his mind, Katrina," said Charlie.

"The whole thing is immoral. Doesn't anyone understand?"

The two men stared at one another's shoes.

"Please," I heard myself begging, "please don't do this to me!"

Neither Charlie nor Donohue was meeting my eyes.

"You're my *friends!*" I was struggling not to cry.

After a long silence, Charlie spoke. "I'm sorry, Katrina, but you have no alternative."

The room was in motion. The windows, the furniture, the rug, all spinning in front of my eyes.

"It's a terrible position to be put into, setting me up to be kicked in the teeth—again."

"Maybe she'll say yes," Charlie gently suggested.

"And if she says no?"

"Well, then we can still have the good-cause hearing," stated Donohue.

I was descending in a whirlpool. Donohue was writing notes again; Charlie was explaining how this approach was intended to save all the trouble of a good-cause hearing. This way was easier, it was quicker, and it was cheaper, too.

"It will all be over," Charlie continued pleasantly, "and you can maybe avoid a hearing altogether. But if not, then you can have it anyway."

Through my daze, I could hear his words. "I'd rather have the hearing *first*," I replied.

"No, Katrina."

Here, at last, was the specific issue. "*That's* what I want. *First*, my hearing." I was rising to the surface again, my breath was returning. "The good-cause hearing is what this is all about, not my mother's opinions. I mean, the question is simply, *do* I, or *don't* I, have good cause?"

Mr. Donohue glanced up and stared me directly in the eye. His voice was soft but firm. "We are concerned, Katrina, that you might not win at a hearing."

This man Donohue astonished me more and more. I turned to Charlie for a contradiction.

"Joe is right," agreed Charlie, avoiding my gaze and nodding toward Donohue. "If there is a hearing, you might lose."

Stunned, I looked from one serious face to the other.

"That's what we are worried about," Charlie continued. "There is no precedent to hang this case on, nothing in your favor. All you have is the doctor's statement, and . . . I mean, he's a nice guy, I like him. But if asked to testify at a hearing, he, uh . . . "

"He is not a strong witness," interjected Donohue.

"A nice doctor, don't get me wrong," continued Charlie. "It's just that he's not going to testify to a life-and-death issue here."

"Of course not." I felt myself rallying. "That's because he's honest."

"The court likes things more clear cut."

"*Honesty* is clear cut," I retorted.

"We want you to win, Katrina," responded Donohue, unimpressed. "You might lose at a hearing. You've got a better chance this way in that your mother might say yes."

"But even if I lost at the hearing, I could appeal, could I

not?" I was pleased with myself for knowing the right legal term.

An appeal, they explained, could take a long time, perhaps even months; it would be difficult, expensive, and of dubious result. An appeal was certainly not the easy next step I had imagined; to the lawyers it was just as unthinkable as the good-cause hearing.

"Look, it's very simple," said Charlie brightly. "A detective can be engaged, a third-party detective, and he can just pick up the phone and call Social Security, and in half an hour they might find her. Why, your mother might be found in an afternoon."

The picture Charlie painted was appealing. I would have liked to cooperate with my lawyers, but the price, as always, was too high.

I let them talk on about this third-party search. They were going to talk about it anyway. I did not want them to regard me as "difficult," so I joined the discussion and contributed what I knew about Tracers.

This search, the men told me, would be paid for by me. Absurd. I did not want it, why should I pay for it? The men, however, ignored that and continued to discuss the details. All the while, Donohue was working on his papers.

"I'm not saying I agree to this, but . . . once she were found, who would then approach my mother?"

"Not the agency." They both spoke at once: "Don't worry." "Someone acceptable to you."

"I could choose?"

"You could have approval, I should think. Yes, I'm quite sure."

"A member of the clergy?" I asked, thinking of Lyn's seventy-year-old nun. The phrase sounded so wholesome. Or maybe one of the ALMA natural mothers.

Charlie rocked back on his heels. "Gee, Katrina, *I'd* do it for you. I'd be *glad* to meet your mother."

Donohue was picking up his papers and asking me to review a draft of the affidavit.

I still did not agree about the search, but I made no comment on that part of the proposal; I needed time to think about it. As for the rest of the document, it was apparent that he had listened carefully. Donohue had written, "I have conferred with the petitioner and have been informed, to my surprise, that the statements made in open court by the agency's attorney were at variance with statements or inferences previously made to the petitioner by the agency. . . . " There followed a meticulous list of the information given me. This information, he observed, did not support the agency's position "that disclosure of the agency's adoption records would invade the privacy of her mother and damage her relationship with her husband, but lend credence to petitioner's claim that her natural mother will consent to have the adoption records opened." He stated in conclusion, "In view of the above, I am now of the opinion that the agency is not the proper party to supervise a search. . . . "

The next thing I knew, the meeting was over. I had been beaten down; but I had not said, "Yes, I agree." Now I must rush home, join the children in the ready station wagon, and depart for our annual family weekend at Lake Mohonk.

I wanted desperately to speak to Florence, to speak to Lyn, to speak to Audrey and Melia and the rest of my friends. If I accepted the judge's plan, I might find my mother, but I would be allowing her to decide my fate. If I refused the judge and withdrew my case, I would lose my only realistic hope.

Standing in the telephone booth at the inn, I dialed long distance on and off all Friday afternoon and evening. But it was not until Saturday that I was finally able to reach anybody.

Search Diary, Saturday, 16 Feb. 1974
    Florence says don't, you'll regret it. Lyn Cobb says go ahead, you're saving time.
    Then the inspiration hit me: That I write my mother a preliminary letter (to be addressed by the Judge).

The idea of a letter for my mother was the loophole that enabled me to accept the unacceptable. This way, the initial approach to my mother could still be made, as it should, by her offspring, not by an agency stooge or a detective in a felt hat. And with this letter I could attempt to plead my own case. I still held one thread of control over my destiny.

At home I wrote Donohue another of my long desperate legal-letters. I was accepting a third-party search, I told him, but with certain provisions. First, I formally stated my objections. I followed with a list of character requirements for the chosen searcher. Then I made the conditions that "the approach to my mother be accomplished . . . with every consideration of protecting her anonymity within her present surroundings," that "a pre-written letter from me to my mother" be "mailed by ordinary mail," and that the "official approach" not be made until seven days after that mailing.

Search Diary, Tuesday, 19 Feb. 1974
Wrote Donohue a four-pager, which his secretary refused to send a messenger for, so I had to mail it. Secretary will make me Xeroxes back.
Called the "other" Judith Williams. She says no calls, remembered me, still has my number, and is still very pleasant.

Lyn Cobb's mother Theresa told her employer of her joyous reunion with her long-lost daughter. Theresa's employer—ironically, a social worker—responded in disgust, "You are sick. What you need is counseling."

I wrote out the letter to my mother, which surprisingly had been not difficult to compose, on my personal stationery. I forwarded it to Donohue later that same day, so that it, too, could reach him before the "Return of Briefs and Court Hearing" scheduled for February 22.

Dear Mrs. "X—"
I have good news for you!—a bit startling, perhaps, so you may want to read this sitting down—but anyway:

Judith is alive and well; she has thought of you all her life; she cares about you; she wishes you well; and she is very, very anxious to meet you.

As you may be guessing, I am Judith. My name is now the one above, but you may call me Judith, or Katrina, whichever you prefer.

What can I say in one brief letter? Obviously, just the essentials. Be reassured, be comfortable, be happy. Know that I realize that the fact of my existence might be an embarrassment to you in your present surroundings, and that I am doing everything I can to protect you from unnecessary exposure.

About myself: Anything you want to know, you may ask, as you now know where to reach me!

About my adoption: I sincerely believe that you gave me up for adoption out of love, out of the desire to do the best for me that you could, and because there was nothing else you could do. I believe you acted out of best intentions and out of love. Please *prove me right*—by *contacting* me now! (I am waiting, literally, by the phone.) Please call me—call collect, if it's long distance—and do it immediately (as I can't bear the agony of waiting). I know it won't be easy; we'll both be awfully nervous. But it's the most important thing in my whole life—and I can't help but feel that the same is true for you.

In case you are wondering, all I want, all I am asking, is to be contacted by you, since I am unable to contact you myself. You see, I have been granted permission by a judge to have this one letter mailed to you, through him. So I don't even know your name, your whereabouts, or anything. If I don't hear from you, anything more I have to say to you can only be said through the judge. And that's a nuisance.

Still, I am hoping you will contact me personally— and I do believe you will. Because I am asking you to; because it's the only *real* thing, and the only *human* thing, to do; and because you do care about me.

So—Looking forward to your call!

With the very best of good wishes to you,

Affectionately,
JUDITH

chapter nine

WAITING FOR
THE COURT'S RESULTS

I had never seen a law brief before. There were two of them, both sent by McKinley and Hart: "Memorandum of Law in Support of Petitioner's Application to Obtain Adoption Records" and "The Children's Aid Society's Memorandum in Opposition." Both had numerous "Statements" and "Points"; both cited cases; both contained quotations and footnotes.

I was bowled over by the "Memorandum in Opposition":

[P]etitioner has not shown or alleged any convincing reasons . . . [*Oh, God.*] This State wants to promote adoption and to protect the privacy of the woman surrendering her child for adoption: People vs. Doe, supra. These mothers' right to secrecy will be worthless if the child caring agencies (hereinafter called the "agencies") are required to search for them at any time in the future. . . .

It was horrible to read, yet I could not stop.

Furthermore, if agencies must search at the request of an adoptee, the social workers' and the agencies' credibility will be totally destroyed. [*That's right.*] For years social workers have been able to gain the confidence of these women by assuring them that they could have their children in peace and be left alone. . . .

The right of this mother to secrecy should not be disturbed especially since . . . the mother has not done anything in the last thirty years to indicate that she would want to waive her privilege. [*Good grief!*] It is doubtful . . . whether such a waiver would be her voluntary act rather than the product of the pressure of the court's asking. . . . [*Am I CRAZY?*]

It should also be noted that this Court recognizes the child's rights to a permanent and stable home.

I dialed the number of McKinley and Hart.

There has been no showing for such a gross departure from a sound practice steeped in a rational public policy of foster adoption.

Wherefore, it is respectfully submitted that petitioner's motion be denied and that the matter be closed.

The matter closed. Was this possible?
"Mr. Perkins, please? . . . Then, Mr. Donohue, please?"

Additionally, today there are 1,000 of [*sic*] hard to place children in care whose opportunities for adoption might be jeopardized by any decision which poses another obstacle to potential adoptive parents. [*No. No no no.*]

Both Charlie and Donohue had already left the office for the weekend.

For a while I was too shaken to even look at the other law brief. When I finally did, I saw that whereas the agency papers had been signed only by Friedman, mine acknowledged the dual authorship of Joseph R. Donohue and Lori S. Odendahl. Well, two was no doubt classier than one, and it was gratifying to have a woman involved in my case.

The paramount interest furthered by adoption in general and §114 in particular is that of the adopted child. In this case, the interest of the adopted child clearly supports the need for disclosure. Petitioner has established in her petition and the supporting affidavit of her psychiatrist, Dmitri L. Thomas, M.D., that she is suffering psychological problems resulting from the denial to her of information about her natural parents and the foster homes in which she lived prior to her adoption.

Not bad, I thought. I began to relax.

Also, as stated in the affidavit of Joseph R. Donohue, petitioner's psychological condition has been aggravated because the agency has seen fit to give her certain facts about her natural parents which have been presented in a vague way or have turned out to be false in light of other statements which have been made to the court by the agency. . . .

Yes, it was easier to concentrate on the comforting statements from my side.

In opposition to this application, the agency, on the return of the citation, argued in open court that the adoption records cannot be opened because they are protected by the social worker privilege. While New York recognizes the social worker privilege (C.P.L.R. §4508), the courts have consistently held that whenever a parent's communications to a social worker are relevant to promote the interests of that parent's child, the claim of privilege to protect the parent must be subordinated to the child's interest, and the communication must be disclosed.

This was good news.

In this case, since the adoption occurred more than thirty years ago, the court files do not contain the information (investigation report, etc.) which petitioner requires. Only the agency has the information and for this reason it has been made a party to this proceeding. Thus, if the current practice with respect to filing adoption records with the court had been in effect here, petitioner would not have joined the agency as a party to the proceeding and the court would simply be required to make a "good cause" determination and full information on the adoption would be disclosed. Domestic Relations Law §114. Petitioner should not be unfairly prejudiced and unnecessarily impeded in her pursuit of information concerning her adoption merely because her court file does not contain the usual adoption information.

Good for you, Donohue.

Noting in his conclusion both my "compelling reasons" and "the absence of any competing needs," Donohue then reiterated the recommendation of a search "by a party designated by the court and acceptable to the petitioner."

It was cool, it was bright; it was wonderful, really. But still it did not proclaim, "Give her the papers, now!"

"Come on," said Lyn Cobb, "I'll drive into the city, and we'll do it—we'll call all the Williamses in the phone book."

"Lyn, there are thousands."

"We'll do it. It'll take time, but there's got to be somebody—maybe we could run off a letter. I've got a machine I can use, and we'll run out letters to all the Williamses. Look, I can even get the paper for free."

Judge Sylvane must read the file. Let there be a person, one reasonably trustworthy person, who knew what this case was really about.

On Saturday, February 23, the editor of the *Atlanta Constitution*, a victim of kidnapping, was freed, unharmed. Arrested and charged with the crime was a William A. H. Williams. The accused kidnapper would be the right age to be my uncle's son, my first cousin. On Sunday there was a picture of William A. H. Williams on the front page of the *Times*. He did not exactly look like me. But he did not look unlike me, either.

When we talked on Monday, Charlie seemed almost to be laughing. "Frankly, Katrina, I wouldn't give their brief another thought. It's too awful."

Charlie's reaction was comforting, the calm sensible papers of my side were reassuring. Still, I wanted to hear firsthand from Mr. Donohue. I wanted to know his reaction to my letters, I wanted to know if he had shown them to the judge, I wanted to know if the third-party searcher had been selected yet.

On February 26, the self-addressed return envelope from the New York State Bureau of Vital Records in Albany arrived. It contained a *real* birth certificate for Judith Virginia Quagliano, born in Mount Vernon, New York, on March 23, 1935. A line was drawn through the typed name, and written above, in longhand, was "Judith Williams—changed by a Court Order."

The names of the parents, Gabriel Quagliano and Antoinette Ponti Quagliano, were similarly crossed out and changed. They were "white"; he was "22"; she "21"; question 7, "Legitimate?", was answered "yes." The hour of birth was given, as well as the attending physician's name. The court-ordered change of name from Quagliano to Williams was dated August 5, 1943.

The birthdate was close but wrong, the parents' ages were wrong; the only full matches were the "Judith Virginia" and the "unusual name." But having in my hand for the first time a real birth certificate for a real Judith Virginia Williams spurred me to develop a scenario in which this could be me.

What if: I was born Quagliano but surrendered as Williams. A few years later, my mother is somehow given reason to believe that the surrender might be invalid because she has used a false name. She returns to the agency in 1943, tells all, and the agency arranges for her to get a court order legally changing the name of her child.

My instinctive reaction was that I was not Judith Virginia Quagliano. But without knowing who I was, I could not be sure who I was not.

The Quagliano mother was described as a housewife, the Quagliano father as a salesclerk in a fruit and vegetable store; hardly Mrs. Meinhauser's portrait of the young publishing secretary and the college-educated "substantial middle-class" older man with a transfer of jobs. But could all that have been an invention to suit Mrs. Meinhauser's concept of what the Kanzlers' adopted daughter might be expecting to hear?

I called Melia, who took down every detail of the Quagliano certificate. She suggested that, because "over" was written in parentheses beside each longhand notation of the court-ordered change of name, all the explanations I needed might lie on the other side of the original document. Melia instructed me to write again to Albany requesting, this time, a copy of the back of the certificate and, as well, a copy of the affidavit for change of name.

I dialed Information. In Mount Vernon, there were no Gabriel Williamses, there were two A. Williamses, and on South 4th Avenue there was a Williams Children's Shop.

In the days of waiting for the further Quagliano papers from Albany, I continued my search of New York City Williamses. I made lists, copied out from the dim photocopies of the 1935 telephone directories, of all the V. and J. Williamses in each borough, of all the G.'s and L.'s. Then I studied the tiny, barely legible addresses, and wrote out the names of any Williams who lived on the same streets as any of these V.'s or J.'s, G.'s or L.'s. I became intrigued by the frequency with which different Williamses *did* appear on a given street. For long hours I mulled over my 1935 lists, concocting relationships; then I cross-checked those lists with Izzie's. There were fascinating connections and coincidences, but there were no conclusions.

In one of our late-night talks, Melia told me about St. Jude, patron of impossible causes, to whom she made offerings and prayed for us, her ducklings. I had not known of him, and his name evoked *Jude the Obscure*, a favorite book of my early teens. Years later, when I saw an adaptation on television, I realized I had forgotten the story altogether. Episode after episode, I recognized nothing until young Jude, the illegitimate son who is reunited with his father around the age of

125

twelve, having been told that there is nothing he can do to help his destitute family, kills his beloved sister and brother and then himself. As the camera focused upon those small lifeless bodies dangling from the beams, I had my first full adult recollection of one of my youth's "favorite" books.

Every day I looked in the mail for a note from Joe Donohue. His secretary had sent the requested Xeroxes of my letters by return mail, but he himself had not yet mentioned them.

Audrey tried to interest the American Civil Liberties Union in the adoption situation, only to receive the familiar ACLU rebuff, "We don't see this as a constitutional issue."

From Melia came another warm note: "I hate to hit you with this, but stumbled across it on search for accidental deaths on another case. Re: *New York Times*—Ja. 9-1937-4:4 'Mrs. L. Williams and daughter—Queens—found dead, victims of coal gas.' Perhaps you should check microfilm at library."

Mrs. L. Williams and daughter—my grandmother and my aunt? A possible explanation for the delay of my mother's surrendering me for adoption? Could *this* be the agency's real reason, to "protect" me from an unhappy family reality?.

Search Diary, Monday, 4 Mar. 1974
Told Charlie that I wanted the Judge to have the file in his custody, that I feared tampering. Charlie said that Lori (the one who worked on the brief) had raised the same query. I brought out the question, why are they fighting me so hard?

The next day, the newspaper carried an obituary for a Mrs. Norman Williams. She was eighty, a possible age to be my grandmother; she had daughters . . . No, she was survived by her husband. My own grandmother had been widowed in 1923.

It was fifteen days since I had written Donohue of my "acceptance" of this terrible search. Still no word from anyone. What was happening?

In daily studies of my lists of addresses, I was concentrating in particular on the Mrs. James and Mrs. Joseph Williamses as potential grandmothers. Although I had not discarded George E. as my grandfather, I was more and more hoping he was not, as he was so exceedingly untraceable.

Another worry reared its head. If the agency papers were transferred to the judge, maybe on the way, in the subway perhaps, there might be an accident. The messenger might be attacked or mugged, and the papers lost forever! It could even be *arranged*. I should warn Charlie and Donohue right away. But if I did they would really think I was crazy.

Lyn's mother Theresa, and her new sister and her new brother—who was, like Lyn, a teacher—were all to spend Sunday at Lyn's house and stay for supper.

"And guess who's coming for coffee!" Lyn chuckled.

"That's too easy, Lyn—your mother Natalie, of course!"

March 9 was my birthday. I did not want to be thirty-nine. Thirty-eight had been pleasant, I looked forward to forty, but thirty-nine was a joke, a squeak of Jack Benny's violin.

Every year on this one day came the chance that someone might be remembering my birth. If only I knew the exact hour I might be able to catch her thoughts. All the hope and anger and frustration released by my reading of Florence's book were with me on the anniversary of my once getting born.

John brought in the cake riddled with candles; the children squirmed with excitement.

"Make a wish," young voices shouted.

I looked at their faces soberly. I knew that they knew. It was their wish, too.

"Hurry, hurry, your wish, the candles, wish . . . "

It was not a wish that my mind was forming, but an oath. Never again, I swore in silence. Next year, I *will* know—*who I am*.

Tennessee Williams, Esther Williams, Evelyn Williams, Ted Williams.

G. Mennen Williams, William B. Williams.

Andy Williams.

I was no longer expecting to hear from Donohue about my letter to him and the one for my mother. Too much time had passed, and it was more likely, instead, that when I did hear from him it would be with real news. He would be calling to tell me that my mother had said yes, I could have my adoption records. Or that she had said no.

My philosophy teacher was urging me to change my academic status from audit to credit. Though I would have liked to, I did not dare commit myself to any endeavor. At any minute, the telephone could ring with my mother's verdict.

Search Diary, Wednesday, 13 Mar. 1974
Becky called. She just found out about Bureau of Child Welfare records: They are destroyed after 12 years.

Also from Becky: When she went back to her agency she was made to sit at a kiddie table on a kiddie chair!

Melia's next letter, handwritten as usual, was of a length—twenty-two pages—previously unequaled. Her purpose clearly was to help me "face" the serious consideration of being Judith Virginia Quagliano. "The possibility has to be confirmed or disproved," wrote Melia. "This is not the first so-called illegitimate birth that becomes exposed as legitimate." Dear, delicious Melia.

The remainder of Melia's letter included a "Mount Vernon search plan" as well as the current Westchester County telephone listings for five Quaglianos, twenty-four Williamses, and four Pontis; in Mount Vernon itself, five Catholic churches, three Episcopal churches, the Board of Education, the hospital, the Health Department, and the public library.

I began with the Mount Vernon churches in search of a baptismal certificate for Judith Virginia Quagliano. I left my personal information; they would call back in a few days. When there were no more churches to telephone, I gazed out the window and imagined going to the Williams Children's Shop in Mount Vernon and looking for a tall, thin woman.

Beginning tomorrow, my children would be home from school for their spring vacation. Vacations. *Spring.* How much longer could this go on? With the children in the house, it would be that much harder to hide from them my increasing inability to perform as a parent.

I struggled to face the disheveled accumulations of paper in front of me. The secretary at such-and-such had said she would call back within a few days. It was over a week, should I call her? Haven't tried so-and-so in a while. If I could muster the strength, I might make the call.

Secretaries with agreeable voices lifted my confidence. Sometimes I cracked jokes and they laughed. These human exchanges gave an aura of vitality. Outright hostile responses, on the other hand, were not totally debilitating. At least I could respond to a rude clerk, if only in my daydreams. The precise cruelty of a random individual was less wounding than the foggy secretiveness of an unknowable institution.

There were many places—churches, hospitals, libraries—which I never called back. Not because they had been rude or rejecting, but because the effort of making a call, any call, was too great.

Audrey telephoned with news of a warehouse in Massachusetts that was reputed to have microfilm records of defunct hospitals. It was possible, she suggested, that my records from Booth Memorial had been sent there and microfilmed before their destruction.

Search Diary, Friday, 15 Mar. 1974
 Called Athenia Microfilm, Worcester, Mass. Nice clerk says fee is $10.00. Must have a doctor's request plus my own authorization. (Apparently there is no need for long "reasons" by doctor.) She doesn't know if they have Booth Memorial or not. She will ask Plant Manager (only other person working there) and call me back collect.

She called me. (Not collect.) No, no Booth Memorial Hospital.

It was heartening, though, that for once *I* was the one whose authorization would have been sought.

I was now almost relieved that Donohue was apparently not going to comment on my letters. If he thought they were childlike pleading, at least I would not have to hear his scorn.

But what was happening? Were any of my provisions being met? Was the judge using the letter I had prepared for "Mrs. X"? It was bad enough that my mother was not hearing my request for help directly from me. Was she to decide my fate without even reading my few words? I guessed the answer, but did not want to know it for sure.

And if she did receive my message and its revealing letterhead, what would happen next? Although I had told my mother who and where I was, I no longer feared bodily harm as I had when I had slipped identifying clues into my book. This time, if my mother wished me ill, all she had to do was refuse me. Letter or no, the result was the same. In one mere communication to a third-party intermediary, my mother had the power to cut off my chance for a future. What irony! The law, which had once stripped my mother of all rights of parenthood, was now giving her a secret second chance to annihilate my history.

My diary was changing again. I could not write even a meager "Today-I-did" entry from the notes on my desk. It was impossible for me to spell out, in dark pen against pale paper, an ordered account of what I was doing. Instead, I attached the scraps of paper—telephone messages, names, stubs of money orders—to the pages of the looseleaf book. The raw evidence of my search told its own story, page following page as day followed day.

chapter ten

RACE AGAINST
THE AGENCY'S SEARCH

I was awakened by an early morning phone call. "This is the Bureau of Vital Records . . . "

The Feds were on to me. I was going to jail.

"About your request for the death certificate of Lillie Williams."

"Yes?" I mumbled.

"We've got two," the voice went on agreeably. "Which one would you like?"

"Oh!" My adoption not having been uncovered, I realized I could speak in safety. "May I please have both?" I was glad I'd sent enough money for three.

"No," the response was cheerful, "you may only receive one certificate at a time. I'll send you a refund; then you can reapply for the second. Which would you like me to send out now, on this request?"

One certificate was for a Lillian from Queens, the other for a Lillie from Brooklyn. Making hasty notes on a matchbook cover, I asked for the names of the informants. The clerk replied that for Lillian, the informant was her sister, and for Lillie, it was a Mrs. Minerva Richards. Mrs. Minerva Richards could be Lillie's married daughter. Richards was hardly an unusual name, but no matter; Mrs. Meinhauser's "facts" were hardly facts, either. I asked to be sent the certificate for Lillie from Brooklyn. Then for the next few hours I telephoned M. Richardses in Brooklyn, without result.

The mail brought a reply from Albany from the Bureau of

Vital Records, State Department of Health: Two more copies of Judith Virginia Quagliano's birth certificate. The information on the back of the certificate and the affidavit for change of name were not included. Damn; no further facts to work with.

Although the likelihood of my being this particular Judith Williams was small, I could not walk away from the possibility. I pulled out my notes of the two A. Williamses in Mount Vernon and dialed the number of the one who lived on Baker Street. A recording informed me that "this number has been changed to an unpublished number."

But it was only three weeks since an operator had provided a number! If this A. Williams *was* my mother, maybe the agency had tipped her off!

I turned next to Melia's list of Quaglianos in Westchester County. They were either unlisted, not available, too old to talk, or obviously not right. I moved on to the four Pontis, again from Melia's Westchester list. I started with the one whose first name appealed to me the most.

"Hello, Mrs. Ponti? My name is Katrina Maxtone-Graham, and I've lost Antoinette Ponti Williams's address. Do you have it?"

"It's in my other book," Mrs. Ponti replied, "Can you hang on while I get it?"

When Mrs. Ponti returned, she apologized for keeping me waiting and cheerfully recited the Baker Street address. Antoinette Ponti Williams was the A. Williams in Mount Vernon whose number had so recently changed!

"Do you want the phone number, too?" asked Mrs. Ponti brightly. "It's a new one."

Antoinette Ponti Williams was within reach. In the space of a telephone call I had climbed over the fence of impossibility and was standing beside the garden of simple reality. I must proceed gently, for Mrs. Williams's sake. I would contact her by telephone, making the call unremarkable to someone who was not my mother, yet informative enough to reveal my identity to one who was. And this was only the first task.

My second would be to ascertain, if Mrs. Williams denied me, whether she was telling the truth or lying. No matter what Mrs. Williams might say, it would be up to me to listen and interpret and ultimately decide.

In preparation, I tried to compose a few opening phrases. There was one Melia had taught me: "I was raised as a foster child." Substituting "foster" for "adopted" forestalled the slamming of the door a little longer.

I thought of my ALMA friends who had located and contacted their mothers. By the time they made their phone calls, they were approaching fairly "certain" mothers. Antoinette Ponti Williams was not that. I wavered a moment— should I wait to know more before I called her? Then I realized that I would never have further documentation for Antoinette Williams; and I knew there was no time for delay. I had to reach my mother before the agency did.

I was ready.

I dialed. The phone rang.

Oh, God, how shall I get through this?

There was a second ring, then a third. In suspended panic, I waited. The phone kept on ringing. But there was no answer.

I dialed again, to be absolutely sure; no response again.

Perhaps Mrs. Williams was at work. I remembered the Williams Children's Shop.

Throughout the day, every thirty minutes or so, I dialed A. Williams's telephone number, each time building myself up for the moment. Always the phone rang and rang; always I dialed twice, in case my finger had slipped. I kept up my half-hourly attempts until, in the late afternoon, I was interrupted by a messenger from McKinley and Hart.

The familiar manila envelope, the blue-on-white address label; inside, a bunch of papers and a short letter with the formal signature of Joseph R. Donohue.

I am pleased to enclose the decision of Surrogate Sylvane which grants our initial application. A private investiga-

tor will be directed to locate your mother and then the
court's adoption investigator, who is an attorney, will
communicate with her regarding your application.

I am very pleased with this decision, as I know you
will be. I feel that it is the best that could be expected,
and I know that Charlie will agree with me on this.

The search had not yet started? All these days of waiting
by the telephone for Donohue's report on the result of the
search, and it had not even *begun?*

Quickly I turned to the judge's decision. There were a
few palatable phrases: "The results of the investigation shall
be made available only to the court in the first instance"; and,
"The investigator shall be retained solely to locate the natural
mother and is not to communicate with her nor be informed as
to the reason for such investigation." I particularly liked,
"This court's adoption investigator is not to reveal to anyone
but the natural mother, the nature of the inquiry," and, too,
that the agency "shall make no attempt to communicate with
the natural mother."

But everything else was infuriating. The decision was
"not to be published." The search was to be made "under the
supervision of the respondent agency." There were no men-
tions of my conditions. Some decision! I made checkmarks in
the margin, seven checkmarks against points that offended
me. It was outrageous, this whole business of asking her permission, of "her rights to refuse to waive her privacy and confidentiality."

"Filed March 15," it said; four whole days ago, and no one
had told me! And if four days had gone by, why was my mother not found? "Just pick up the phone and call Social Security,
and in half an hour . . . " Was my mother dead?

After supper with the children, I telephoned Antoinette
Ponti Williams again. She still did not answer.

I tried every fifteen or twenty minutes. At 9:45, still no
answer.

At 10:00, I wondered if I should even try that late. There
was no answer.

134

10:10. I tried again.

When I dialed at 10:20, the phone was picked up.

"Hello."

"Mrs. Antoinette Williams?"

"Yes?" Her voice was guarded.

"Hello, Mrs. Williams. My name is Judith Maxtone-Graham and—"

"How did you get my number?" she demanded angrily. "It's unlisted."

"Yes," I said lightly, "the operator slipped and gave it to me, she said it was a mistake and she was sorry . . . "

"I see." Mrs. Williams accepted the absurd explanation. "Just the same, it's late, you know."

"I'm sorry. Would you rather I . . . ?"

"Go ahead then. Why did you call? Make it quick!" This woman who might be my mother was plainly a crotchety, crabby old bag.

I started in. "I was born Judith Williams . . . raised as a foster child . . . "

"I don't know anything about it," pronounced Mrs. Williams with hostility.

"And when I asked for a birth certificate, I was sent . . . "

If Antoinette Ponti Williams was my mother, she ought to know by now who her caller was.

"It's late," whined Mrs. Williams, "I'm very tired."

There was little time left.

"Mrs. Williams, you do have a daughter named Judith, don't you?"

"I might," replied Mrs. Williams cautiously.

"Well, uh, since I have the certificate," I paused, "maybe you would like to send it to her?"

"I don't know where she is," pronounced Mrs. Williams with irritation.

Did Mrs. Williams mean adoption? Or had I happened upon some other, unrelated, separation?

"You see, since I was born in March, 1935 . . . " I repeated my statistics, then waited, hoping Mrs. Williams would say more. She offered nothing. "Gee, Mrs. Williams," I fum-

135

bled for words. If she was the wrong person, I did not want to press her about an unhappy situation. "Well, what do *you* think I should do with the birth certificate?"

"Do whatever you want," Mrs. Williams sighed. It sounded as though she meant what she said.

"If it's not mine, then of course I don't need it. Would you like it?"

"I don't care," she replied blandly. "It's late."

"Yes, you're right." This was not my mother, I was pretty sure. The conversation was running dry. "Well, I'm awfully sorry to have disturbed you—"

"Is this some kind of crank call?" Mrs. Williams broke in with sudden spirit. "I get home from bowling and the phone rings, and—you never know these days. There's a lot of crazy people, and the whole neighborhood has changed, and you never know who's out to do what to—"

"Oh, no, Mrs. Williams. Oh, my goodness, *no*."

"I certainly am glad to hear that. You just can't tell anymore." Mrs. Williams was becoming considerably more relaxed. "I was afraid you were one of those funny types, you know, they're all over the place nowadays."

"Please don't give it another thought, Mrs. Williams. I'm sorry to have disturbed you."

"No trouble, not at all," replied Mrs. Williams, cheerfully, "I was up anyway and I only just got in, so I wasn't . . . "

"I sure do thank . . . "

"But not at all!" insisted Mrs. Williams, "I *enjoyed* it."

The conversation over, I decided—as well as one can decide these things—that I was not Judith Virginia Quagliano.

Then I telephoned my ALMA pals. We all agreed that the Quagliano episode was finished. Tomorrow I would write Mrs. Antoinette Ponti Williams a reassuring note, enclosing one of the birth certificates—and covering the one percent chance that my conclusion was wrong by providing her with the means to contact me.

The next morning when I spoke to Donohue, he gave the impression of not even listening to my comments on the

judge's decision. He seemed rushed, and I had so many questions: What if the agency had already contacted my mother?
Who was the court's adoption officer? Could I meet with the
judge and the adoption officer, so that they could see what
sort of person I was? How could I ensure that the adoption
officer approached my mother with discretion?

Donohue interrupted to ask what ceiling I wished to set
on the amount of money to be spent. "Five hundred dollars
won't pay for much of a search," he suggested. "You'll probably have to go at least to a thousand."

Yes, it was easy to imagine the agency declaring they
were unable to find my mother because of insufficient funds.
Better too much than too little. Two thousand? Three thousand?

"Will Tracers be used?" I asked.

"Can't think why not," replied Donohue. "The court has
no objections."

"Do you think that by my suggesting Tracers the agency
might go out of its way to *not* choose them? Are we taking a
risk by mentioning them?"

"I don't see how. No. It's up to the court, and the court
has no reason to object."

Riding on the Madison Avenue bus I noticed a woman,
thin and fairly tall, with straight blonde-brown hair and an
angular high-cheekboned face that rather resembled mine.
The woman was too young to be my mother; indeed, she
looked several years younger than I. Suddenly it struck me
that this woman, certainly not my mother, could be my *sister*.

I had never considered the existence of a sister. Or a
brother. Blood relatives had been utterly alien to me. Now
that I had recognized the possibility I could not push it aside.
Before, every stranger a generation older than I had been a
possible mother or father; now my contemporaries, too, posed
an unanswerable question. There was no longer any unknown
person, older or younger, from whom I was free.

Again I was waiting for news of the search. And again I

was to learn that it had not yet begun. It turned out that the judge's decision of March 15 had been only a preamble to the writing of the court order for the search. My lawyers had not explained this to me, and it was like pulling teeth to get the information from them. Apparently the court order had yet to be drafted; furthermore, it would be drafted not by the judge, but by the lawyers for each side, working independently. Each side's draft, favorable of course to its own position, would be submitted to the judge, who would "pick" the "better" one. I was appalled. Although perhaps I was not understanding fully, I could not help thinking that the judge was getting someone else to do his homework. I wished Charlie and Donohue would tell me things rather than just put up with me. Whatever was going on, I wanted to understand it.

At the end of the week, two sets of papers arrived. One was by McKinley and Hart; the other, by the agency's law firm, Curry, Pell, Byrne, Lundberg, and Stein. Each document opened with a lengthy first paragraph summarizing the case and was fairly similar to the other in content. Each continued with several more paragraphs, all beginning with "ORDERED." Starting at the "ORDERED"s, the two sets of papers became very different. I read through the papers prepared for my side first.

NOW, on motion of McKinley and Hart, attorneys for petitioner, it is

ORDERED, that respondent, the Children's Aid Society, be, and the same hereby is, directed to conduct an investigation as to the whereabouts of petitioner's natural mother; and it is further

ORDERED, that said investigation shall be carried out by Tracers, Inc., 515 Madison Avenue, New York, New York, a private investigative agency licensed by the State of New York, which agency shall be authorized to incur disbursements and render services which shall not exceed the aggregate sum of $3,000; and it is further

ORDERED, that said investigative agency shall be directed only to locate the natural mother and not to communicate with her in any way nor to inform her as to the reason or purpose of such investigation, and said investigative agency shall report the result of the investigation to the court.

Another two paragraphs followed about the adoption investigator's role and my mother's "rights," including the statement,

Prior to communicating with petitioner's natural mother, the Court's adoption investigator will confer with the petitioner in the presence of respondent and the Surrogate to obtain the information which the parties desire to impart to the petitioner's natural mother.

I felt proud, and grateful, and excited. There was Tracers' name at last. It *was* going to work out. And Donohue had worded so well the part about letting me meet with the court's adoption investigator. The adoption investigator and the judge would be able to see for themselves that I was not a criminal, nor a crazy, nor whatever it was that made me an object to be feared and fought.

The "ORDERED" portion of the agency's document consisted of only two paragraphs. The first was basically similar to mine, although once again the agency was speaking of receiving the investigator's report and "informing" the court of the results rather than having the investigator's report be directly delivered to the court. I read on, and the agency's second "ORDERED" was a bolt of lightning:

ORDERED, that all parties are proscribed from revealing anything regarding this proceeding or relating to it so as to preserve its confidential nature and to protect the rights of all persons and organizations directly or indirectly involved.

I had never imagined I might be legally deprived of my right to speak.

chapter eleven

AN IMPENDING COURT ORDER

"Just because the agency asks for something," said Joe Donohue, "does not mean the judge will give it to them."

He so calmed me that I was able to laugh at the transparentness of the agency's, "All parties are proscribed . . . " "All parties" meant me, my mother, and the agency. My mother, knowing nothing of the case, would not be discussing it. The agency had no intention of doing so. Only I had to be silenced.

The court hearing was on Monday. Joe called the following day.

"It doesn't look as though we are going to get Tracers," he began in a somber tone.

"Why not?"

"The agency objected to our having any say in the selection."

"But they *could* choose Tracers, anyway." I wished Joe Donohue would not be so bloody pessimistic. "They know its reputation, they know it's the detective agency I prefer—"

"They made a crack about that," murmured Donohue.

"What sort of crack?"

"They said, uh," Donohue's voice was strained, "you were probably 'in collusion' with Tracers."

"Collusion—that means sort of like hanky-panky? Like I'm dishonest?"

"That's the general drift."

"In front of a judge?"

"Yes." Donohue seemed frustrated, as angry as I.

"But how can they say something, when it's not true?"

"I don't know how," he sighed, "but they said it."

Donohue then told me the good news: He had fought for and won permission for me to meet with the court's adoption officer. I felt newly hopeful. The conditions of my letter—which still Joe never mentioned—might be met after all.

Suddenly I remembered the agency's final paragraph. "The no-talking nonsense, did you squelch that?"

"The agency didn't want to give that up," replied Donohue.

"Really?" I was almost surprised. "So what happened?"

"They tried to get it 'in perpetuity.' "

I gasped.

"But I argued them down to 'during the pendency of these proceedings.' "

I was so horrified I could not speak. Finally I was able to get words out. "I'm glad you did that, Joe."

"So was I." Donohue's voice was tired. "They sure don't like this case."

I called Sylvia, a long-time friend and the children's pseudo-grandmother, and spilled out the story of the court's impending order. Even as I was speaking, I was torn between urgency to tell what was happening to me and fear of getting myself into trouble by talking. Without intending to, I kept muttering phrases like "I can't say, but . . . " Afterwards I felt silly about being so cautious. Now, quickly, while it was still legal, this was what I *should* be doing: Building conduits of understanding to protect myself from the deadening silence that was about to engulf me.

But I did not have the energy to repeat my story often. It was more peaceful to pick up the newspaper and read the obituaries.

A day went past, then another. I had learned by now that research suspended in the belief of a near resolution of my case would be regretted later. I forced myself to continue.

I turned to Melia's shortened list of female Williamses born in 1916 and 1917. From the total of 187 births in those

141

two years, 94 were eliminated as being already nineteen or still only seventeen at the time of my own birth; there remained 93 baby girl Williamses born between March, 1916, and March, 1917, who would therefore have been exactly eighteen years old in March, 1935. Lyn meanwhile had sent in for the birth certificate for Virginia M. Williams, who had been not the third, but the first child in her family. So, down to 92 eighteen-year-old possibles. For the next, I chose Viola W. Her birth certificate number was a scrambling of the digits in mine. "I believe the above-named person to be a close blood relative of self," I wrote. "Reason for request: To verify my relationship to above, for legal cause."

Summer seemed far away, but John and I were making plans. We recognized that the older children were growing up and becoming increasingly independent, and we suspected that this could be our last summer as a sixsome. As John had written a book about transatlantic liners, we decided to make a voyage on the S.S. *France*. The trip would be a fitting celebration of our family's final summer together. We made reservations to sail on July 11.

Lorraine Dusky, a natural mother at ALMA and also a writer, had written an article about adoption that had been accepted by the Op-Ed page of the *New York Times*. We all waited for it eagerly; if our mothers read the *Times*, they would *know*.

From Audrey I learned that there was a Family Court judge called Joseph B. Williams. We wondered if he were my uncle.

ALMA moved a step closer to realization of the dream of bringing a test case before the Federal courts. Cyril C. Means, Jr., a professor of constitutional law at New York Law School, was impressed by ALMA's arguments against the present state laws and had had several conversations with Florence; he wanted to hear more from the other adoptees. Florence, who was hoping that Professor Means would agree to act as counsel for ALMA in a constitutional case, arranged for him to talk with a group of its members. The meeting took place on the afternoon of March 30 in the home of doctor-lawyer-psychiatrist Judianne Densen-Gerber. We—Audrey, Becky, D'Arcy, April, myself, five or six others—represented "some of the people from ALMA."

Florence, Professor Means, and Dr. Densen-Gerber did most of the talking. Dr. Densen-Gerber told of having arranged the placement of some children for adoption, and she described her procedure. It was understood by all parties that the adoptee would, upon reaching maturity, be given all information. During the minority years, Dr. Densen-Gerber remained in contact with the child and both sets of parents. She sent an annual report on the child's health and welfare to the natural parents. Particularly impressive was Dr. Densen-Gerber's assertion that she had encountered no objections from the adopting parents; indeed, she had a long waiting list of couples who would happily accept this arrangement.

There was a great deal of discussion of the medical problems arising from sealed adoption records. Dr. Densen-Gerber described instances where adoptive parents had been refused medical information about their adopted children. She said, "It was only when I, as a psychiatrist, intervened that their agencies would give help to the child. In New York, you have to be a *psychiatrist*, if you want to get information about a child."

"At my agency, even a psychiatrist is not enough!" I exclaimed, speaking for the first time.

"What do you mean?" The doctor regarded me intently.

"Tell them what they're doing to you, Katrina," urged Florence.

"I don't know if I can."

Florence leaned across to me. "You've *already* put your foot in it."

I started slowly, awkwardly. "I'm not allowed to speak. But the court order isn't signed yet, so I think I can."

"What sort of court order is this?" Professor Means asked gently.

"It has to do with finding my mother and asking her permission if I can have my records or not." Everyone was listening, looking. "I'm sorry, I shouldn't say more, I don't want to lose my case." I wished this moment would end.

Professor Means nodded sympathetically, then quietly addressed the group. "I think that one adult citizen is being given rights over and above another adult citizen. It appears as though some constitutional principles are being overlooked in the case of this young lady."

I could hear the compassion in his voice; he did not press me further. There were murmurs of agreement, and then the meeting continued.

Vivian Raminer, an adoptee, read a letter from the adoptive mother of her recently found brother and sister, now in their twenties, from whom she had been separated in childhood when their own mother died. The letter threatened Vivian with a lawsuit if she did not "mind her own business." Vivian's story exemplified the threat adoption as presently practiced posed to any family: No parents wanted to think that if they died, their children could lose their names and their heritage, be separated from each other, and be forever forbidden to know of one another or of their family which once had been.

The meeting went on for nearly four hours. By the time it was over, there was no doubt in our minds about the desirability of Cyril Means as counsel to ALMA.

"Any day now," repeated Donohue impatiently. "It could be signed today, even. Maybe already this morning, certainly some time soon."

"It makes a difference, knowing when. What's going on, whether I can talk to my friends . . . "

"I'll keep you informed."

Each time Joe Donohue hung up, I knew it would be another three or four days, at the earliest, before I could call him again.

Among the papers scattered on my desk were the notes

about the Lillie and Lillian Williams for whose death certificates I was still waiting. I would have liked to be sending in for more certificates, but I did not dare. True, it was said that the Bureau of Vital Records received over a thousand requests a day, but still I was afraid of being noticed. I was beginning to wonder: Were all abandoned people as fearful as I?

Jack X came into my life early in the week of April 1. I never saw Jack nor did I ever speak with him. Although I knew his correct name, he did not know mine, nor my address, nor my telephone number, nor anything else about me. All Jack knew was that there was someone with a job to be done, a need for extreme speed, and a willingness to spend $500. Jack had access to New York City marriage records.

Jack's assignment was to search the marriage records for women named Williams, born between 1915 and 1917, white, and married between 1938 and 1943. His results were to be delivered by the end of the working day, Friday, April 5.

Now I was hoping for *no* news from the court. I prayed for *no* phone calls from Donohue. This time the law's delay could work in my favor. I might get to my mother before the court did. I might beat that bloody document yet.

Midweek, I learned that Jack's research was not going to include all marriages in New York, only those that had taken place in Manhattan. Jack did not have access to the other four boroughs.

Friday morning brought Viola Williams's birth certificate. The second child born to her mother, but the only one surviving. Wrong again, ninety-one more to go. Wait a few days and try . . . who? Alice V.? Inez Harriet?

Early in the afternoon, through an intermediary, a messenger delivered the report from Jack X.

To Whom It May Concern:
    In the period, 1938 through 1943, more than 400 marriages took place in New York City involving brides bearing the surname, Williams.

145

The enclosed information pertains to those twenty marriage applications which were made by females of the Caucasian race, having the surname, Williams, and born within the period of 1915 through 1917.

My hands, my arms, my whole body, were shaking as I turned to the list.

Each entry included name, age, and address of both bride and groom. The date of the application for a marriage license was given and, in some cases, the couples' places of birth and their occupations. Here was the break I had been dreaming of. Thank heaven it was a Friday, I thought; I had two full days in which to study, decide, research, contact—and possibly to win!

I rushed through the names first, looking for J's, V's, and unusual married names.

There was a Jillick, a Spotonick who was a year too old; a Raber, Themis Raber—that was pretty unusual. I liked a Sybil who had married a marine engineer and who had been born in Wales. A Jane Williams, "student," born in New York, who had married an architect twenty years her senior. Was John Stymers an unusual name?

There were no Jillicks nor Spotonicks in any of the five boroughs, nor in Westchester, Nassau, or Suffolk counties. Raber was not listed in either Manhattan or Bronx, but there were several in each of the other boroughs and counties. No Themis, though. My friend Sylvia was married to an architect; he would find out about John Stymers. Sybil, unfortunately, offered no clues for search.

I read through the list again, taking more time and weighing the details more carefully. One woman was increasingly standing out: Ann Moore Williams, who had married Jason Henry Ardsley. Jason Ardsley was several years older than his bride and a professional man. Ann Williams had been born in New York City, and her residence on East 36th Street would have been very close to Booth Memorial Hospital.

There was only one Jason Ardsley in the telephone book.

Twenty names on Jack's list, and perhaps none of them right. At least nineteen *had* to be wrong—nineteen certain errors, nineteen intrusions into the personal worlds of nineteen strangers. I could not bear another Quagliano episode, yet there was no escaping. I had to call Mrs. Jason Ardsley. If Mrs. Ardsley was the right one, I would beat the agency, the court, the licensed private investigator. I had to call Mrs. Ardsley, now, before any of those other people messed the whole thing up for us both.

I dialed Mrs. Jason Ardsley, the former Ann Moore Williams. She answered immediately.

I gave a cheerful hello and introduced myself. "This is Katrina Maxtone-Graham. I'm calling about something personal about myself, and I wonder if you could help me."

"Yes," responded Mrs. Ardsley agreeably. "*Try* to."

"I was raised as a foster child, and I'm trying to establish my identity in a Williams family." I stopped; the following line was the crucial one.

Mrs. Ardsley was waiting for me to continue.

"My name at birth was Judith Virginia Williams," I spoke the facts as slowly as I could, "I was born at Booth Memorial Hospital on March 9, 1935—"

"By the way, how did you happen to call me?" broke in Mrs. Ardsley.

"A friend of mine who's helping me led me to this branch of the family."

"Well, I don't see *how!*" exclaimed Mrs. Ardsley. "I was only a Williams for two years while I was married to that rotter Williams! I've been Ardsley for thirty-three years now. Moore before that."

Shit. I had thought Moore was her *middle* name. "You mean you were never a 'Miss Williams' at all?"

"Moore was my maiden name. Williams was my first husband—what a mistake he was!"

"Then I'm so sorry. There must have been some mix-up." For a mistake, at least it had been painless and fast. "I'm awfully sorry to have disturbed you."

"You were a foster child?"

"Yes."

"Did you get adopted after that?"

I was startled by her quickness. "Actually, yes, I did."

"Where did you grow up?"

It seemed only fair to be responsive. "In Michigan," I replied. "From the time I was three."

"I hope they were nice to you."

"Yes, they were nice." What an extraordinary woman. Again I started to say good-bye.

Mrs. Ardsley interrupted. "So you're calling me because you think I'm your mother."

"Well—I don't *now*, Mrs. Ardsley. But you're right," I acknowledged sheepishly. "I was calling just in case you were."

"Well, I'm not, darling," she said. "It would be easier for you, wouldn't it, to have it be over with?"

"Yes." Her directness was staggering.

"I hope you find your mother."

"Thank you, Mrs. Ardsley."

"But I'm not. You've got to understand that. Do you understand that?"

"Yes, Mrs. Ardsley."

"I am *not* your mother," she repeated more firmly. Then her voice became gentle. "I don't mean to sound unkind."

"I know, I appreciate it." There was something quite tender about her denial. "Please don't give it another thought, Mrs. Ardsley."

"I don't know how else to convince you."

"But I am convinced. Believe me. You're not my mother, I know that."

"Are you *sure?*"

"I *promise.*"

"It's interesting," mused Mrs. Ardsley, "I haven't even thought about that rotter Williams in thirty years. And just this afternoon there was this man, a sandy-blond man, outside on the street, and he looked like Williams. Williams was

good-looking, I'll say that. But he was no good. And I was a
fool. Still, I was thinking about him as I rode up to my apartment, only a few minutes ago. And then you called. Are you
blonde?"

"Light brown."

"Sandy," pronounced Mrs. Ardsley. "Are you tall?"

"Yes."

"So am I."

Oh, dear, now she is going to think that *I* am going to
think . . .

"How tall are you?" Mrs. Ardsley went on. "I'm five foot
eight myself."

I could not lie to her. "I'm five foot eight, too."

"That's interesting. But don't get the idea that means I'm
your mother."

"No, I don't."

"That's good. Now, tell me, what did you do after you got
adopted? When did you leave Detroit?"

"Detroit?" Shivers of tension shot down my back. "I
didn't *say* Detroit, Mrs. Ardsley."

"Oh, I thought you did. What *did* you say, then?"

If Mrs. Ardsley was not my mother, then how had she
known Detroit? "I said 'Michigan,' actually."

Now I was obliged to let the conversation go on, in case
there were further slips.

"Listen," Mrs. Ardsley told me suddenly, "you've got to
get it out of your head that your mother's name was Williams.
I think it was your father's name. Could easily have been that
rotter I was married to. Why are you so determined it's your
mother's name?"

"Well, the agency said . . . "

"Oh, those agencies! You can't believe what some social
worker says."

"True."

"They'll say whatever serves them. Nothing but a pack
of lies. They pretend they know everything, and they don't
know beans!"

This Mrs. Ardsley was a delight.

"Listen, dear," she went on earnestly. "I want you to think seriously about your father being Williams. From a large family, from Massachusetts, there's sure to be lots of them still around."

Mrs. Ardsley insisted that I note "the rotter's" name and former address, as well as the names of his several brothers and sisters. She gave advice on how to search: "You've got to do it on your own. Go to the library, study old phone books, school records, yearbooks." It was an echo. "Julia Richman High School was around then. Did you ever hear of it?"

Lyn's mother Theresa had gone to Julia Richman; Lyn and I had both called there during Lyn's search.

"It's near where I work," continued Mrs. Ardsley.

"It's, uh, it's sort of in my neighborhood, too."

"Oh, really? I work across the street from the Foundling Hospital."

Coincidences and points of contact were revealed at every turn in the conversation.

"What year were you born?" Mrs. Ardsley asked.

"'35."

"My daughter was born in '34. But she's married now and has a family. Do you have children?"

"Yes, four."

"Four. Vicky has four also. Vicky's my daughter. Judith Victoria, I call her Vicky."

That was uncanny. Perhaps to escape the parallelisms of our lives, our talk moved away from the personal, to politics, to philosophy. Again we were confronted with agreement. Mrs. Ardsley and I had mutual acquaintances, mutual interests, mutual attitudes. We talked for nearly two hours. As we finally said good-bye, Mrs. Ardsley had one last suggestion: I should pray, she told me, to a saint of whom, surely, I could never have heard . . .

" . . . St. Jude," we said together.

The phone call over, I was totally exhausted. Although it had been wonderful to come in contact with this kind and forthright woman, two hours of non-stop forthright kindness were more than one's body was accustomed to receiving. I felt grateful, and rather attached, to Mrs. Ardsley. But I swore to myself that I would never again telephone an "uncertain" mother.

The following day, Saturday, was the April ALMA meeting; the speaker was Lyn Cobb.

Time was passing, and no one was telling me what was going on.

Michelangelo's *Pietà*—did all adoptees feel drawn to this statue depicting an adult child of thirty-three dead in the arms of a mother of eighteen?

When I next tried to reach Donohue, his secretary informed me curtly that Mr. Donohue was "a very busy man."

Donohue scared me, his secretary scared me; one snippy reply and I was washed out for the day.

There was no question in my mind but that an adoptee's mother owed the adoptee one complete meeting. Absolutely, and without exception. An hour together—which would consume three or so hours—this was the minimum obligation of mother to child.

But what of the proposition in reverse? Did the adoptee similarly owe three hours' time to the mother?

The ALMA stance was that the adult adoptee had the right to make a choice, yes or no. The mother, however coerced, had already had a moment of choice in the signing of the surrender. Similarly the adoptive parents, by adopting, had already made their choice. Only the adoptee, then a child, had never yet had a chance to speak. Should that chance finally come in adulthood, it would seem fair and right that the adoptee at last have the same freedom to choose as the others had. And that included the freedom to say no.

Logically, it might be so. But humanly, I could not accept this. I believe the adoptee does *not* have the human right to say no to the mother. Whatever the situation, the individual

151

who alone holds the salvation of another's life does not have the human right to refuse. I believe, with utter conviction, that we are *all* obligated to give that other person three hours of our time. As adoptees, as parents, as anyone at all.

That was the price of being human, I guessed—three hours. It did not seem exorbitant.

chapter twelve

WITHOUT FREEDOM OF SPEECH

When I finally got through to Donohue, he was very brusque and brief. No news.

Ordinarily, I would not "use up" two lawyers, one right after the other. But I was desperate. I needed Charlie's voice right now, his warmth, his unhurried manner, his willingness to hear me out.

I could not bear this much longer, I told him. It had to finish. I had to have the papers, everything, before another two weeks had passed. Charlie, will it be over in two weeks?

Charlie said he did not really know anything, I should be discussing these matters only with Joe. But, I said, Joe did not seem to understand . . .

Charlie now made it clear that I had gone too far. Charlie was correct, professional, loyal; nothing could break the bond to a fellow lawyer, to a partner. He did not know anything about the situation, Charlie told me firmly, I must talk exclusively with Joe. The walls closed in yet tighter.

Easter weekend was here. No detective would be looking for my mother over a holiday weekend. And even if one were to find her, there would be no bureaucrat around to pass on the good news.

On Monday, April 15, the Bureau of Vital Records finally responded to my request for death certificates for Lillie or Lillian Williamses. Instead of the certificate promised on the telephone in March, the envelope contained my check and a letter informing me that there was *no* death certificate during the years I had named for *any* Lillie or Lillian Williams!

On Tuesday, the request for the birth certificate of Alice V. Williams, sent in for me by my babysitter, was returned to her for "insufficient information."

Rather than going to philosophy class, I stayed in the house, catching up on homework. It seemed I could not even get a book read on time.

As I sat at my desk reading, a letter arrived from Joe Donohue. Inside was the court order. This was the real one. It had been signed on April 3, Joe wrote, but "not entered in the clerk's office until April 11." April 11 was now five days past, five days for searching. Did no news mean bad news?

Donohue went on to say that our proposal for the court to receive the detective's report was granted; "however, the Court has also required that the agency receive a copy. Otherwise, the Order contains all that we wanted with the exception of the designation of Tracers, Inc. The last ordering paragraph contains a provision with respect to confidentiality during the pendency of the proceeding *only* rather than as the agency requested—permanent confidentiality."

The bulk of the judge's order was almost identical to Donohue's submission, and it contained two further points which had been mentioned in the judge's decision. These, too, were welcome restrictions on the Children's Aid Society: "[N]or should the investigative agency be informed of the reason or purpose for the investigation," and "The respondent shall not contact the natural mother." I hurried on. Yes, the feared paragraph was certainly there:

> ORDERED, that all parties are proscribed during the pendency of this proceeding from revealing anything regarding this proceeding or relating to it. . . .

It might be true, as Florence had said, that an adoption agency could not put you up for adoption again. But an agency could certainly hurt you again.

Deprived of the freedom to speak, I thrashed at the enemy with renewed search.

I asked my babysitter to send in again for the Alice V. Williams birth certificate, this time adding the phrase, "This request is being made for legal purposes," and notarizing her signature.

I wrote to Staten Island for a five-year search, 1938-1943, for the marriage certificate of the Virginia E. S. Williams born in that borough.

I called Lyn Cobb and asked her to send in for the death certificate of potential grandfather Joseph P. Williams; I asked Sylvia to send in, the next week, for that of James. Both men had died in 1923 in Brooklyn at the age of forty-two.

Three days passed. Still no word about my case. I called Joe.

"What do I do? Can I speak to the kids? At dinner, they ask me—"

"Don't worry about it."

"But what am I allowed to say?"

"I wouldn't take it too hard."

"It's a court order."

"Well, these things . . . listen, I've got someone on the other wire—"

"Just one thing," I spoke hurriedly, "if they find her, will we know?"

"The court will notify us here. Absolutely."

He hung up.

It was Friday afternoon. Another weekend.

"There's got to be a way," Lyn exclaimed. "All we have to do is think what it is."

"Maybe if I went up on the George Washington Bridge—"

"I *like* it, Katrina."

"I threaten to jump off unless the agency gives me my papers."

"It's good publicity for ALMA, too. You'll get the TV cameras there. It'll be great, the ten o'clock news . . . "

155

"The rescue squad will come, file in hand—"

"Listen, people watch these things, and the TV will go for anything crazy. You know, poor people don't buy the *New York Times*, they watch the news on TV. ALMA's too square. My mother Theresa never heard of ALMA, and she lives right in Manhattan. What we should be doing is dropping leaflets on the city."

"You mean handing out pamphlets at subway stations?"

"Better yet, drop them from an airplane! I've got a friend, and she's been going with this guy who's a pilot in a traffic helicopter—he'd do it for us, Katrina, I'm sure."

"It'd make one hell of a mess, Lyn."

"Listen, there's mothers out there, thousands of them."

"What am I going to do if I'm hanging out from some bridge, freezing my tail off, and then there's a bloody damn bank robbery?"

"You're *right*, you've got a problem. Listen, Katrina, let me think about it."

There was "no record" in Staten Island of a marriage by Virginia E. S. Williams. Well, at least I would not have to send for her birth certificate. Ninety left. What should I do now?

I did nothing.

After the brief flurry of requests for certificates, I did no more research. I had lost strength for everything except communicating with friends. At night, between 7:30 and midnight, I came alive again. I talked with Audrey or Becky or April. Sometimes I flipped through my index of ALMA friends and called whomever I had not spoken to in the past few days. They called me, too, in the same fashion. We knew what we were doing: We were hanging on. The bonds between one another were our links to sanity.

Becky was going for another appointment at her agency. Barry was still waiting for his mother to answer his letter. Sister Barbara, a fifty-year-old nun with terminal cancer and a life expectancy of sixteen months, was putting off contacting her agency—the Children's Aid Society—for fear of being lied to. Nanny was researching retired teachers' associations. Luther had discovered that his mother had been a resident of a mental hospital. Naomi had been disowned by her adoptive parents. Myra learned that the mother she was searching for was an adoptee, too—a three-generation adoption cycle, for Myra herself had given up a child. Molly, a natural mother who had given up a daughter thirty years ago and whose letters to her agency were always answered with assurances "that your daughter grew up happily, and as an integral part of the family," had received a very different response to her last letter: The agency could not forward Molly's news of her diabetes and multiple sclerosis to her daughter because the family had moved when the daughter was one year old and "there has been no further contact."

By day, I sat hoping for that other phone call, the call of my dreams: The lawyers were phoning to inform me that the agency had relented and was now wanting to help me. The agency was going to hand the file over to me; and I could do my own search my own self.

I was supposed to be reading Hobbes's *Commonwealth* for my next philosophy class, but I could barely concentrate. Hobbes's lines transposed too readily into my own situation: "Whosoever has right to the end has right to the means."

On April 22, there was an explosion on East 45th Street. I feared that the explosion might have been in the Children's Aid Society building and my files destroyed. Would the agency go this far to stop me?

On April 24, my babysitter received a second rejection to her request for Alice V. Williams's birth certificate. The door was certainly being slammed in my face.

On April 25, I sent in myself for Alice V.'s certificate. I signed my request, "Mrs. John Maxtone-Graham, née Williams."

That same afternoon, as I was about to leave for my phi-

losophy class, Joe Donohue telephoned. This time he had a lot
to report.

The agency had not yet begun to search for my mother.
The agency did not intend to search for her. The agency
claimed that they had "absolute power to keep Mrs. Maxtone-
Graham from learning her mother's name." The agency was
not going to comply with the court order that it had, in fact,
helped to compose. The agency was going to appeal. I thought
of Hobbes: "It belongs therefore to him that has sovereign
power to be judge or constitute all judges." Donohue would
file for contempt of court papers. He was furious. I felt
nothing.

I rushed to class and listened to the discussion of Hobbes.
The discussion made my scalp tingle. I kept silent and stared
at my shoes. My shoes were very ratty, I noticed.

The next day I opened my search diary. Six weeks had
passed since the last written-out entry. I reached for a pen.
Unconsciously, I chose a red one. As I wrote, I had a faint
awareness of using my recent daydream language, the phras-
ing of the law, to describe my situation.

> *Search Diary, Friday, 26 Apr. 1974*
> *Having been informed, yesterday, that the Chil-
> dren's Aid Society (allegedly against the advice of
> counsel), intends to not comply with the Court Or-
> der; and further, intends to appeal from the Court
> Order; and having been informed, to boot, that the
> Children's Aid Society considers their position to be
> of "Absolute Power to keep Mrs. Maxtone-Graham
> from learning her mother's name," plus a lot of other
> shoddy accusations; and having, at last, learned the
> lesson that the Children's Aid Society will attempt to
> delay and frustrate me beyond human imagination;
> and having every intention of remaining, myself,
> within the law of Surrogate Sylvane's Court Order,
> but continuing with my life-long freedom to search;
> and having my sanity jeopardized, I have, today,*

*one year to the day since my first visit to the agency,
contacted Ed Goldfader of Tracers, Inc. He is coming here on Monday, April 29, 1974, at 10:30.*
*Got a card from Melia, and a Saint Jude in
plastic.*

What Melia sent was a card, the size of a playing card,
laminated in plastic and having crinkled edges, with a picture
of St. Jude on the front and a pathetic rhyme on the back. I
put it in my wallet. Whether I believed or did not believe—
and I was open to anything—the preciousness of Melia's St.
Jude in his plastic robe was certain. I knew I could believe,
without question, in Melia's love.

Saturday's mail brought documents from Joe Donohue.
The agency was asking for a stay of the judge's search order,
explained Donohue in his covering letter, and this motion was
returnable on May 7. "You clearly are injured by each day
that passes without location of your mother," wrote Donohue,
"and we intend to make these points clear in our opposing
papers."

Joe Donohue was getting better and better, I thought.
Friedman, on the other hand, was his usual self: "Petitioner
would not be harmed thereby, whereas the agency and the
natural mother might suffer irreparable damage if the order
were enforced." Wait until May 7—then I would be in that
court myself telling the judge what I thought of Mr. Friedman's nonsense.

There was another affidavit enclosed. It was three pages
long and written by a new name, Mathilda Stern. I had no
idea what this might be.

Mathilda Stern began by identifying herself as an admin-
istrative supervisor with the Children's Aid Society and a social worker for twenty-five years. Her "casework experience
predominantly was with natural parents," she declared. "The
petitioner's records and the casework responsibility for her
are within my direct supervision and I am fully familiar with
the facts of this proceeding."

Here at last was the agency. Now I would finally hear the charges against me. I could oppose them, defend myself. Reading this affidavit, I would be in court at long last.

In order to understand and appreciate the agency's opposition to a search for the natural mother, the surrender process has to be considered. Women faced with unwanted children [*What is unwanted is not the children but the pregnancy, the poverty, the helplessness*] or children they cannot care for [*more accurate*] come to the agency (or other agencies) to discuss the alternatives available to them. [*No, they come for help in caring for their children.*] Surrender for adoption is only one of the various courses of action. [*It's an irrelevant and inhuman suggestion. Why not offer the mother a job, a place to live, money, training, understanding?*] If surrender is decided upon, it is after the mother has concluded that it would be in her best interest and in the best interest of her child that the mother be relieved of all future responsibility for this child. [*Whatever the mother concludes is meaningless; she has not been informed of the true effects of surrender and of adoption.*] The women selecting this solution customarily ask the agency for the following assurances: that the child will be cared for; that they do not have to be further involved; and that the whole matter be kept confidential. [*No, not true. The agency assures the mother nothing. The mother hopes her child will be cared for, but has no way of knowing if this is done. The mother is not allowed "to be further involved." And as for the "confidentiality": The mother expects the agency will not tattle on her to her parents, her friends, or the newspapers. That is all.*]

Until this case, the agency's social workers could freely assure such mothers that the confidentiality of the proceeding was absolute and they would be left alone. Now in face of this Court's order, the latter is not true and the social worker's position will be seriously undermined. [*No loss.*] How can the social worker give assurances that the natural mother will be left alone when an investigator can be hired thirty years later to track her down and turn her whereabouts over to an officer of the court? [*"Assurances" again. And always you are assuring our mothers either of something they don't want—to be left alone—or of something not yours to give away—our feelings and actions.*] For thirty years this woman has elected not to communicate with the agency responsible for her child's adoption. [*Of course not. She would have gained nothing but hogwash.*] Who knows what effect a simple inquiry will have on this lady? [*None of us knows. But she's a big girl now; let her tell us herself.*] We do know that for thirty years she has lived (if she is living) with absolute confidentiality and no contact. [*This sentence provides information. It's probably even true. Of course, I can't know for sure.*]

While there are no surviving adoptive parents herein, it can be reasonably assumed that such an order in a case involving adoptive parents would be very disruptive to them. [*To some, yes; because they have been miseducated. Because they have swallowed your lie that our interest in our past comes from their failures; and that our wholeness would wipe out our affection for them. But your myths are simply not true. Those parents who have devoted years to nurturing their children's selfhood are not benefited by your secrecy; they are thwarted by it and deprived of their goals.*] The possibility of this sort of proceeding might deter people from adopting. [*Not really. Adoption has existed throughout history; sealed records for not even sixty years.*] No one wants to compete or enter into a contest, now or in the future, for his child's affection. [*Who is setting up this competition?*]

Who was she, this Mathilda Stern? Did she really imagine that secret files were guarantees of a child's—or of a thirty-nine-year-old's—affection?

It was all twisted. The entire affidavit was based on presumptions. Mothers who did not care, adoptive parents who did not understand—fictional characters, from a past which was incorrectly described or a future which had not come. Adoptees were not even considered; let alone this adoptee in this case presenting this application of good cause. Was Mathilda Stern really opposing Judge Sylvane's order? Or was she opposing the existence of any law permitting the opening of any record?

Or was she opposing me, personally? I remembered Charlie's words, "They made the decision: *We're going to fight this one.*" Did Mathilda Stern have some special private hate for *me?*

Was Mathilda Stern *my mother?*

chapter thirteen

LAST FLAILINGS

All my search materials were spread out on the dining table.

"Okay, what we've got here," declared Ed Goldfader, "is a Miss Williams who we know to have been in New York City on the 9th of March in 1935."

"And who we think was also from this area—"

"Thinking it doesn't make it a fact," Ed corrected. "A fact is not a fact until it's confirmed as a fact. All we have as fact is that she was here on March 9. Probably a few days before. But not necessarily." He smiled. "You don't have to look so worried. All I'm telling you is that it isn't so easy as you see it on television."

Ed had a manner that was both friendly and businesslike. He studied my documents and lists. Obliquely I referred to being involved in a legal action which could not be discussed but which necessitated a rush.

"Williams. You could have picked something easier than Williams, you know."

"Yes, uh . . . "

"But you never know until you try. I had a Jones, John Jones, once. Supposed to be in Georgia, but I found him in Montana. So these things can be done. The trick is: You've got to know where the information is. It's probably sitting on some shelf, collecting dust, and people don't even know what it is. My job is to know where the information is. There, I'm telling you my whole business!"

163

I asked him if he had access to Social Security records.

He laughed. "Nobody, but *nobody*, has access to Social Security!"

The price for his services, Ed announced, was $1,500, flat rate, in advance, and with no guarantees.

"Good grief!"

"I know. But it's fair. And I don't come back asking for more. No extra charges, the way some detectives do. You know, just $200 more? Flat rate, that's how I operate. And I keep on working as long as there's work that can be done. I give written reports."

"And what if you've spent $1,500 and you still can't find her?"

"I keep on trying. Of course, I'd like to find her *tomorrow*. So would you, right? Then you're happy and I'm ahead. Get it?"

"This is the craziest arrangement I've ever heard."

"Sometimes I'm lucky. And sometimes I lose. But that's the breaks of the game. Now, don't you get the idea I'm softhearted. I like you adoptees, but I'm in this for business." He smiled. "Yes, the law is all wrong. I met Florence Fisher. I'm on your side. Don't worry, I *want* to find your mother for you."

Ed confirmed my suspicion that the private detective's methods were the same as those I had learned from ALMA: Genealogy, research, fact, intuition, imagination, common sense. But what the amateur spent hours in the New York Public Library waiting to have sent up from the stacks, Ed Goldfader had right in his own office.

"I can't help worrying," confided Audrey, "what if she's poor?"

"Or a bitch, or dying . . . "

"As it is, I can barely make ends meet."

"Yet still we go on looking!"

"Katrina, are we crazy?"

"A lot of headaches. That's all we want, the right to a lot

of headaches. And we've known it from the start, Audrey."

"Yes, I guess I'd find a way. After all, if she's in need . . . I mean, she's my own *mother*."

A twenty-four-hour miracle by Ed Goldfader did not come.

On Wednesday, May 1, Melia received a letter from Izzie, saying he had completed his work on the 1917 military census and was starting to research Manhattan marriage licenses. He planned to write out every Williams marriage beginning with 1935. Sweet, but useless. Jack's list had already covered the relevant part of this ground. Izzie would now be occupied for weeks, maybe months, at something I no longer needed. That evening, John and I went out to dinner. I got drunk.

May 2. Only five more days until the return date in court. Yes, sir, Your Honor, sir. Give me liberty or give me death. Ed Goldfader telephoned to inform me that he had to go to New Orleans for four days on another case; he hoped I would understand.

On May 3, at long last, the birth certificate for Alice V. Williams arrived. She was the first child born to her parents, and therefore not my mother. Alice V. had consumed the month of April; and there were eighty-nine more female Williamses born between March, 1916, and March, 1917. I knew I should try next for Inez Harriet. But I did not have the strength.

Two Watergate articles on the Op-Ed page of the morning's *New York Times* caught my eye. Tom Wicker wrote, "How easily the phrase 'national security' can be trotted out for almost any purpose"; James Reston commented on the continuing games-playing from the White House, "still trying to keep the lawyers and the technicians from checking the tapes."

Tapes, files. Executive privilege, social worker privilege. Secrecy was power, power was secrecy.

On the shelf between my desk and the window was an empty blue looseleaf notebook. It would be an excellent note-

book, should I ever try to write again. I inserted a thick handful of clean, lined sheets. I stared at their emptiness. I felt
utterly useless.

Lyn called to tell me she had received the death certificate for Joseph P. Williams. She tore open the envelope as we
talked. "Okay, listen: We have 'male,' 'white,' 'married.' No
birthdate. 'Born USA. Father's name, Peter S., born USA.
Mother's name, Margaret, born USA.' They sure aren't much
help on birthplaces! We got 'Resident of New York, 24 years.' "
"Great!"
" 'Borough, Brooklyn. Address, 238 Jerome Street. Type
of dwelling, tenement.' Katrina, that's a style of building, tenement, it doesn't mean a slum or—"
"I don't mind."
"It's those row houses, some are very nice homes."
"What's it got for cause of death?"
"Damn, I can't make it out. 'Hallucinations'? No. Do you
die from hallucinations? Maybe 'Poisoning'? You won't believe
this handwriting."
"Acute indigestion?"
"No, no . . . give me a minute. Here, it says, yes, it says
. . . 'Suicidal'! Suicidal—shit, Katrina, but that's what it
says. And down here, I don't *believe* this, Katrina, but, for
contributing cause of death, they put 'his head.' It says, 'Contributing cause, his head.' "
"Lyn, he's *got* to be my grandfather."
If my grandfather had been a suicide, it would be easy to
imagine that my mother, then age seven, might have been
told her father had died of "a stomach ache." Perhaps that
was how the "acute indigestion" had gotten into the agency
report. Or, my mother might have known the truth but had
purposely lied to the agency. Or, the agency had known the
truth but had lied to my adoptive family. Or, the agency, to
"protect" me from this "bad" news, had invented the "acute
indigestion" for my ears. Well, I *liked* his "suicidal"; I felt akin
to Joseph P., poor man.

Checking the 1935 Brooklyn phone directory for Williamses on Jerome Street produced nothing helpful, but when Lyn forwarded Joseph P.'s death certificate I noticed a detail she had not mentioned: The undertaker was named. Adam Walker Harmon, almost next door, at 224 Jerome Street. In the current Brooklyn directory there was still, fifty years later, a Noel Harmon at 224 Jerome! Most likely he was the undertaker's son; he might have old records.

There was no answer at Noel Harmon's number.

Outside, the Mother's Day munitions were being stockpiled in store windows. Blonde mamas with blonde babies, black mamas with black babies. A mother was someone for another person to look like, one half of a matched set. It seemed that the satin hearts and chocolates of biological warfare were attacking with new viciousness this year.

Donohue would not allow me to attend the return date proceedings on May 7.

Search Diary, Tuesday, 7 May 1974
Another Return Date in Court. Highlights of which: Sylvane told Friedman to the effect that "his client and/or he would look like asses, if the mother were found and were delighted *to so be."*

Apparently, also, the agency is considering gathering other social workers' affidavits—in which case, so can I! (—and we'll know within 48 hours whether or not they'll do it.)

Agency is calling this "precedent setting," and, it seems, if they're stupid enough to go to the Appellate Division and I win, then it will *be precedent setting! It seems that by opposing me in the first place, they'd started digging their grave; but now they seem bent upon digging a grave the size of New York County. God, what asses! Anyway, it's exhilarating—some of the time. There's talk of a "hearing" on this issue! Good grief! And, to be sure, there's another Return Date for next Tuesday, the 14th of May.*

167

Maybe I could go to *that*, I told myself.

If the agency appealed, the proceeding would be in open court. At last my dealings with the law would not have to be in secret. Anybody could attend Appellate Court hearings— the press was often there, Florence told me—and I could be there. Florence and Audrey could be there, too. But would I dare ask them? I was afraid of Donohue's anger if he saw me with ALMA friends in attendance.

The fiercer the agency's battle, the more fervent my pursuit of an explanation. I knew the agency's supposed reasons for keeping me from my file. What was their *real* motive?

My doctor put me on tranquilizers.

"So maybe your mother *is* Mathilda Stern," declared Audrey, "But what if—I mean, what if *my father*—were *Richard Nixon?* And the agency would think they were protecting *him!*"

How different was an adoptee's real concern from the agencies' imagined fears. Our fathers might be "criminals," they told us. This was old hat; adopted people have been living with the cliché "terribles" since first hearing of them in early childhood. We had progressed, by now, to our own individual worsts. But these, too, were unimportant. What mattered was simply that a parent be a human being. A criminal, a president, a social worker; even Mathilda Stern was a bearable prospect. Any end to the mystery lightened the burden. For if my mother was the head prune at Children's Aid, at least she would not be, at the same time, also the head prune at Spence-Chapin and at Louise Wise.

My adoptive father had believed in adoption's credo of secrecy. But would he really have believed in what was going on now? Ernie Kanzler had been an intelligent man and loving of his children; he had also for a time practiced law. I could not possibly imagine that the agonies of this court case were what he would have wished for his daughter.

Thinking of my own children, I went to my desk so that I would not have to face them.

Florence prepared a list of several social workers around

the country whom I could call on for supporting affidavits. A few were in total sympathy with adoptees' rights; the others were middle-of-the-roaders who favored "mutual consent." Even the middle-of-the-road position was sufficient to defend me against the agency's appeal.

But how could I ask someone to write a supporting affidavit without talking about my case? Donohue told me that for the purpose of soliciting an affidavit from a social worker, I was allowed to speak.

Still fearful, I asked, "But are you sure?"

"Of course I'm sure! You're allowed to defend yourself!"

Saturday's ALMA meeting was the final meeting of the season. I had never seen the room so crowded. Although we seemed more exuberant than ever, underneath we were frightened, aware that we would not be together again until October.

After the talks, I sought out those friends who were social workers. There were quite a few: Becky, Wendy, Seymour, Nanny. Although soliciting affidavits, I was also making use of the opportunity to pour out my story. The release was wonderful. But how silly, that it was legal for me to seek the solace of friendship provided the actual ears I addressed belonged to someone who might be able to help me in court.

Nanny, who lived in Philadelphia, wrote an analysis of the adoption agencies there, whom to contact, and a description of each social worker's attitude. Rumor had it, added Nanny, that one of the most sensitive to adoptees' feelings was a Miss Archibald, who was high up in a major Philadelphia agency.

Search Diary, Monday, 13 May 1974
Nanny called. Told me that Miss Archibald will write an affidavit. Her policy is to contact the mothers and ask them. She has been dying to know which is my agency, but Nanny wouldn't tell.

Called Miss Archibald to tell her the whole story. She says she can't understand why they're fight-

169

ing this search. Says she, "We have confidentiality not to give descriptive material to the adoptee, but we certainly don't have confidentiality between ourselves and the bio family." I'm too shaken up to really describe what happened.

Anyway, she's going to call Miss Becky Smith at Child Welfare League, and tell her to look into what's going on. She offered to call Mathilda Stern herself and look into it!!! I said I was too scared of her, and would rather she wait. I told her I'd get back to her, when I knew what was going on, in whatever event. She's a nice woman, and also sympathetic to "the need to know the bio-parents."

Miss Archibald had been stunned when I had read aloud Mathilda Stern's affidavit. Then, when I had added, "And they won't even tell me my foster mother's name," Miss Archibald had exclaimed, "They won't? How cruel!" She had been speechless for a moment, and then she had repeated softly, "How cruel. I wonder why not."

Search Diary, Tuesday, 14 May 1974
Called Annette Baran of Adoption Research Project, Los Angeles. Called Natalie Stephenson, San Francisco. (The latter has 35 years of experience, 10 years in Court, will supply info re natural mother's feelings, with documentation.) Former has access to a lawyer.

Must tell Donohue: Just in case C.A.S. is released from Court Order, I want release, too!

No one will know the truth—until we see "the tapes"!

My dream is, they will call it off.

I had a dozen copies made of Mathilda Stern's affidavit, bought a dozen mailing envelopes, and spent the next two days conferring with social workers who would champion my cause.

I asked Miss Archibald to describe her agency's policies, how she would deal with a good-cause case, and whether in fact natural mothers ever changed their minds about interest in their offspring. I asked Judianne Densen-Gerber to write about how she handled adoptions and what she told the adoptive parents. A co-worker of Becky's who had been employed for many years by the City of New York offered to submit an affidavit about hard-to-place children who, customarily older, already knew who they were; she wanted to point out that people secure enough to adopt these children were not troubled by the fact that the children had identities. Becky herself wanted to write about the attitude of many of her fellow social workers toward adoptees, whom they regarded as "sick." Nanny and Seymour would both write something "ALMA-ish." A total of eight professionals would support my cause.

Search Diary, Thursday, 16 May 1974
> *Early A.M. call from Miss Archibald. She'd talked to a "Miss Gardner" at Child Welfare League who "knew nothing about the case," to which I explained the confidentiality bit, and (oh, what a good girl am I!) asked her to respect this confidentiality! What a jerk I am, but fortunately she isn't. And she, most graciously to me, implied as how this was bullshit and she would make her own decisions.*
>
> *Anyway, she wants Donohue's formal request in writing; and then she's leaving for London on May 23.*

I was busy all morning with Guy. The previous day we had received a call from his school to say that he had had a small scratch on his arm and wouldn't we like him to be seen by a nearby doctor. John had met Guy as he emerged smiling from the doctor's office, his right arm wrapped in a large white bandage. There had been a few stitches, that was all; he

171

should keep his arm in a sling and skip school the following day. Guy was feeling fine but was concerned that having to wear a sling could mar his upcoming performance as the king in the second grade's play at the school fair on Friday.

Guy and I were just finishing lunch when two sets of papers arrived from McKinley and Hart, apparently from the last court meeting. Skipping the heavy legal stuff, I skimmed through to see if there was anything new from Mathilda Stern. There was! I had better save that for last; once I read it, I might not be able to read anything more.

To fortify myself, I began with the affidavit written by Joe Donohue. It was full of strong words about the agency's delay: "[T]he agency has failed and neglected to carry out the provisions and requirements of the order and has wrongfully refused to comply with same . . . even though the agency's attorneys participated in the formulation of said order."

Joseph R. Donohue was so good in print; I wished he were not always so rushed on the telephone.

Next I squirmed through the worst of Friedman's affidavit: "[T]here is a substantial burden on the party attempting to open the records which has not been met here." Did he know how much his words could hurt? "Here, the mother is a stranger, she has kept herself from the child and done nothing to indicate anything other than her desire for anonymity." What "ought" she have done, Mr. Friedman? Let us hear what realistic options are available to natural mothers. But no, Mr. Friedman was busy with "the ramifications of this type of relief and the possible effect it would have on agencies who are asked to conduct such searches in the future."

Then I noticed a further affidavit in the envelope. This one was by Dennis Rennick, Executive Director of the Children's Aid Society. His statement was a reiteration of the agency's concern for the "policy of this state," the "thousands of children in this city who are hard to place," the "potential adoptive parents" who might be "reluctant to take a child who could later petition the court," and, of course, for "the word of its social workers becom[ing] meaningless." I was almost get-

172

ting used to sentences that declared, "Certainly, the order entered herein breaches the protective wall of privacy and is not consistent." But I was taken aback by what followed: "I am certain that other agencies would similarly view this matter and this Court could obtain testimony from various sources as to the detrimental effect of such searches." Would Spence-Chapin and Louise Wise join the battle against me?

Enough. The time had come to take on Mathilda Stern.

It was no surprise that she still opposed me. This time, however, she did deal with my specific circumstances rather than just setting forth agency beliefs. Wittingly or not, she gave me useful information. "The natural mother was 18 years old at the time of petitioner's birth. . . . " "She immediately committed her child to the Department of Public Welfare" (this was footnoted, "Thus, the mother never took care of petitioner"). "[T]hereafter on August 10, 1937, surrendered the child for adoption." "[C]ame to the predecessor of this agency on June 30, 1938, and signed a second surrender." (Again Mathilda Stern added a negative interpretation, "Thus, she twice was able to conclude that she should free herself of responsibility for petitioner.") "[S]he volunteered that she married in 1940. . . . "

I was glad to have these confirmations of dates and the firm knowledge of the earlier surrender. Today's information was not just chat from a social worker in her office; these were real facts, written, and sworn to in an affidavit. At last I had something I could accept as true.

"18 years old" was crucial; Melia and I had guessed right when we had narrowed our Williams birth list from the vaguer 187 to the precise 93 who were eighteen-year-olds. But the marriage year of 1940 was disconcerting. Jack had found no relevant marriages in 1940.

I hurried on, looking for more information. Mathilda Stern told quite a lot about my mother's return visit to the agency, including mention of that missing photograph, here called "pictures for the adoptive parents." My mother, Mathilda Stern observed, "indicated at that interview that she was pleased that her child had been adopted." I wondered what Mathilda Stern might have been expecting my mother to say—"That's too bad; I hoped you'd lose her in the street"?

Mathilda Stern continued, "The worker who recorded this meeting noted the following remark in the casework record: 'She thinks it would be happiest for [petitioner] if she could believe her own mother is dead.' Thus, in her last visit, more than 30 years ago, the natural mother clearly indicated that she had made a life for herself and had no desire to have contact with her daughter."

While I was not feeling hurt by Mathilda Stern's suggestions of my mother's lack of interest, I was nonetheless fearful that the *lawyers* and the *judge* could be impressed by these prejudiced interpretations. They might even accept as fact Mathilda Stern's concluding hypothesis, "She made peace with life in the 1940's but if we contact her now, we could disrupt or destroy her and her family."

There; I had read it all, and I did not hurt worse. No, I still felt the same. Methodically I returned the papers to the envelope.

I wanted to fight back, to make some motions on my behalf. But there was nothing left for me to do. I had already contacted everyone there was to contact for affidavits. Still, I somehow had to flail my arms against the agency, I had to show them I was real.

Telling myself that a statement for Joe Donohue would somehow benefit my case, I took a deep breath and began writing.

First I pointed out the many discrepancies between Mathilda Stern's insistence that my mother had disposed of me as hastily as she could and Mrs. Meinhauser's report that my mother had breast-fed me, had visited me frequently in the foster homes, had been in a "dilemma" about keeping me, and had provided a picture of herself for me. Then I responded to Mathilda Stern's declaration that my mother had "freely decided to surrender her child." How free, I asked, is a decision made under the pressures of poverty, overcrowding, so-

174

cial stigma, family opposition, and no resource for help? Next I challenged the agency's alleged concern for adoptive parents' potential competitive instincts by noting how easily photographs of my mother had been sent to my adoptive parents. By contrast, I went on, the agency had not passed on the fact of my mother's inability to absorb calcium. "It seems that the 'protective wall of privacy' disintegrates upon whim," I wrote, "but is rebuilt when confronted with potential medical purpose.

"In sum," I concluded, "whether or not my mother would wish me well, at age 39, or would wish me dead, is irrelevant. I see no reason why my health should be victim to her whim. I am asking for my records as an adult with medical needs, and I am asking for relief and for justice. If, however, by asking my mother and obtaining her permission, I can obtain this medical relief more rapidly and more certainly, then I beseech this Court to sustain its order."

I sealed the letter without a rereading, grabbed my notebook, and left the house for my philosophy class. Hearing my letter thump to the bottom of the corner mailbox, I wondered what would become of it next. All these intense, passionate communications, drifting into nowhere. In an unpeopled forest, did the falling tree make a sound?

Today was the last class of the philosophy course. So much was ending, just as it should have been beginning.

Friday came again. Again, the last chance for news before a news-less weekend.

The morning's mail brought a packet from Melia, mostly Izzie's research of Manhattan Williams brides. He had noted every Williams, regardless of age or race, starting with 1935; he was now up to 1937. Six pages of minute details, and how many more before he got to 1940? Melia, ever valiant, had highlighted all those which for some reason seemed a possibility as my elder aunt. It was too much even to look at. Along with Izzie's list, were notes from Melia about Jillicks, Rabers, and John Stymerses in each of the five boroughs of New York, plus Westchester, Nassau, Suffolk, Essex, and Passaic counties. There were no Jillicks whatsoever, which was good, and no Stymerses named John. There was no hot lead on either list, not even a somewhat warm one.

Then I went to Guy's school fair.

Guy was a brilliant success as the king, of course; the sling did not bother him. But the other parents looked at me strangely.

After a while, from a few casual, frightened questions, the full story of Guy's accident came out. It was not the simple story John and I had been imagining. The narrative emerged in fragments: A hook seven feet above the floor . . . a boy, suspended, screaming . . . blood on classmates' shirts . . . hysterical children unable to sleep . . . a teacher too upset to come to school the next day. Our son's little scratch on his skinny arm had been a two-inch tear of whatever meager fat he possessed. Cutting no nerve or muscle, there had been a miraculous near-miss on the right arm of a righthanded boy.

Now it was over. The boy, the arm, the classmates and teacher, were all fine. And I had never known.

It was 97 degrees outside—and I was in a winter shirt. My children had no summer clothes, yet they were about to start their summer vacation. I had not even known. Our family trip was going to come, and where would I be?

Looking around at the vital faces and active cottoned bodies of the other parents, I knew I did not belong with them. These people knew who they were; they were all somebodies. I belonged with no one. While they chatted among themselves, I simply watched from outside. I was barely functioning, I could only stare.

The weekend was terrible. We had a house guest, Timmy King, a school friend of Ian's whom we had not met before. Timmy seemed a nice boy. Ordinarily I get along well with my kids' friends; but this was a different sort of weekend. It was only when I did finally address Timmy to say good-bye that I realized this was the first time I had spoken to him. For twenty-four hours and three meals together I had uttered no word to our guest.

In Monday's mail was an invitation to a benefit for the Salvation Army. Listed as a member of the Board was a Walter R. Williams, Jr.—my Uncle Walter? For $100 a ticket, I could gaze at male trustees to see if one were tall and thin.

Noel Harmon, the undertaker's son, still never answered his telephone.

Search Diary, Monday, 20 May 1974
Called Miss Archibald, spoke with her v. nice sec'y—the one who asked how to file hyphenated names. Miss Archibald is full of meetings today, it may not be till tomorrow. I left the message that there were "inconsistencies" in Ms. Stern's affidavit.

Called Ed Goldfader re Walter R. Williams on Salvation Army Advisory Board. He wants me to send him the invite.

Another week had begun. It was Monday afternoon, and still nothing promising. Nothing for me to be doing. No prospect, no potential. All I could do that day was gaze out the window at the passersby.

The following morning I took the largest knife in the kitchen and brought it to my desk. For several hours, I sat staring at the knife in my hands or staring out the window. Then I called Dr. Thomas and told him I wanted to terminate my therapy. Whatever the doctor said to me, I told him I didn't care. Finally, I asked him to please put me in a hospital. He replied that if he did, I would get there and then feel he had rejected me. I told him he was wrong. Having nothing more to add, I clicked the end of my knife into the mouthpiece of the telephone.

Next I telephoned Donohue and clicked my knife at him, too.

Then I called Florence.

chapter fourteen

OTHERS' ACTION

Florence, like me, had had enough. But unlike me, she was mobilized.

"Tell me I have your permission, Katrina." Her words seemed to be coming to me through some distant haze. "I've stayed out of this, Katrina, for a very long time. Now they've got to listen. Donohue, and the doctor too—both of them. They have to know how far this has gone."

"I don't care," I murmured.

"Just tell me I can go ahead. I won't do anything, unless you agree."

"I don't care."

"I *know* you don't care. But do you say yes?"

She asked several more times. "I don't care," I kept repeating; finally, even that was too tiring. "I don't know," I said.

"That's not an answer, Katrina."

Yes was a shorter word. "Yes," I said.

"Are you sure?" asked Florence.

"Yes."

Florence was now the personification of me, the figure that arises from the sleeping body, goes out and acts. I sat there, still paralyzed, and felt my angry spirit take form in her voice. Her actions were my actions.

An hour later, everything was changed.

Search Diary, Tuesday, 21 May 1974
Florence called Donohue, talked at least 20
minutes. ("You brought me into this case, when your
firm showed Katrina my book.") She called Dr.
Thomas. (Said he, "But she won't talk to me.") She
told him I would not commit suicide!! And she told
me he was "very sweet" and to "call him and patch it
up."
I cleaned all the kiddies' bookcases, then made
arrangements to get help on fixing their summer
clothes. Oh yes, first I went through the boxes of par-
ty favor toys in basement for the upcoming birth-
days. John asked, "O.K., where's your Dexedrine?"
Florence is my, all of our, Dexedrine.

The next morning I received a letter from an absolute
stranger in Sarasota, Florida. Peg Lawrence was an adoptee
in her late forties, and through the familiar self-effacement
and discreet euphemisms, I recognized that she was asking if
I were her mother. I wondered how she had come to consider
me; perhaps an ALMA volunteer, noting that Peg Lawrence
was a fellow adoptee of the Children's Aid Society, had sent
my name and address.

How existence jumped about from one day to another.
Alert and cheerful, I promptly called Peg Lawrence and we
shared our frustrations with the Children's Aid Society. Peg
had seven children, four grandchildren, and an agreeable,
alert eighty-nine-year-old adoptive father who lived in an
apartment in her house. She read me two letters—twenty-
two years apart—that she had received from the Children's
Aid Society. The 1952 letter professed that her mother "was
employed at one time as a telephone operator" and that her
father was "of Swedish descent, though born in this country."
The contemporary letter, from Mathilda Stern, stated merely
that her mother had "a pleasing voice" and that her father
was "of Northern European descent—probably Scandinavi-

an." Peg and I agreed that we trusted the more specific 1952 letter over the vaguer one of 1974.

Donohue and Dr. Thomas were at last communicating with each other. And another court hearing was set, just two days away, for Friday, May 24.

I announced to Donohue my intention of coming to this hearing; this time, nothing was going to stop me. Donohue answered firmly that he would not let me. My presence, he said, would put him, and therefore my case, in a bad light, as it would appear that he was inviting me to court "to hear how upset I was."

There was some sense to what Donohue was saying. But was I forever to be locked out of my own trial?

"I really do not want you there, Katrina!"

Donohue had never been so vehement. I realized that he was going to succeed in keeping me away.

Search Diary, Thursday, 23 May 1974

Received Annette Baran's affidavit. Pretty good. Am having messenger take it to Donohue.

Call from Sylvia, re 1923 death certificate for James Williams—"male, white, married, age 42 years. Watchman, born U.S. Parents: William & Margaret. Cause of death: Lobar pneumonia. Residence in N.Y. City: 4 months." Four measly months. Good-bye, Grandpa James.

Copy of Judianne Densen-Gerber's statement arrived—direct and strong, not a single phrase of pussyfooting.

Dr. Thomas called. He can't keep my Friday (tomorrow) appointment, as he'll be meeting with the judge!!!! Now, all I'm doing is shaking. I told him to be forceful. He'll call late on Friday to report. Now I have fantasies of seeing my file: I'm real, I'm real, I'm real.

Midnight, Natalie Stephenson's powerhouse affidavit arrived. She is fantastic.

The telephone rang around noon. It was not Donohue, but Dr. Thomas.

"I testified to suicide," he said quickly.

As I took in his words, I thought how scary it must be for a doctor to tell that to his patient.

The judge had been very angry with the agency, Dr. Thomas said, and had refused to grant a further stay of his order. As of June 10, the agency would have to begin searching.

Mathilda Stern had not been present. And the lawyer who spoke for the agency was not Jerry Friedman but a new one, a Mr. Silver. The doctor was particularly impressed by the judge's understanding, for the judge had seemed as frustrated with the agency's attitude as we were. There had been quite a scene, apparently, as the judge had let loose a tirade at the agency's lawyer. Silver had had to stand there, quietly accepting it. It was a terrible experience for Silver, said Dr. Thomas sympathetically. Dr. Thomas thought him a nice person. I tried to feel sorry for Silver, too, since the psychiatrist seemed to be telling me to; but I could summon up no pity at all.

When Donohue finally telephoned, I asked about the agency's new lawyer. Yes, they had brought in Mike Silver, one of the partners at Curry, Pell; he was very highly regarded.

How had the judge liked the affidavits?

"We didn't use them."

"Why not?"

"It's better." Donohue seemed not to want to explain. "Listen, I'll send you a copy of the transcript. On June 10 they've got to start looking. That's not very far away."

"Just one more thing, Joe."

"Yes?" He was more patient, actually, than he used to be.

"I will have won by July 11, won't I?"

"July 11? Hmmm. What's happening then?"

"We're going away with the kids."

"I don't know." He paused. "Actually, you might not."

"That's four whole *weeks* after they start searching," I objected. "With names and addresses, a search can be done in two *days!*"

The court transcript arrived on the morning of May 28. The judge's tirade at Silver was not included—"Discussion off the record." Although Dr. Thomas said that the transcript did not begin to give an adequate impression of the intensity of the judge's ire with the agency, it still seemed marvelously strong. Dr. Thomas's testimony, moreover, was firm and clear:

> In the last three to four weeks my patient has undergone a very marked personality change. Prior to this time she has never shown any evidence of such gross emotional instability as she shows today. This is in direct association with the delay and attempt at a stay of your order. She has become anxious, she has called me frequently. . . . She has made allusions to suicide repeatedly. And I think that if there isn't some movement and some conclusion made with respect to your order, I sincerely believe that she will become so depressed that I will have to hospitalize her.

The judge had concluded:

> Now, after fifteen days from today, if an Appellate Division justice does not further stay my stay, the agency will be compelled to go forward, or we will have to take very strict measures to get your records, and then the confidentiality won't be there anymore. . . . We will make it June 10, a Monday. By 4 P.M. my stay is over. . . . [To Dr. Thomas:] If after your testimony the Appellate Division justice grants a further stay, he is taking somebody's life in his hands. I don't think he will do it.

I made photocopies of the court transcript and sent them to the eight people who had written supporting affidavits, telling them that even though their statements had not been used, I was appreciative of their efforts. Even the two who had retained their commitment to "mutual consent," Annette Baran and Miss Archibald, nonetheless had certainly supported my own case. And Miss Archibald, who had sent copies of her affidavit to both the Child Welfare League and Dennis Rennick at the Children's Aid Society of New York, had sent a particularly sympathetic covering letter to Joe Donohue: "Without knowing all the facts with respect to Mrs. Maxtone-Graham but basing my judgment on telephone calls from her and data in affidavits, I feel great compassion for her efforts to search for and find her birth mother. I will be interested in the outcome of this most interesting situation."

Maybe it was just as well that Donohue had not used the affidavits; the agency might have manipulated them into one more excuse for delay. As it was now, there would be a whole month between the beginning of the search and our family departure to Europe. Surely that was ample time.

That same evening, May 28, 1974, Professor Cyril Means formally agreed to be counsel for ALMA's constitutional case. It would be presented as a class action, and Professor Means would begin work immediately.

I wondered what Mathilda Stern looked like. I found myself searching for her among my fellow riders on buses. Might I spot her? Would there be some giveaway, a large manila envelope with a name and address? She would smile at me—social workers were always smiling at you—and I would scream back, "I'm the person you're torturing! I'm 'the petitioner,' Mathilda Stern, I'm . . . "

But I did not know how to complete the fantasy. If other passengers heard me, would I have broken the court order? "Mrs. Maxtone-Graham goes around telling everyone on buses." Could I silently leap at her throat? "The petitioner is obviously unstable. She should not be trusted with the files."

God, even in my mind I did not have the freedom to behave like a lunatic on the crosstown bus!

"And when June 10 comes, how do we know they really will search?"

"Oh, they'll do it. They have to, like it or not."

"But how can we be sure? And that they'll do a halfway decent job? That they genuinely will try?"

Donohue was silent for a moment. "They have to—they have to act in good faith."

"And can we be *sure?*"

Perhaps I was suggesting something which Joe Donohue had never before imagined. When his words came, they were slow and thoughtful, his voice was filled with conviction: "One *has* to act in good faith."

Izzie called to say that while going through marriage records for 1939 and 1940 he had uncovered some Williams brides not included on Jack's list. Of particular interest were three whose husbands had marvelously unusual names. The first, a Joanna from Maryland, had married a Canadian seaman, Joseph Urbain Rousseau. Yes, Rousseau would be nice: "The fruits of the earth belong equally to us all and the earth itself to no one." There was a Virginia from Hoboken, who had married an Alex M. Ceralde. And there was a Ruth with a Spanish mother, who had married a Russian called George Severian Ketiladze.

But Izzie's findings were no better than Jack's. Unique though their husbands' names might be, none of the three women had reached eighteen by the time of my birth. Still, I scribbled everything Izzie gave me onto the margins of Jack's list.

The rest of Izzie's finds had less exotic names. Of the fifteen additional Williams brides, there were only two real possibilities: Sue E., who had married Patrick Bobbin, and Moon, who had married Frank Eliot Ladler. Both Sue E. and Moon had married in 1939, both were the right age, and the name Moon seemed particularly intriguing. Studying the details, I discovered that Moon's address in 1939 was the present address of McKinley and Hart! And, as if this were not coincidence enough, her husband's then home address was Charlie's present one!

I called Ed Goldfader with the news. Reading off my notes, I realized that today—May 30—was Moon Williams Ladler's thirty-fifth wedding anniversary! This was getting wilder every minute.

Ed called back within an hour: The Ladlers had stayed in New York until 1951. They had lived on East 37th Street, just a block away from my publishers. But in 1951, the Ladlers disappeared, and so far Ed had been unable to trace them further. The name was uncommon in New York, but there were many—too many—in New England.

The second of Izzie's possibles, Sue E. Williams, I recognized from last October's compilation of Williamses listed in the 1935 Manhattan telephone directory who lived near Booth Memorial Hospital. A few phone calls disclosed that there were no Bobbins at all in the five boroughs of New York, but there was a P. L. Bobbin in Nassau County. Lyn Cobb, who lived nearby, offered to stake out the Bobbin house for me, taking her ten-year-old in the car with her. Maybe, Lyn suggested, she could approach Mrs. Bobbin by pretending to sell magazines.

But the next morning, when Lyn arrived at the Bobbin address, she had no need to invent a ruse to get inside: The Bobbins' house was the very one in which Lyn's adoptive grandmother had lived throughout Lyn's childhood!

Mrs. Bobbin, unfortunately, was not at all the right age to be my mother.

Search Diary, Monday, 3 June 1974
Appellate Division has refused to grant a further stay. The bad news, though, is that the Appeal will not be argued until June 19.

Denial of the agency's request for a further stay meant a round won by me. But what a long time it would be until the search began at 4:00 P.M. on June 10.

On June 4, the *New York Times* carried a feature headlined, "Lepers Sad but Hopeful in Giving Up Children for U.S. Adoption." The article was accompanied by photographs of some of the families being severed. The non-leper children were being taken from their leper parents not for medical reasons but for "the promise of a solid diet, pleasant housing, good education . . . a much better chance." The arranger of the adoptions was quoted: "What I am trying to do is liberate the children." It sounded like wanting to liberate apples from other people's orchards. "For the parents, it is love for their children that lets them send the children away," continued the adoption arranger. "That is, for them, the meaning of true love." I composed letters of objection to the editors of the *Times* and stared at the picture of a little girl named Hae Sook, almost three now. One day she would be thirty-nine.

Joe Donohue sent over copies of the agency's motion for a stay and his affidavit in opposition, together with the order from the Appellate Division.

I was now known as "Petitioner-Respondent," I noted, and the Children's Aid Society was called "Respondent-Appellant." And the agency, although denied a further stay, had been granted by the Appellate Division "preservation of the confidentiality of this proceeding, including not publishing any order."

The agency papers were written by the new man, Silver. Although he avoided Friedman's "these women," Silver was nonetheless infuriating, especially when he pronounced that "the agency is sympathetic to the anguish Petitioner-Respondent feels. . . . "

Donohue's opposing papers again contained some nice moments. I especially liked the line, "From the inception of this proceeding, it was the agency rather than the court which requested confidential treatment." At last Joe Donohue was fighting the secrecy! His conclusion was neat, too:

"In complying with the first phase of Surrogate Sylvane's order, no prejudice whatsoever could conceivably flow to the agency or to the natural mother since the investigator who will be hired to ascertain her whereabouts will not be told about the existence of the proceeding."

It was June again, the season of doctor check-ups and dental visits and children's birthday parties.

Each day I arranged to talk with Ed Goldfader or Melia or Donohue, but never with all three. I was spacing my comforts out, always holding something in reserve.

I thought about running away, but where could I go? Afraid of airplanes, afraid to be alone, afraid of the dark . . .

Each morning when I woke up I noticed that my face was salt wet.

Divining a motive for the agency's opposition remained a constant preoccupation. If all this battle *was* "in the best interest of the child," from what was the agency's secrecy protecting me? For the first time I considered a possibility that filled me with genuine terror: To find myself in an incestuous relationship. Being the product of incest, although not pretty, was bearable news; I was not, after all, responsible for the acts of others. But supposing I myself had committed incest, had unwittingly married my own brother, the guilt would then fall to me.

I wondered if one of John's parents could be my mother or my father. I thought of John's mother: Were she my mother, too, she would have known so in time, and would never have allowed the marriage. But what of John's father, who had lived in England and did not meet me until a year after the wedding? Where had he been in 1934? Had the agency lied about my father being Irish? Had they told me he died thirty years ago so that I would pursue no further? Yet if kindness were the agency's motive, why did they by their secrecy leave me still committing my incest?

It was reasonably clear that my in-laws in no way could have been my parents and that my husband and I were not

187

brother and sister. And I certainly doubted that the agency's motive was kindness. Still I wished I could be sure that the agency grasped the issue: I did not want protection from any truth, however horrible. Whatever the facts of my past, I would rather know them than not know them.

Izzie had now progressed to the 1941 marriages. But despite his efforts, the best he was coming up with was the same Welsh Sybil whose husband was a marine engineer, plus a Carol Marion. Carol Marion was the daughter of John and Virginia Ruth—a J, a Virginia; she was a dancer, her husband was an artist, and she had been born in Oklahoma. But Oklahoma was so far away. Wales was so far away. Everything was far away. Only summer was near.

Again, I noted Izzie's additions. I noted them all as they came. Like Izzie, I was eliminating nothing, writing out whatever I received. All these people, all these useless people, I was neither forgetting nor remembering, but simply holding. And there were now masses of names on reserve for an inspiration.

"You know, Audrey, one day this will all be past."

"Do you *really* think so?"

"Oh yes. The records will be open, the secrecy gone . . . "

"Adoptees won't have to go through what we've been through." Audrey paused, then giggled. "And no one will *believe* it was once this way."

"We'll all sit together on our rockers at the old folks' home and talk about 'the old days.' "

"No one will understand it. They'll think we were *crazy*."

Ian went to stay for a few days with his friend Timmy King at Timmy's grandmother's summer cottage. I was glad for Ian's sake that he was having a chance to get away from the tension at home; and I was amused to hear that Timmy's grandmother was named Florence Fisher.

On June 9, my Florence Fisher left on a speaking tour of

six cities, concluding with a visit to her natural father in Los Angeles. Florence gave me the phone number at each of her stops. I should feel free to call her whenever I wanted, she said, and she would be back at the end of the month. The end of the month? Could, would, the month ever end?

The morning of June 10 came. Joe Donohue telephoned: The detective would be going to Curry, Pell that afternoon at four.

And there was more good news. My file, he said, was now with Curry, Pell. Curry, Pell would certainly not destroy a file. Mike Silver had a fine reputation. Dr. Thomas said he was a nice man.

This time it was *not* a dream. This time, it would *really* happen.

chapter fifteen

THE AGENCY'S
COURT-ORDERED SEARCH

It was now two days into the agency's search. Finally there was a reasonable possibility that my mother was being found.

Cyril Means visited me at home, wanting to talk about my case. He intended to use my experience with New York's Domestic Relations Law §114 as a part of his argument and to include me as one of the plaintiffs in ALMA's forthcoming class action. The enormous difficulties with which I had been confronted, said Cyril, would demonstrate that New York's adoption law was unworkable. With "Matter of Maxtone-Graham" before them, the Federal judges would not be able to rule that the state's law had already provided an adequate remedy for adoptees and that therefore the Federal courts need not be involved. The way Cyril described it, all my misery had not been wasted; on the contrary, the force of the agency's opposition, the gross expenditures of time, money, morale, might truly serve a purpose.

Despite the confidential aspect of my own case, Cyril explained, I was completely free to speak with him inasmuch as he was acting as my counsel in the constitutional case. We talked at length about both cases, and when Cyril left, he took my complete file of legal documents away with him for further study.

Soon after Cyril's departure, three items arrived from McKinley and Hart, all in baby blue covers. Two of these looked like the usual law brief, but the third was a great packet, actually bound like a book. On the front of all three items was printed, very important and formidable:

Appellate Division—First Department

In the Matter of the Application of Katrina Kanzler Maxtone-Graham pursuant to the Domestic Relations Law, §114, for access to and inspection of sealed records pertaining to her adoption by Ernest Kanzler and Josephine C. Kanzler, his wife.

Petitioner-Respondent

against

THE CHILDREN'S AID SOCIETY

Respondent-Appellant

"Against." I liked that best.

I had not been expecting to receive any legal papers before the hearing of the appeal on June 19, nor had I wanted to; the appeal seemed simply a further device by the agency to harass and delay me. Besides, the premise of the conflict was ridiculous: I would be asking to have the order—which I despised—upheld, while the agency would be asking to be excused from the order they had helped to write. Anyway, since my mother would have been found before June 19, there was no need for me to face the subject.

Still, I was curious. The big blue book, entitled "Record on Appeal," was ninety pages long, but I saw at a quick glance that it was nothing more than a rehash of a lot of papers I had seen before and, moreover, placed in the wrong order. The two much thinner booklets bore the titles "Petitioner-Respondent's Brief" and "Brief for Respondent-Appellant." These were clearly more interesting.

I opened the agency's brief. It was even worse than their previous papers. "The petitioner seeks to learn the identity of her natural mother (and apparently enter into some form of relationship with her) in order to help cure an 'identity' problem which she has been experiencing." "Petitioner has been under care for 15 years. Her doctor cannot guarantee that

191

communication with her mother will cure her." Where would they ever stop? I read on, trying not to absorb the tides of innuendos and insults, but merely to catch the general drifts. "The only relationship which existed between petitioner and her natural mother was a biological one. . . . " "The natural mother told her husband she had a previous child that died." "[C]lear evidence that the natural mother wanted no contact with her daughter." When it was over, I felt washed out. Washed out, washed up, waterlogged, awash.

After about fifteen minutes of sitting and staring, I picked up Donohue's brief. Immediately a footnote caught my eye: "The agency is in error when it states that petitioner simply seeks the married name of her natural mother (A. Br. p. 2) or to have her natural mother communicate with her (A. Br. p. 9). Also petitioner, who has a husband and four children, has never intimated that she would want her natural mother to become responsible for her (A. Br. p. 10)."

Although I could barely read anymore, barely think, barely feel, I could see that all of Donohue's points were terrific. He neatly knocked down the agency's assertion—at this late date—that we were arguing in the wrong court. He took care of their references to social worker privilege by repeating his refutation of last February, "[T]he courts have consistently held that the claim of privilege to protect the parent must be subordinated to the child's interest." He even made a nice reference to the paucity of "authority which construes 'good cause' " being the result of judges' specific requests that their opinions and orders not be published. And one particular paragraph stood out from the others. This one was really heartening to read:

> In its brief and the record on appeal the agency has repeatedly asserted that a parade of horrors including the destruction of the whole adoption process will result if petitioner is given information surrounding her adoption. [*Bravo, Donohue.*] None of the agency's sociological discussions are relevant to this case because the petitioner is an adult, her adoptive parents and natural father are all

dead and her natural mother, under the safeguard of court imposed confidentiality, will simply be asked by an officer of the court whether she will waive her privilege in favor of the relief her daughter seeks. Since the facts in this case are so unique it would appear that the agency's real objection to the order appealed from is the desire of the agency, rather than its client, to keep completed adoptions closed. [*Joe Donohue said it, he really said it!*] In refusing to communicate with its client, the agency has made its own interest paramount to that of its clients.

The truth at last was going to be heard!

But I was too weak to hang on to the comfort. Cyril Means came back to borrow the three blue books. I was glad to have them out of the house.

Now there was nothing left to do but wait for the detectives' news.

To be stripped of even the pretense of personal power is to face despair. My family watched, concerned but ineffectual. Dr. Thomas told me, "You feel very angry." Donohue was busy, Charlie was "not up on the case," Florence was away although she telephoned every few days—"They have no right to do this to you." Ed Goldfader had another lead to look into, Lyn Cobb had leaflets to distribute from helicopters, Audrey had religion, Melia had heart and fifteen more pages. They were all wonderful, really. They all gave me time and patience and warm voices. But none of them could bring any sense to what was going on.

My fantasies were getting more violent. Now I imagined that in my earlier life I had murdered little children. *This* was the agency's reason for keeping me from my records.

Talking with Donohue was the one action I could take. "Tell them, Joe, tell Mr. Silver. They've got the husband's name, profession, their addresses—it's all in the agency file. If they provide just *her* name, that isn't everything. And the grandfather's name, grandmother, aunts, uncle—the agency has everything."

"I'm sure Curry, Pell . . . "

"Tell Mr. Silver that the agency *knows* how to search. They've read Florence Fisher's book. It's been a week, Joe. If the detective doesn't know how, I'll tell him, for God's sake. I've got packets of lists, Joe. Why don't they call me, do you think that their detective might call me for my help?"

"They're not going to call you, Katrina."

"Why not? I could help, I've got—"

"They don't even want you to know who they're using."

"How dare they? What do they take me for?"

"I really don't know." He sighed. "They haven't told me, either. Unfortunately, I can only do so much. But they promised me they would conduct a good search. And Curry, Pell is a good firm, Mike Silver is a nice guy."

"Tell him about the uncle's name, and the grandparents, how you use old records, tell him about Florence's book, tell him that their detective has got to do a decent job—"

"Listen," Joe interrupted. "Do you want to come to the hearing on the 19th? I'll meet you, if you like."

"Really?" Suddenly I felt alive.

"Just do me one favor?"

"Sure."

"Don't bring Florence Fisher!"

Then the phone call was over and I was back to waiting. Through my fog, I gave a birthday party for Guy and sixteen second-graders—balloons and hats and secret agent pens— and went to Emily's school commencement.

Search Diary, Monday, 17 June 1974
    Florence called, from Cleveland, to say an ALMA article coming out in Time *mag. on 18th.*

Maybe the appellate judges would read the article before coming to the hearing.

Melia told me that her husband's plant was closing and he was being relocated to Nebraska. He would make a trip out this month to look for a house; she would leave for Nebraska in August.

Into the second week, and still no news of my mother.

"What are you going to wear?" asked Donohue.

"What do you mean, what am I going to wear?"

"I don't want you to appear in something outlandish."

"Don't worry, I'll be fine," I assured him. There were more important matters to discuss. "Why is it taking so long, Joe? Are they delaying until after the appeal?"

"Even if they found her, they'd still have the hearing."

"Then what's taking so much time?"

"Maybe she really *is* hard to find," Donohue suggested.

"I'll bet if they'd hired Tracers, they'd have found her by now!"

"Listen, I'm due down in court . . . "

"Just one thing. You know what I did?"

"What?"

"I hired Tracers, myself."

"Really?" Donohue sounded startled, then excited. "Did they come up with anything?"

"Nope. How can they, when they've got no information!"

On the day of my hearing before the Appellate Division, Joe Donohue met me in the lobby of the courthouse. He was accompanied by an exceedingly young man with pale blue eyes and pale curls who "will be listening with you in the courtroom to gain some experience." It was immediately obvious that this junior lawyer had been brought along to babysit.

The three of us crossed the lobby to a bench near the courtroom door. Donohue was particularly lively, talking as he worked on his papers, scribbling notes in the margin and drawing long arrows for insertions.

"You'll hear a lot of strange words, and it will seem very confusing to you," the young lawyer was trying to explain. "But you don't have to concern yourself, Mr. Donohue comes here often."

I glanced around the now-filling lobby. The junior lawyer kept on talking. "This court is one of the most interesting in the city, it's called the Appellate—"

"He saw you!" Donohue suddenly exclaimed. "There he goes."

"Who?"

"Silver. We should never have brought you in by the front!"

"I'm allowed to be here!"

"I wish he hadn't seen you." Donohue turned to the boy lawyer. "I hope he doesn't make something of it."

"Maybe I'm your secretary," I suggested cheerfully.

"You're *not* my secretary. We shouldn't have met until after."

"I *know* I'm not your secretary. But *he* doesn't."

"He knows, I could tell."

Donohue left us, and the junior lawyer led me into the courtroom. It was huge, awesome. We walked down a side aisle, talking in subdued voices as if we were in church. In the distance, I could see the altar at which the five judges would sit. The boy lawyer led me to a side seat in the very back row, the farthest possible place from the action. It was just like a church pew.

"I won't be able to see, this far away."

"This is where Mr. Donohue wants you."

We sat. Mr. Blue Eyes made polite conversation about the ceiling beams, I muttered appropriate "aahs" and stared eagerly around me. A party of middle-aged women wearing corsages and nametags declaring "Acme Tenant ·Group" trooped past us directly to the front seats. The room was suddenly very full.

The judges were announced. Everyone stood up and was quiet, as though for the processional hymn, and five figures in black robes filed in.

The judges went to their seats in a prescribed order, less like ministers now and more like schoolchildren coming on stage for a commencement exercise—number one to center, two to stage right, three to left, four to far right, five to far left. It was all very imposing.

The first case seemed to be about some cartons sitting on a New Jersey pier. People wandered in and out; the talk went on.

"Matter of Katrina K. Maxtone-Graham" was called.

I felt proud; at least my name could be spoken aloud.

"Mr. Donohue wants you to be quiet," whispered Blue Eyes, "just as though you weren't here."

I nodded sweetly. Over his shoulder I saw Cyril Means walk in. Winking, he took a seat in the row immediately in front of us, and looked straight ahead toward the judges. I noted with pleasure that Blue Eyes had missed him.

Donohue and Silver were beginning. Like the previous two lawyers, they stood side by side, facing the judges. They looked exactly like the bride and groom at a wedding; I wondered if they didn't feel silly.

Donohue was impressive and articulate. I leaned farther forward.

"Sit back," whispered Blue Eyes.

"Shhh. I can't hear."

The judges were lighting into Silver: Did he know if the mother's husband was even living? How did he know the mother did not want to be found?

They were asking all the right questions. It was fantastic. They were saying all our side's lines.

"The only thing the petitioner-respondent does not know is her mother's married name," Silver stated. "All previous information is known."

"Bullshit," I muttered, glowering at Silver's back.

Blue Eyes nudged me. I moved back in my seat a few inches to calm his nerves.

Maybe her mother would be very happy to see her, a judge suggested to Silver. Maybe the husband was dead. Maybe the mother was yearning for her long-lost child. Then, suddenly, one of the judges was extolling the beauty of motherhood, the sanctity of this closest of all human relationships. There was silence in the room. The audience, 90 percent of them men, listened reverently. The hymn to maternity seemed to go on forever, but it probably lasted only three or four minutes.

Now a decision would be made, concluded the chief judge, adding lightly but clearly, "Let's hope we are not blinded by our tears."

The hearing was over.

Cyril stood up, shot me a big grin, and went out. The boy lawyer, looking immensely relieved, indicated that we could depart.

Donohue, Blue Eyes, and I met in a nearby coffee shop. Donohue was pleased with the hearing; but Silver had, indeed, said something to the judges about my being present in the courtroom, and Joe was annoyed and concerned. As he talked on about the case, I realized how disturbed Joe Donohue was by this battle, and how much effort he was putting into it. Football frame sprawled out over the cramped coffee shop booth, he was no longer the cool preoccupied martinet I had met in February, nor the rushed, unlistening voice on the telephone, nor even the taut performer ad-libbing before judges. He was a warm, friendly person.

"When this is all over," said Joe, "you and I ought to open a bottle of champagne."

Cyril called shortly after I got home; he figured I had won the appeal, possibly even unanimously. Cyril's only uncertainty was over the chief judge, who had made the crack about "tears." The remark had probably been intended to counteract the feeling for my side and maintain a semblance of impartiality. But it could also have meant that the judge was opposed.

"Yet I don't think so," Cyril said. "He's an excellent man."

Cyril scored each judge's attitude and complimented Donohue's performance. There would be no transcript, he explained, as the Appellate Division used a tape recorder. "And poor Michael Silver," he said, "they certainly gave it to him!"

"I guess so, but how can you have sympathy for him?"

"It's no fun to stand up there and have to defend a ridiculous position," Cyril replied. "They all have to do it once in a while. But no one wants to do it too often."

That afternoon Audrey went down to Worth Street once again. At the Bureau of Vital Records, she made a wrong turn and found herself in an unfamiliar corridor. Directly in front of her was a sign: "Sealed Records—No Unauthorized Personnel." Clerks were moving in and out of the forbidden room, and Audrey could neither go in nor even linger. Unwilling simply to move on, she made a pretense of looking for the ladies' room. To her surprise, a rather seedy looking man offered to show her the way. Inside, alone and safe for the moment, Audrey tried to calm down: It was a shattering experience to be physically so close to the papers she desperately sought.

When she came out of the ladies' room, the man was still there. He stopped her.

"Maybe I could help you in *another* way," he said.

Audrey wondered if it was possible the man worked here. He was a short, slight, black man of approximately fifty-five, wearing a red shirt, jeans, suspenders, and a shiny belt that might be a chain. Was he offering access to the sealed records?

The man handed Audrey a card and disappeared.

The card read, "Victor Frost, 960 West End Ave., Apt. 83D, Women's Clothes, tailored to suit. Free home demo. At all prices. Even free. Pants from $8, ensemble from $16, skirts from $6. Made while you wait. Park at 106th & B'way. Leave precise message under door. 8th floor, Name, address, when you will return, etc. Mention your size."

Tailor? Pervert? Con artist? Clerk? The possibilities echoed the childhood rhyme. Or perhaps he was the adoptee's white knight on the golden steed. Neither of us had the courage to find out.

The following day was Thursday. The hearing past, the reports of it heard, now I was back to waiting.

Search Diary, Thursday, 20 June 1974
Peg Lawrence is putting up ads for the 3 of us—

herself, Audrey, me—("Judith Williams, in Foster Care 1935-1938, seeks Foster Parents . . . "), in Laundromats, Sun-City, etc.! Peg has talked to Mathilda Stern. (She had her husband do it, for her.) Plans to see Stern in August. Has 19-year-old son, who wants to come to New York, flirt with social workers, and con the info. Told her social workers unflirtable.

The day ended without news of the detectives' investigations.

I awoke the next morning with the mounting sense that the agency was about to spring a new, and worse, surprise upon me. I had no idea what the blow would be, but I was increasingly convinced of its imminence.

I called Charlie and asked if there were any means whereby I could assure that if I died the agency's role would be investigated. Interestingly, Charlie did not object nor argue. Instead, he informed me matter-of-factly that he could draft a codicil to my will.

Feeling a little better, I telephoned Donohue. "There has to be some result, Joe, before the 11th of July. Something."

"I'll call Silver and see if we can't get them to move over there."

"There's not much time."

"Okay, let me see if I can arrange a hearing. I think that's reasonable."

They were going to *not* find her—was that what the agency had in store? Here it was Friday. Another Friday; they had been searching for two whole working weeks. It was the 21st of June already, another Friday and another empty weekend threatening. I did not know how I could get myself through it.

I considered committing myself to a mental hospital, and I thought of Bellevue. But then I remembered hearing horror stories of people being drugged on Thorazine. I did not want that. The Payne Whitney Clinic was a possibility; what did they do to you there?

Suicide was not an option. On the contrary, survival was crucial. I had to live through one more day, every day to live through that day, if only to defy the agency's desire for my "silence in perpetuity."

I called the Suicide Prevention Bureau and asked if there was a mental hospital I could go to where I would not be drugged.

"We do not have that sort of information here," snapped an irritated voice. "Consult your local Community Council."

"But—"

"In your own community." Suicide Prevention disconnected my line.

Donohue telephoned that evening around 5:30. Silver had told him that after two weeks of searching for my mother it "has been established that she is not in New York State." Beginning on Monday, they "would start looking for her in other states."

This was the first news I had had, and as such it was exciting. At the same time, of course, it was non-news. I wondered how the detectives would proceed now—checking retirement states, centers of activity of her husband's profession? Or would they begin with Alabama and go dumbly through the alphabet?

Donohue went on. The agency, he told me, had not hired a detective firm with the resources of a large organization, as I had assumed. No, the agency had engaged only a single individual. This individual, in his two weeks on the job, had spent $500.

This was the blow of defeat I had felt coming: The generous allowance of $3,000, intended to insure a superior job, was instead guaranteeing the slow drip torture of delay. Ten more weeks would pass before the agency's detective would even acknowledge failure. Ten weeks!

"And what if they don't find her ever, Joe? What then?"

201

"I asked Silver that. I asked, if they don't find her, and the money was spent, whether you could then have the files."

"Good for you, Joe."

"He told me, 'I'd say yes. But the agency will no doubt require a good-cause hearing. And if they lose, they will probably appeal it.'"

After I put down the telephone receiver, I realized that all this delay over the search was only the beginning. The agency was sure to pull another procrastinating performance when my mother was located. Another three months could be spent haggling over each detail of what could be said, how it could be said, and when, where . . .

I wanted to tell someone, to let people know. I should be going to the press with this story. But here was the rub: Communication, which was my only means of winning, was also my certain way of losing.

Never had my powerlessness been so clear. Three months, hell; how would I get through the next three minutes? I thought of Florence away on tour. I had resisted disturbing her, but now I was desperate. She was at her father's in California. I called her, and I felt all right for quite a while afterwards. I ate dinner, washed dishes, talked with the children. The okay feeling lasted for almost an hour and a half. Then I began to crumble again.

Maybe Judianne Densen-Gerber could do something. She was away, but the ex-addict on the switchboard at her drug rehabilitation center was eager to help.

I did not want to turn to yet one more person, to involve yet one more unrelated stranger. I wanted to die, really.

But the man would not let me off the phone. He really wanted to talk to me, he insisted, he really would be happy if . . .

The nicer he was, the more I cried. "I'm not worthy of your time."

"It don't matter what you done," he insisted.

"I'm worthless."

"Look, if someone got a rap on you, we'll get you law-yers."

"Not lawyers!" I choked.

"Good lawyers," he asserted. "The best. There's no cost."

We talked for a very long time, and after the call I went straight to sleep.

On Saturday, we celebrated Emily's eleventh birthday with a family party. On Sunday, our neighbors, the Andersons, were having a wedding at their home and we, who never entertained, gave the bridal lunch.

Somehow I was talking, doing, continuing, but the appearance of functioning was a sham. And what of the future? Time was pressing me forward, but no roads were open. I could not leave on that ship in July and be a participant in my family's life, and neither could I cancel the trip and crush their dreams. Either way, I would see my failure reflected in the eyes of my children. There was nowhere to go.

On Monday, I was back at my desk, waiting. The only news was from ALMA friends: Peg Lawrence, whose adoptive father had told her her original name—Agatha Car, spelled, unusually, without a second "r"; Nanny reporting that she might have found her mother—dead in 1966—a Catholic nun! and Lyn Cobb, giving her phone number in Florida where she would be visiting her adoptive father. In the evening, Audrey and I spent three hours discussing, as though for the first time, the possible significance of those extra unexplained numbers on our certificates of birth by adoption.

Charlie's codicil arrived on Tuesday: "I authorize my executors to bring such legal proceedings against the Children's Aid Society of New York City as they may in their discretion deem advisable." Blah-blah lawyer talk. "I further authorize my executors to retain Florence Fisher as an adviser and consultant." No, this was merely a shadow of what I really wanted to say. Even in my will, the truth of my predicament was not going to be clearly and forcefully stated.

No means of attack, no means of defense. No right to say so.

On Wednesday morning I telephoned Joe Donohue and spoke to him with surprising assertiveness. I told him he must do something.

He replied that he had, that a hearing was scheduled for July 10. This was the day before we were to sail on the *France*. Something would happen in time, I told myself.

I was grateful to Joe and thanked him profusely.

I wondered what to do next. A long time ago Melia had told me that one of her other cases had told her that there was a form—Form 935. If you went to Surrogate's Court, paid a fee of about $20, and filled it in, you would then be given your records. Just like that.

It was too ridiculously easy to be true. Now it occurred to me that I at least ought to try. I could call the Surrogate's Court, not use my name, and make a simple inquiry.

Form 935—"Order Breaking Seal and Directing Production of Original Birth Record"—required a court order signed by a judge, a pleasant man informed me, but it was of no use to anyone adopted through an agency. The man, a lawyer, did not rush off the phone. We kept on talking, both of us nameless, about adoption and agencies and the law. The friendly man insisted that I did not sound at all as though I were falling apart. I tried to convince him, but to no avail. Indeed, he proclaimed with admiration, he was extremely impressed by my clarity and strength.

As soon as the conversation was ended, I stripped my wallet of all identification and put four cold Tabs and a carton of cigarettes into a shopping bag. Then I left the house, hailed a taxi, and went to commit myself to the Payne Whitney Clinic.

chapter sixteen

COUNTER-SEARCH

With bland noddings and the suggestion that going home would be "sensible," the emergency room psychiatrist at Payne Whitney had refused to accept me. I had left his office and taken up residence on a chair in the hospital waiting room.

Eternity was beginning. It was cold. I was aware of sitting, of being cold. Now I was waiting for time to be over.

Six hours passed. Darkness came.

Nine hours passed. Ten.

It was midnight. The director of the emergency room, frustrated by my continuing presence, summoned another psychiatrist. This one was a woman, young and pleasant.

The doctor's warmth was compelling, and I was focusing on that rather than pleading my cause. Thus I was startled when she told me that, yes, she would accept me into the hospital. She was willing to admit me, she said, but she would not commit me; that decision was mine.

Suddenly I had freedom of choice. I was no longer bashing my head against a stone wall, helplessly begging to be let in. How different it was.

"Thank you," I heard myself say.

After a minimum stay of seventy-two hours, the doctor was explaining, I could leave at any time—provided, however, that a panel of doctors did not decide it was in my best interest to commit me. This panel of doctors could, if they decided I was truly crazy, force me to remain in the hospital.

It came to me in a flash that the price of my present acceptance at the hospital was to yield control of my destiny to someone else. Too much control had been taken from me already. I would not intentionally, willingly, relinquish yet more.

With relief, I left the hospital and returned home.

The enormity of my mistake in leaving Payne Whitney struck me the instant I awoke the next morning. Nothing was changed. Today was the same as yesterday, except that one more day had passed, and I was one day closer to July 11. If only I had stayed at the hospital I would have been waking up to a fresh start, in a different place, with unfamiliar faces, new concerns.

And today held the additional grimness of preparing the children's suitcases for the trip—letting down hems, sorting hand-me-downs, dragging impatient youngsters through the buttonings and unbuttonings. Tomorrow we were to leave the city for a week's courtesy visit to my mother-in-law's on Cape Cod. Upon our return there would be only a useless weekend and a hasty Monday and Tuesday; that Wednesday would bring the new court hearing Donohue had arranged; and Thursday, our departure on the *France*. My time had already run out, I realized abruptly.

The telephone rang.

"Katrina? Joe Donohue. I'm on a boat, sailing, how are you today?"

Goddamn sailboats, I hated them. "Just for the day?"

"No, through the weekend. We'll be cruising."

So Donohue, my final straw, was going to disappear into the sunset.

"I just checked in with the office," he went on cheerfully. "There was a message that the agency's detective has made an oral report about not being able to find your mother. He says he's looking very hard."

"Oh, yeah, I bet." By the time Donohue returned, I would already be on the Cape.

"Even though she's got an unusual married name, he has not been able to trace her in New York after 1955."

"After 1955!"

"He has her in the New York area until 1955, and then she disappears." Donohue's voice was calm. "He says he can't find her after that."

"Those fools, Joe! They may have *helped* me! That's terrific! 'The New York area, and disappears after '55.'"

"I thought you'd want to know. And that her married name is unusual—did you get that, too?" he asked.

"Right. Now it's for *sure*. Was there anything else?"

"Just that he's going to keep on looking."

"I'm going to call Tracers immediately. Joe, you're wonderful. If they say anything else, no matter how trivial . . . "

"I don't expect to hear from them again, Katrina, not before the hearing on the 10th."

"Thanks again, Joe, and have a nice sail!"

Dialing Ed Goldfader's number, I realized that for two months I had been telephoning him every second or third day, chatting on about Williamses and ALMA and bringing up children, and yet this was the first time I actually had news to impart.

"What's up?" Ed asked immediately.

"How can you tell?"

"Your voice. Shoot."

"The unusual name—it's confirmed! Plus, 'in the New York area until 1955.' She disappears after 1955."

"Wow!" Ed exclaimed. "What happened?"

"The detective gave a report."

"Well, I didn't think you got an index card in the mail!"

"Anyway, I've got Jack's list. If we could select the five most unusual names, and then we see whether . . . "

"Fire away."

"Spotonick, Stymers, Jillick—"

"Spell 'em."

I did, slowly.

"Others?"

"Themis Raber, R-A-B-E-R. Wife is Lois. She's the right age, and born in New York. I've found Rabers, but not Themises."

"Sounds Greek."

"Then, from Izzie's additions, I've got George Ketiladze, K-E-T-I-L-A-D-Z-E; Patrick Bobbin, B-O-B—"

"Forget Bobbin. There's three Bobbins on the Island, right near me."

"Then I think that's all." I flipped hurriedly through my lists. "I still like Moon Ladler, but you say it's common. There are a few other names that are sort of unusual, but not as much. I don't think we have the time to pursue more than a couple—"

"We're talking about the early 1940's, right?"

"I figure my mother got married sometime between '38 and '43."

"When do you sail for Europe?"

"The 11th."

"And you want to find your mother by the 11th, right?"

"But of course!" I laughed. "Actually, by the 10th. There's a big hearing on the 10th."

"You know that next week's a holiday. It's a short week. Ketiladze—is George?"

"George Severian Ketiladze. Born in Russia, wife is Ruth. It's a great name, but there's one snag: Ruth works out to have been seventeen when I was born. Mathilda Stern said in a sworn statement that my mother was eighteen."

"Maybe Mathilda lied."

"That's perjury, isn't it?"

"Okay," Ed said, "while we've been talking, I've been doing a little work here. In the period we're talking about, 1938 through 1943, of the names you've given me—Spotonick, Stymers, Jillick, Raber, and Ketiladze—Spotonick, Stymers, Jillick, and Raber never lived in New York at all."

"Oh, no."

"They must have rushed in for the wedding and cut town. But I do find a Ketiladze in Manhattan, in 1941 and 1942. Lose him in 1943."

"Shit!"

"Hang on, let me look a little further." Ed was silent for about twenty seconds. "He disappears from Manhattan in '43, but in 1949 reappears in Queens! Wonder why he moved there. He stays in Queens. Now, this is interesting: He stays in Queens until 1954, and I'm not picking him up after." Ed paused. "This is only a brief look, Katrina. But, so far, I'd say your George What's-his-name is disappearing from this area in 1954."

"Not in 1955?" I asked glumly.

" '54, '55, that's no big difference."

"Are you telling me that even if he disappears one year off, even if it's '54—"

"I'm saying one year's difference is not important."

For a moment, I could not speak. "Ed?"

"I can hear those wheels moving around in there, Katrina."

"We've either got Ketiladze or . . . Ed, it's Ketiladze or *nothing.*"

"That's about the size of it. You sure haven't given me my easiest case!"

The air between us was standing still. It was up to me to say something.

"What do you think, Ed?"

"It *is* an unusual name, all right," Ed drawled. His voice was warm and kind.

"Let's do it, Ed! Let's go for Ruth Williams Ketiladze! Mother or not, let's you and me find her!"

Ed laughed, "But do me one favor—"

"Yes?"

"Pronounce that name for me again—"

"It's 'Kay-til-AHD-zay.' Wait! I'm just guessing, myself."

"You sound very impressive. Let me find out what I can about George, and I'll get back to you. Do you think it's Slavic?"

"It's Russian. You're not too worried about the '54 being wrong and her age being wrong?"

"Those are the least of our problems. I'll see what I come

up with this afternoon and get back to you."

"Thanks, Ed. You're a brick. And I'm sorry, if it turns out to be just a wild goose chase."

"I don't mind."

Ed called back around four. "Here's the poop on George Ketiladze: Born in Russia in 1903—"

"That makes him older than she—great." I grabbed a notebook and made notes while Ed talked.

"In early 1940 he was at 3 Park Avenue in Mount Vernon; that's a large apartment building. He only stayed a few months. By late 1940 and 1941, he's in Manhattan on East 39th Street. In 1942, still Manhattan, at 220 East 52nd."

"John used to live at 434! When he first came to New York. Friendly area, and the buildings are still there."

"This building's there, but it's now a Chinese laundry. No apartments. Have been doing a trace on the owner of the building, but she disappears a year after George moves out. From 1943 to '49, I lose George completely. Can't imagine where he went. He doesn't turn up again until 1949, at 71st Avenue, Queens, telephone BO 3-5835. It's a two-family rental dwelling. Ketiladze is downstairs, Fields is upstairs. Fields moved out in early 50's, then disappeared. Present tenant, downstairs, is Becker, been there just two years. Lots of tenants in between. Same story in the houses next door. The sort of neighborhood that people move in, stay four or five years, and then they move on. Very transient. Have also checked every year since 1954, and he never shows up in New York again. That may be why the agency's detective can't find him. But I've got some ideas for tomorrow. When do you go to your mother-in-law's?"

"Tomorrow, at three."

"Well, I'm leaving the office now. We're having a cookout on the beach with the kids. But we'll talk tomorrow, okay?"

When I reported every detail of the sudden development to Audrey, she was very excited and offered to contact some Russian churches for me. While she made her calls, I dialed the Ketiladzes' 1954 phone number. I was startled when it

210

rang. I had forgotten to plan out what I might say, and I was almost relieved that no one answered.

In the evening, I felt sufficiently relaxed to concentrate on my family. They did not mention my strange absence of the previous day, nor did they treat my enjoyment of them now as something unusual. They acted as though they had not even noticed my withdrawal of these past months. It felt strange to be relaxed and affectionate and pleasant; I was surprised, actually, to observe that I still knew how.

Before going to bed, I dialed Information for Ketiladze in a few key retirement sites: Miami, Tampa, Tucson. No Ketiladzes. Tomorrow I would try another bunch. It struck me that I would never have received Joe Donohue's telephone call had I accepted admission to Payne Whitney.

Around noon, Ed called with further news: George Ketiladze was a teacher.

Everything about this man Ketiladze was coming out right. A teacher, Russian—Tolstoi, Dostoevski, Rachmaninoff . . . He *was* the one. Oops! I stopped myself short: I had forgotten that even if George Ketiladze's wife were indeed my mother, George himself would not be a blood relative.

Ed and I made guesses about George's teaching. Maybe he had taught Russian at a local college, perhaps he had given private lessons in his Queens home. Sylvia, who was a linguist, preferred the information that Ketiladze sounded like a name from the Georgian Republic of the U.S.S.R. Then I gave the children lunch and called Information in a few of the major university towns. I called Nanny, who offered to pass on her research on retired teacher associations. Nanny's own search, meanwhile, had returned to zero; the nun had been a spelling mistake on a death certificate.

Ed Goldfader telephoned me at my mother-in-law's on Monday as promised. This time his startling news was that George Ketiladze was an engineer. As early as 1928-29 his name appeared in New York City as an associate of the American Society of Electrical Engineers although, strangely, there were no more recent listings. George Ketiladze entered the U.S.A. through Canada, married Ruth A. Williams in 1940, and became a U.S. citizen in 1943. Ed had even acquired a physical description: Six foot one inch, 220 pounds, brown hair, brown eyes. Ed had also learned his birthdate: March 8, 1903.

The 8th of March—one day before my own birthday! Oh, yes, I did feel akin to this Russian, wandering man. But what of my mother? The knowledge of these consecutive birthdates would have to have affected her.

Ruth's birthdate was June 1, 1917, Ed was continuing almost monotonously; she was seventeen at my birth, twenty-three when she married. I was thinking how, from all these facts, I had hoped to make a find, not another collection of facts. Ruth's mother, Ed was saying, was Alicia Navarro and her father was Albert Tell Williams. No Virginias and no J. Indeed, the only piece of trivia that corresponded to a prior hunch was that Ruth had been born in Brooklyn.

What was the use of all this information, I asked Ed. We were still accomplishing so little.

"We've only just started," Ed said confidently.

"We don't even know for sure that we've got the right person."

"Look, it fits: A man of thirty-seven marrying a girl of twenty-three. He's been around, he's traveled—Russia, Canada, New York. Now, he's not going to go marry just any twenty-three-year-old. She's got to have had some special maturity. Your mother had been through something, she'd had a lot of life."

The initial exhilaration of the first days' searching was wearing off, and now I was seeing the underlying reality: If Ruth and George Ketiladze were indeed the right couple, then the agency's detective must have known that for over three weeks. Their detective would have known as well my mother's address when I was born, plus all the crucial data on my grandparents, my aunts, and my uncle. Ed Goldfader, with a fraction of the information held by the agency, had only a few days in which to succeed where the agency, with more data and more time, had failed. The situation was as bleak as ever.

Tuesday was a difficult day. Ed's not calling seemed confirmation of the absence of a breakthrough. Finally, I telephoned him.

Ed's voice was, as always, warm and reassuring, but his news was duller. He was now researching Navarros—a Navarro who had managed a cafe, a Navarro clerk, a Navarro who owned a candy shop. I wrote them down, but I was not really interested in Navarros. I wanted Ketiladze, Ruth. It was July 2 already.

"And I'm wondering if we shouldn't be looking into a change of name," continued Ed. "Ketiladze is impossible."

"No, it's beautiful. Besides, it begins with a K."

"Change of name proceedings are open records, but it means a visit to the Queens courthouse. That's a long trip."

This was boring, exhausting, defeating. What had started so excitingly with the snap selection of an unusual name was now subsiding to the same endless researching to which I had already devoted so many months. And I was growing panicked at the passage of time. Tomorrow, the 3rd, was Ian's birthday; the 4th was a holiday; the 5th would be consumed with the long drive home, and then there would be the lifeless weekend. Not until Monday the 8th of July could I even return to serious research! There would be just two days left before the hearing. Then came the day we were supposed to sail . . . I realized I had forgotten to think of packing my own things for our trip. I wondered when I would do it.

To kid myself into feeling useful, I called Information for the New York boroughs asking for Ruth, Albert, and R. A. Williamses. "There's no place in this world where I'll belong . . . " snatches of Phil Ochs's song rang through my head. I was scribbling the numbers on matchbook covers. "And I won't know the right from the wrong . . . "

Nothing was going to happen over the July 4th weekend. Kind Ed, who would be off with his family the entire time, discussed my case with his associate, Bob Eisenberg, and left me his home phone number "in case." The holiday passed in superficial cheer; the children had a wonderful time. On the long drive back from the Cape, I looked in local phone directories at gas stations for Ketiladze and, on behalf of Peg Lawrence, for Car, without success. Then we were home, back with the familiar scents and honks peculiar to New York streets. Nothing was different from before. And the final countdown had begun.

In the heap of mail awaiting us was a notice forwarded by Joe Donohue. On July 2, the Appellate Division had reached its decision on the agency's appeal from Surrogate Sylvane's court order: "It is hereby unanimously ordered that the order so appealed from be and the same is hereby affirmed." In simple English, I had beaten the agency, unanimously. I was glad for a victory; but it changed nothing.

The same mail held a note from Melia. Her message was the briefest she had ever sent: "Dear Katrina, Please call when you get a few moments; I'm anxious about you. Love, Melia."

It was a couple of weeks since I had last spoken with Melia. I had been avoiding the contrast between her warm encouragements and the cold realities of my situation. Now I called her and quickly summarized the fizzling Ketiladze project. In response Melia gave me the names of engineering firms in New Jersey, California, Massachusetts, the locations of major government missile centers in White Sands, El Paso, the Mojave Desert.

John came in and made the astonishing suggestion that we should go out, tonight, to the old Queens address, to get a feel of the place where the Ketiladzes once had lived.

It was sweet of him to offer, but what was the use? No one was left there. Besides, John had just finished a seven-hour car drive. I stayed on at my desk, trying Information for Toronto and Montreal, in the chance that the Ketiladzes had returned to Canada. No luck.

I called Peg Lawrence, to learn that she had been at-

tempting to telephone me all day because she had just received a certificate of birth! It was not, as she had expected,
her amended certificate but rather her original, birth-by-
being-born certificate. Back in the 1920's someone had forgotten to seal it.

Just for the heck of it, I took out the original list of female
Williamses born in 1916 and 1917. Yes, Ruth A. was there, at
the end of the Brooklyn 1917 page, one of the original 187. Yet
Ruth's certificate of birth was one I would not have considered requesting until I first had disqualified all those on the
shorter, more likely, eighteen-years-old-at-my-birth list of 93
names, of which there still remained 89.

John came back, again suggesting we go out to Queens.
The children were in their pajamas; the babysitter was free to
stay with them.

"You've got nothing to lose," John said.

There was certainly no reason to stay home.

As we set off in the car, I had a slight feeling of adventure. It was a balmy evening, and it was pleasant being out
with John, just the two of us alone. Speeding through Queens
toward 71st Avenue, we passed a sign to Booth Memorial Hospital.

The block between 70th and 71st Avenues was friendly
and residential. Trees lined the street, the houses were neat
and well kept. There were children riding bicycles on the
sidewalks, teenagers talking on the corner, and, at the far end
of the street, people buying ice cream from a busy Good Hu-
mor wagon.

We parked at the corner and walked slowly toward the
Ketiladzes' 1954 address. A boy wheeling a bicycle smiled as
he passed us. Approaching number 146, I was feeling both
nervous and exhilarated.

The first doorbell we rang was the Beckers', the very
apartment in which the Ketiladzes had lived in 1954. Becker
children raced through the doorway as I explained to Mrs.
Becker about "some close family friends who lived here in the

'50's, and was there anyone who had been in the neighborhood for about twenty years?" Mrs. Becker suggested we ask Mrs. Radkin at 149. Mrs. Radkin told us to try her downstairs neighbor, who directed us to the people at 161. The questioning grew more comfortable; I called out to faces in the windows, or addressed passersby on the sidewalk: "Know anybody who's been around for twenty years?"

The possibilities narrowed until there remained no untried names except "Esther." Esther lived up the street, near where we had started, almost directly opposite the Beckers'.

Esther's porch door was open to the evening air, revealing a warm orange glow inside. We were already partway up the steps when we realized that Esther was outside on the porch sitting in a rocking chair. Now she rose, a tiny woman in her late sixties or early seventies, with grey-blonde swirling hair and twinkly eyes.

I asked Esther if she had lived here in 1954 and if she had known Ruth and George Ketiladze. George, I said, had been an engineer.

Esther had not moved in until 1954. She cocked her head. Or was it 1955? It just could have been 1954, but, no, that seemed too long.

"What was your friends' last name again?" asked Esther.

"Ketiladze. Ruth and George Ketiladze."

"I don't think I know that last name." She paused. "Did you say he was a magician?"

I tried not to laugh. "No, an engineer. Electrical engineer."

Esther was busily trying to establish whether it was seventeen years, or nineteen or twenty or twenty-one years, that she had been in this house. Probably seventeen, though she might be wrong. She was very understanding about trying to find someone, however. She herself had searched for forty-five years for a man she had known as a girl in Poland— and she had found him at last in New York. Then she told us about her son who didn't visit much anymore. And would we like some coffee? When her son had been a boy, he had grown so fast that Esther had had to save every penny for new shoes. Always she had managed to buy him the shoes; but now he didn't come to see her very often.

I interrupted as gently as I could to ask if there were anyone else to whom I should speak.

The only long-term residents of the neighborhood were herself and the people next door, Esther said. Following Esther's gaze to the unlit porch next to hers, I saw two elderly women in the darkness, listening intently. As though having suddenly been introduced, the two women chimed into the conversation. They had bought their house about five years after Esther, they said, and they did not know Ruth and George Ketiladze either. The three old ladies then spent several minutes debating the exact year of Esther's moving in.

"What you should do," Esther returned her attention to me, "is you should talk to Juliet Goldman. She works at the cleaning store, Marshall's on Main Street."

"If anyone knows," concurred one of the neighbors, "it'll be Juliet Goldman."

"Tell her that Esther—that's me, Esther Winterstein—and you say that Esther told you to call; and you ask about your friends. Juliet knows everyone, because they all go to Juliet with their cleaning. And Juliet *has* to give the right clothes to the right customer, so of course she has to know everyone's names, too."

Esther bid us a hearty good luck and told us we should stop by to see her any time we wanted.

John and I ambled back to the car. Darkness had fallen, the street had grown calm and quiet. The younger children had gone into their homes; the older ones were talking softly on the corner. From open windows came subdued sounds of TVs and family voices. This was a neighborhood that was both tranquil and continuing.

Before we went home we drove the two blocks to Main Street, then slowly right along Main Street. I wrote down the names of every shop and building that might have been stand-ing twenty years ago.

When I telephoned Juliet in the cleaning store the follow-ing day, she was very hurried. "Ruth and George, they went out West. And he died and was cremated," Juliet replied quickly. "But how come Esther says she doesn't know them? Of course Esther knows them."

"Esther knows Ruth and George?"

"Of course, very well. And who are you?"

"I'm Katrina Maxtone-Graham. Do you know where ex-actly in the West?"

"Why do you want to know?" demanded Juliet.

"They were old friends of my family," I told her.

"I'm very busy here. It was California. I have to go now. And after he died, they brought the ashes back, but they stayed in the West." Juliet hung up.

Esther's phone number was listed, and when I called she greeted me warmly and began talking about last night. Gin-gerly I broached the fact that Juliet had contradicted her claim of not knowing Ruth and George.

"Ruth and George? Oh, you mean *Ruth* and *George!* Why didn't you *say* Ruth and George? Oh yes, I remember them. Right across the street from me. I can see their living room window right from my porch. I'd see her walking out. I'm not too good with the last names, but I remember her."

"Was she tall and slim?" I interrupted eagerly.

"*Lovely!* She was *lovely!*"

"But was she tall?"

"The loveliest one on the block! Not like so many. She was always friendly and nice and had a pleasant word for ev-eryone." Esther's voice became conspiratorial. "Now, did you see those two old birds on the porch next to me? *They're* not friendly. Not a nice word to say to anybody."

"Oh, I hadn't realized that."

"But me, I like to be friendly, and I like you young peo-ple, you're so young and you're friendly. I'm glad you called.

Of course I remember Ruth and George. He wasn't around so much, being a magician. But I remember her very well."

Magician again. I wished she would say "engineer," or even "teacher," so I could feel sure of this being right.

"She was different from the rest. She was lovely. And they went out West. And they had the car, with the mattress up on top. You would think that car would never get there."

"Where did they go out West?"

"They went to Mexico, and they had the car.—"

"Might it have been California?" I suggested.

"Might be. California, Mexico, one of those places. And they had the car, and everything on top of the car, everything they owned on the roof. And the mattress on top of it all."

"Did she have children, too?"

"Oh, yes. Some boys, some girls. Maybe a girl and a boy. I remember the baby in the window. She piled the children in, too, after all the belongings."

"Do you remember their names?"

"There was a girl, maybe Sandy, and she came back for a visit. Some boys—I can see the baby in the window, too. Must have been three children. Maybe four. As a matter of fact, I have a dish that she gave me."

A *dish?* A dish meant far more than fantasies, stories, hypotheses. A tangible, visible, *dish*, from my own *mother!*

"Very generous she was. I still have that dish," Esther continued. "And he died of a heart attack, some years ago. And when the girl came back, she said her mother got all the way out West. The other drivers, they saw that car coming, with the mattress on top, and they just stopped and let her pass. Every crossroads, they let her pass through. Very fine woman. People aren't the same anymore."

My mind was swimming with clues, images, words. Magician. California, Mexico, out West. Could it be that Juliet's "California" was simply the Easterner's assumption that every state "out West" was California? The ideal compromise, I was thinking, between Juliet's "California" and Esther's "Mexico" would be *New* Mexico.

Suddenly I remembered a detail of research from long ago: That list of male Williamses dying in 1923. In the excitement of this new name, all the old Williams names—George E., Joseph P., James, the Lillies—had been mentally discarded and, with them, the related research. But now it was hitting me: Ruth Williams Ketiladze's father, Albert Tell Williams, might be on last November's listing of Williams deaths during 1923!

I dashed to my desk and threw open my search diary. It fell straight to the right page. There were George E. and Lazarus, with stars, and James, Harry, Thomas . . . no, Albert was not there.

The next page was for 1930—the "disappearing" hypothesis of a listing seven years later. No Albert.

The only other year I had copied out that day long ago, "just in case" because I had had some extra time, had been 1924. I turned the page again. Five names were starred. All were forty-two years old. Then, under "Bronx," alone and without a star, I saw "Albert T. 43y Jan. 17 #442."

Albert Tell! This Albert T. Williams must be Ruth's father. Albert T., dying in 1924 at the age of forty-three, was my grandfather! *Ruth Williams Ketiladze was my mother!*

"Sorry, Ed, you know I wouldn't disturb you at home unless—"

"Fire away."

"The person we're looking for *is* the right one." I explained about the death listing. "I'm certain she's my mother."

"Hold on. Nothing is certain, until it's a fact. You have to *know*."

"Oh," I sighed.

Ed relented. "Between you and me, Katrina, it seems pretty good."

"Ed, it'll take six bloody weeks for Worth Street to get around to mailing me a certificate. I haven't even got six *days*. Is there anything you can do?"

"Not on a Saturday."

I laughed. "I meant on Monday."

"I've already made a note." Ed was laughing too. "All the facts written down. Bronx, January 17, 1924. Monday morning, first thing."

To think I had almost forgotten to check for her father's date of death! If I was right, if Albert T. really was my grandfather, then Mrs. Meinhauser had certainly led me astray. By giving me "age forty-two in 1923" rather than "age forty-three in 1924," she had caused me to believe that, of those twenty-five names, Albert T. had been about the least likely. I would have spent another two years sending in for other death certificates before—if ever—I would have "wasted my time" on Albert T.

Over the weekend, I got out the atlas and pored over the map of New Mexico. Whenever the children were occupied, I would dial another town in New Mexico.

"Ketiladze. K-E-T-I-L . . . "

"What's the first name for K-E-T-I-L-A-D-Z-E?"

"*Any* first name."

Albuquerque, Roswell, Santa Fe, Carlsbad.

"I'm sorry, we don't show any listing for K-E-T-I-L-A-D-Z-E."

Raton, Los Alamos, Silver City, Tucumcari, Gallup.

Then I had an inspiration—could I call Mexico City Information for free?

"Yes," said the operator, "I'll put you through."

There was no Ketiladze at all in Mexico City. Shit. I had really thought I would find one. I felt stripped of my final possibility.

Ed Goldfader telephoned Monday midday. "Katrina, I've got the word on Albert T. Williams, dying in 1924, residence 4026 Dyre Avenue, Bronx; widow, Alicia."

"Ed, what did he die of?"

"Don't know if I have that."

"You've *got* to!"

"Oh, here we go. Cause of death, acute gastric indigestion."

"That's it, Ed! He *is* the one! Mrs. Meinhauser told me 'acute indigestion.' And she also told me that he died without a death certificate—"

"I like this Dyre Avenue," interrupted Ed. "I've been waiting for something solid."

"Ed, we have the right people, at last. And now that we've got them, we can't find them." I told Ed about going to Queens, and about Esther and Juliet, and about the journey out West. "I've tried all over the West, even Mexico City. I mean, where the hell is she?"

"Right now, I'm interested in Dyre Avenue."

One more isolated clue was not enough to lift my spirits, not now. "If George is dead, and she's remarried, what do I do?"

"Let me try a few things."

"But if she's got kids, Ed, there ought to be a Ketiladze *somewhere*. I've even tried Toronto and Montreal."

"None there. I checked."

"You too?"

"Listen, Katrina, this is where I go to town. If we don't talk earlier, I'll call you before I leave to go home. 5:15?"

"You're a brick, Ed."

I took the children down the street to the barber's. When we got home, there was no message from Tracers. In spite of myself, I had been expecting something. *"There's no place in this world where I'll belong, when I'm gone."*

Florence telephoned. She had been talking with a reporter from the Associated Press, a reporter whom she liked; the Associated Press was very big coverage. She asked if I wanted to give an interview.

"But I can't speak, Florence, you know that."

"I could kill Judge Sylvane for doing that to you."

"No, not him. Get the prunes. Mathilda Stern. And her buddy-prunes. God, I hope none of them is my mother!"

"Katrina, you can talk to her now, and she'll hold it. And then when this whole thing is over she can use the piece on you." Florence's voice was infectious with strength and determination. "Her name is Cathy Browning; I trust her."

"Florence, I really shouldn't. I mean, this is breaking the court order."

"Not if you don't *release* it. Look, you're strong. You're not going to let Mathilda Stern destroy you, are you?"

I gave a feeble laugh. "Stupid, isn't it?"

"Listen, just talk to this woman. I've already explained there are reasons you can't release your interview yet. You'll tell her when you can meet?"

It was hard to hold off Florence. "You trust her?" I asked feebly.

"Definitely. Very sympatico."

Florence put Cathy Browning on. I liked her and agreed to meet the next day for lunch, suggesting a restaurant that was only two blocks from my home. Then Florence was back on the phone.

"One day you'll be *really* free, Katrina."

"I don't know."

"I feel it in my bones."

But what if I *never* were? What then?

> There's no place in this world where I'll belong
> When I'm gone
> And I won't know the right from the wrong
> When I'm gone
> And you won't hear me singing on this song
> When I'm gone
> So I guess I'll have to do it
> I guess I'll have to do it—
> I guess I'll have to do it
> While I'm here.

Near the end of the afternoon I had a sudden brainstorm, and I called the American Embassy in Mexico City. When I asked for the passport office, I was immediately put through.

223

The clerk I spoke to was extremely pleasant and made note of the names, Ruth Ketiladze or her husband, George.

"What's your relationship to the party?" she asked agreeably.

"I'm her niece," I responded quickly. My God, I'm doing it!

"What's her birthdate?"

"June 1, 1917." How fantastic to *know* it. Here was I, replying to a personal question with a known fact!

The clerk checked her files. In less than a minute, she returned. "No, we don't have Ruth Ketiladze registered here. We don't have any Ketiladze at all."

Another stroke of genius that was only one more blow of hopelessness.

Ed's promised phone call was a further disappointment. He chattered details, but none represented progress. The Williams family had still been on Dyre Avenue, in the house next door, at the time of my birth and during the years of my foster care. 4024 Dyre Avenue would surely be Mrs. Meinhauser's "house that was too crowded."

There were no new names in the voting records; grandmother Alicia had moved to Mount Vernon by 1940; after 1943 there was no trace of her. Ed could find no Ketiladze births listed in the entire period of 1940 to the present. Nor could he find any Ketiladze deaths since 1950. There were no Ketiladzes anywhere. All these resources, yet no leads at all.

I told Ed about the American Embassy, then we chatted some more about Queens, about the car with the mattress on the top, and Esther's no-good son—

"What do you mean, no-good?" interrupted Ed. "He's a very fine fellow!"

"Esther's son?"

"Winterstein; sure, we talked to him."

"You've been out to Queens, too, Ed?"

"No, we spoke with him on the phone. He didn't remember George, but he remembered Ruth well. He was sixteen at the time and noticing only the females."

I was having a sudden comical image of the three search teams—me, Tracers, and the agency's detective—all converging on the tree-lined corner of 71st and Main.

"He thinks she went to Mexico," Ed was saying, "maybe to be a radio announcer, but says he doesn't know for sure."

"Ed? How come the agency has not been talking to the same people we have? If they had gotten to Esther before me, I can promise you I would know it."

"Maybe they don't know what they're doing! I'm still hoping we'll turn up something on Dyre Avenue."

"But the agency's got Dyre Avenue, too, Ed. For four weeks, they have known exactly what we just got today! Plus they've got her brother's name, her sisters' names, her mother's. They've got *everything*. And *they're* stuck. No wonder they can't find her either. She's unfindable."

"You know something, Katrina? I think I want to find your mother as much as you do. I'm not adopted, but I feel I understand you people. Of course, don't get me wrong, I'm looking at the business angle, too."

"I always told you, Ed, you should charge by the hour."

"No way. So I luck out once in a while. But I don't mind. I like talking to you."

"Thanks, Ed."

"When do you leave?"

"Thursday. Two more days."

The doorbell rang. It was a distant acquaintance, with whom I had never had much in common, carrying a bag full of gifts for the children and inviting herself to dinner. For the next two hours I struggled unsuccessfully to be cordial. I was too exhausted even to explain my silence. The visitor's presence was ghastly, but when she had gone my sense of guilt was just as terrible. I went to my desk and telephoned Florence. We talked for an hour, then I talked to Audrey for another hour.

It was still only ten o'clock. Time was hanging heavy. I stared out the window until it was midnight and too late to telephone anyone. Of course Melia would still be up; but I did not want to hear Melia's voice. There was something about Melia's faith I could not face.

It was good that I was going out to lunch tomorrow. It would be a way of killing time. While I should be at home, packing, getting organized, readying myself for the trip, I would be *showing* them—whatever that meant. I would kill time and I would keep on killing time until there was not any time left to be killed.

July 9, and tomorrow would be the 10th. In twenty-four hours I would be at the court hearing. Your Honor, I am not an adopted child; I am thirty-nine years old. My own children will soon be old enough to vote, to marry, to divorce, to kill foreigners in the name of freedom, all without asking my permission. But I have to ask my mother's permission to know my ethnic origins and what time of day I was born.

At the end of my session with Dr. Thomas that morning, he wished me a good trip. I did not reply. He asked that I call him after the hearing to tell him how it went.

"No messages," the babysitter announced sympathetically as I walked in the door.

Everything seemed to be coming to an end. No phone call from Tracers. My last psychiatrist's appointment. Nothing further I could do. There was nothing to hope for at all. I decided to cancel the lunch with the reporter. I dialed her number, but there was no answer. Obviously, she had left already. As soon as I hung up, Florence telephoned.

"Just checking to make sure you didn't change your mind about talking to Cathy Browning!"

"I couldn't reach her," I confided.

"I'm glad. You'll have a great time."

"Mmm."

"Cyril's in town, to research our case. I'm meeting him downtown, and I'll be out until about three. So you won't be able to reach me before. But I'll call the minute I get in. Okay?"

"Say hi to Cyril."

"So we'll talk around three, Katrina," repeated Florence firmly.

In the middle of the lunch with Cathy Browning, I suddenly was aware of what I looked like: Hair straggled, shirt and jeans filthy. My concentration was vague, my conversation disorganized. Truly a mess. When I spoke, I was switching back and forth from monosyllables to disconnected rambling. I pulled myself together enough to mumble an apology. It was all right, Cathy answered, Florence had explained that I was pretty upset. Cathy seemed nice, I thought; she could be trusted. She would not publish anything unless I regained my freedom of speech. Do it while you're here, was Phil Ochs's message; hang on, stay, don't quit when there is a job to be done. I began, finally, to speak with purpose. The words, rehearsed in my brain these past months, now frothed in my mouth. The narrative line was not arranged, but I kept on talking.

When Cathy offered to walk me the two blocks home, I was grateful for the gift of another few minutes of company. Talking, talking; I had not appreciated the free use of speech until I had lost it. I invited Cathy into the house. To talk to a reporter was to stay alive; to return to the realities of home was to return to death.

The babysitter had a message. "Tracers called," she said. "He called twice."

"Twice?" I searched her face for her estimate of the event.

The phone rang, the babysitter answered. Then she turned to me. "It's a Bob Eisenberg for you."

"That's Tracers!" Halfway up the staircase, I realized that Cathy Browning was still in my kitchen, standing by the stove. "Sorry, Cathy, very busy," I stammered, "nice meeting you."

I grabbed my desk phone.

"You've been keeping us pretty busy these past couple of days," Bob began chattily. "Ed had to go out. Left a message for me to call you."

"That's nice, I always like hearing your voice." Even when they had nothing to report, Ed and Bob made the minutes worth surviving. "Got anything new?" I settled back for a pleasant conversation.

"We've been making discreet inquiries, you know, in the Dyre Avenue area. And we've got a little information. Ruth and George went to Mexico. He died in the late fifties. There's a sister, Mrs. Anderson."

"That's funny. I've got some best friends whose name is Anderson."

"There's a brother, Howard, who may be dead. It seems that Ruth stayed on in Mexico and is probably still there. And there's a younger sister, Clare, who married a Frank Englehardt from Mount Vernon." Bob paused. "And Clare lives in Mount Vernon still." He stopped. "So what do you want to do?"

I was confused. "What about?"

"I was thinking you might want to go out there tonight."

"Bob, I don't take airplanes."

"An airplane to Mount Vernon? It's just thirty minutes by car!"

"I was thinking of Mexico."

"We wouldn't know where to send you in Mexico. We don't have Ruth's address."

"Oh, right. So why—"

"But we're hoping Clare Engelhardt does."

"Oh, Bob! I get it! You found my aunt!" My mother's little sister—a person with a name and an address.

"What do you want to do?" repeated Bob gently.

"Do?"

"Do you want to pay your aunt a visit?"

"Oh no!" I exclaimed, "I don't want to involve my *aunt!* She may not know about me, she was only ten years old."

"Katrina, someone has to contact your aunt. It's the only chance we have of getting your mother's address."

"Oh, my God, what do I do?" At last I had absorbed Bob's news. "This is it!"

"Take it easy now. Relax." Bob spoke slowly and gently. "Ed was sorry he had to be out, he would have liked to handle this himself; he's been working on it all morning."

"I'm calmer. Bob, I'm terrified."

"Well, here's your options. You don't want to blow the story to your aunt, right?"

"Exactly."

"So you've got to call her on some pretext; then try to get her to give you Ruth's whereabouts."

"Good grief."

"Or, you could let us do it our way."

"You? Contact my aunt?"

"We'll be very discreet."

"I feel it should be me."

Bob sighed. "Katrina, can I give you my advice? Let me tell you what I'd do in your position."

"Okay," I replied. He was treating me so gingerly, so sweetly. "I'll listen."

"If you call your aunt, the way you are now, you'll blow the whole thing."

"You mean it shows?"

"I mean, you're a *mess*."

"Damn."

"Just give me twenty minutes, okay?"

"Do be careful."

"Don't worry. I'll be discreet. And if it doesn't work, then you can try yourself."

"You won't be more than twenty minutes?"

"I'll get back to you."

"Well, all right—and, Bob?"

"Yes?"

"Uh . . . good luck."

chapter seventeen

IN CONTROL

I had not yet begun to measure the passage of time when Bob Eisenberg was calling back. He had spoken to her.

"Mrs. Engelhardt was at home. Ketiladze died in 1959, a year after moving to Mexico. He died in Michigan."

"I grew up in Michigan."

"There are some children, but not in Mexico. Ruth is still there. She uses a different name, but she's not remarried. Do you have a pencil?"

"Right, I've been taking notes."

"Her name is Ruth Jason. 47-2 Rio San Lucas. Mexico 5, D.F. That's Mexico City."

"Ruth Jason, 47-2 Rio San Lucas, Mexico 5, D.F.," I repeated mechanically.

"The telephone number is 624-7562."

The number was almost a recombination of my own.

"Your aunt has no idea what it's about. At first she wanted to mail the information—"

"Bob!" I burst out, "You did it!"

"But I kept on talking and talking, and finally she said, 'Oh, well—' "

"You got it *all*, Bob!" I raved, aware and now incredulous at the news. "You got everything! Even the phone number! We actually *found* Ruth Ketiladze!"

The search had been accomplished. From a wild moment of decision to a telephone number in Mexico City.

"Well, it's all yours now," said Bob. "This is where we bow out."

"You've both been wonderful."

For a moment neither of us spoke. Then Bob said, "Good luck, Katrina."

"Thanks for everything."

I told John the good news. Quietly, calmly. Then I checked on the children: Guy was busy reading, the others were out and not due home until five. John would keep his eye on Guy and also fend off all phone calls. I would let John know when I was going to dial Mexico City.

Closing the door behind me, I went to my desk and opened my search diary. The last entry had been the one made just before my trip to Payne Whitney. I turned to a fresh page. I would open my conversation with, "May I please speak to Ruth Jason?" I wrote the name, "Ruth Jason."

Then I wondered what to say next. I was going to call, but what on earth was I going to say?

I dialed Lyn Cobb in Florida.

"First," said Lyn authoritatively, "you've got to make sure you've got the right Ruth Jason."

"Oh, I'm sure . . . "

"Yes, but you don't want *her* pulling that it's some other Ruth Jason. 'You got the wrong Ruth Jason, another one down the block,' or some such. You say the whole name: Ruth Williams Whatever-Else. Say 'daughter of so-and-so and—' "

"You're right. And if she rejects me, I've still got my cafeteria—"

"There's just one thing I don't get, Katrina—you said you were going to find your mother before the 11th of July, and you know what date this is? It's the 9th today."

"No, I never—when did I tell you that?"

"All the time. 'I gotta find my mother before July 11th.' I thought you were bananas."

"Why didn't you say something?"

"Well, we're all bananas during this."

Next I telephoned Audrey.

"When, exactly, do you think you might be calling?" Audrey asked. "If it's all right with you, Katrina, I want to be praying, at the right time."

"No, I'd be glad—thank you." My answer should be accurate for Audrey's sake. "After I hang up. Then about five minutes."

I went to John in the next room. "I'm about to call."

John handed me an index card on which he had written the schedule of flights from Mexico City to New York: Aeromexico at 4:45 this afternoon, Eastern at 9:00 tomorrow morning.

"Just in case," he said, matter-of-factly.

I nodded. Together we walked back to my desk. We smiled at each other, squeezed hands. He went out. I sat at my desk. In front of me was the white page with my notes. To my left was the black telephone. In about two minutes.

The house was quiet. I mouthed my opening line. I took in a deep breath and then another.

Sitting up straight in my chair, I turned slightly to the left. Then, just as my hand was moving toward the receiver, the sudden thought blazed across my brain: Though it is true that all natural mothers care for their children, *what if mine is the one-in-a-million exception?* A minute from now I could be hearing, "I hated you then, and I hate you now," followed by a click and then silence.

My hand touched the telephone. I took one last breath. I dialed.

Two rings.

A man's voice answered. "Hello."

I had not expected a man to be there.

"May I please speak to Ruth Jason?" She was probably out.

"Yes, just a moment please."

"Hello," the woman's voice came on quickly.

"Is this Ruth Jason?"

"Yes," the voice was relaxed, pleasant, "it is."

"Is this Ruth Williams Ketiladze Jason?"

"Yes, it is."

"I'm calling from New York." Everything was moving so fast.

Her voice was suddenly excited. "Is this Winifred? Is this Winifred Hewitt?"

Oh dear, I'm not the friend she's hoping for. "No," I spoke deliberately. "No. It's not." I tried to put some heaviness in my voice, some lead-in of preparation. "Is this a good time to talk?"

"Just fine," Mrs. Jason responded cheerfully.

"Are you *sure* it's a good time?" I tried again to alert her. "You've got people there . . . "

"No, it's quite all right."

"And you might prefer to take this call," I went on, "in another room."

There was quiet at the other end of the phone wire. Then Ruth Williams Ketiladze Jason answered, slowly and unevenly, "I hope . . . this is . . . what I think . . . it is."

The waiting and wondering were over. It was finished. Home free. I had done the impossible.

chapter eighteen

REUNION CONTINUING

We were both spluttering. I was trying to say the name "Judith Virginia Williams"; she was gasping something sounding like "I hope I've found my little girl." We were both talking at once, wildly, excitedly; then she grew fainter.

"Actually, I can't *hear* you," I exclaimed.

"I'm sorry, I'm moving the phone. I'm very excited—my little girl, at last!" She was audible again. "I read an article, just five days ago, in *Cosmopolitan*, telling how the adopted person feels. I never knew before. I always thought the suffering was only on my side. That was the 4th of July." She was speaking, I realized, about an article by Lorraine Dusky, the natural mother from ALMA who was a journalist. "And I wrote a letter to an organization called ALMA. I haven't mailed it yet, but I've been crying ever since. The address for ALMA was given at the end of the article."

"I'm a member of ALMA."

"I hoped you would be."

We talked about the article, that its author was my friend, and about how a visitor from the States had brought this issue of the magazine to Mexico City. The visitor had known that my mother enjoyed *Cosmopolitan*, which was banned from sale in Mexico, but was unaware that she had given a child up for adoption. Then my mother asked if my name had been changed.

"Yes. It's Katrina now. But you may call me Judith, or Katrina, whichever you prefer."

"Katrina," my mother enunciated the name with flair. "That's pretty."

Quickly I explained the urgency: I had to leave the country on Thursday and would she come to New York to see me. Her response was an immediate yes. But it was too late to make this afternoon's flight; she would take the one tomorrow morning. I would meet her at the airport tomorrow afternoon, Wednesday, at 3:15.

Our line suddenly was disconnected.

"I've just found my long-lost mother," I shouted at the operator, "after thirty-nine years—and now we've been cut off!"

The operator, unimpressed, instructed me to replace the call.

"Ruth?"

"We were cut off," she answered. "It happens all the time here. But now you're back. That's fine."

She asked for my phone number. "Oh," she exclaimed, "your number is practically like mine." Then her voice became quizzical. "Did you call me 'Ruth' just now?"

"Yes."

"Why not 'Mummy'?" She sounded a little offended. "Or 'Mother'?"

"If someone else had answered . . . " I was wondering what I was going to call her.

"My other children call me 'Mummy.' I had a daughter—another daughter—ten years later. Did I tell you? You have a sister, a wonderful sister. And three brothers."

"Wow!"

"Yes, they're great people. Your sister is twenty-nine, and your brothers are twenty-six, twenty-three, and twenty-one. They call me Mummy, or Mother—you know, 'Mo-ther!' You could call me Ruth, though, if you like."

I was already "Mummy" myself; the name "Mother" had belonged to someone else. "How about, uh, 'Mum'?"

" 'Mum'! That's nice." She was quiet for a moment. Then in the intense, sincere voice which was already becoming familiar, she said, "Thank you for finding me—thank you, thank you!"

It was unimaginable. And this was not me composing fantasies, me inventing the lines.

"May I write that down?" I asked.

"Do you write things down, too?"

"I also wrote what you said first—'I hope this is what I think it is.'"

"How did you find me, by the way?"

"That's a long story." I was wondering how it ever could be told.

"I understand. Yes, we have lots of time now." Then she said, "I don't imagine the agency gave much help . . ."

"No, they sure didn't!" I laughed. "A detective helped me, though."

"I'd like to hug that detective."

I thought of Ed's big grinning face. No doubt he would like to hug this success, as well.

We were cut off a second time. Before redialing, I rushed in to John with a quick bulletin. "All's well. Sounds very nice, too."

"Is she coming?"

"Tomorrow, it's too late for today. And she said, 'Thank you for finding me'!"

I hurried back and dialed the now memorized number.

"I've been thinking," my mother immediately began, "that if I take the morning plane, we'll only have twenty-four hours together." She went on quickly, "But if I rush, right now, I may still make the 4:45 flight. That way, we'd have thirty-six hours."

"Terrific!"

"It does mean that I'll have to get off the phone."

"John and I will meet you."

If she got in tonight, there was a chance she might come to the hearing tomorrow. No, I told myself, to dream so much was crazy; and selfish, too, not fair to her.

"If I don't make it in time, I'll call you. Forgive me for

rushing now. If you don't hear from me, I'm on the plane. And tell that detective I think he's wonderful."

"He is. See you at eleven tonight."

"Good-bye, dear. And thank you, thank you!"

I was staring at the replaced receiver. "Dear"—she had called me "Dear"! It was the first time in my life, it seemed, that anyone had called me that. What a nice sound. And how extraordinary that she had used such a word. I had not been expecting her to behave in a maternal fashion, I realized. It was almost as though I had forgotten she was my mother; I was regarding her as a "pal." Now, by her use of one word, she had reminded me.

I had found my mother!

I had better tell Audrey first. "She's so *nice*, I can't believe it . . . she really is nice . . . "

"But I *knew* she would be nice," interrupted Audrey with conviction.

I reminded Audrey about the hearing, and she promised to be at the courthouse tomorrow morning at 9:45.

Quickly I told John about the change of flights. Allowing for the time difference between Mexico and New York, we figured that we could not be certain of my mother's being on the airplane until 6:45 New York time. Then I returned to my desk and the telephone. I called my friends: "This is Katrina and I found my mother and she's very nice."

Lorraine, as it was her article, then Tracers, where Ed and Bob both got on the line; Lyn in Florida; then Florence, who was calling in to see if I was all right and, hearing such excited confusion, feared that I had flipped; Melia, of course; and Dr. Thomas, but he wasn't in. All the time I was babbling wildly, and my friends were crying, and they had me crying, too.

Very soon, Dr. Thomas called back. I narrated, word for word, the opening lines of the reunion dialogue.

The doctor made a response that was unintelligible.

"What?" I asked.

"Mrs. Maxtone-Graham," he said, "I'm all choked up."

237

Then I went into the bedroom, where Guy was enjoying the treat of watching TV cartoons, permitted today to keep him busy through all this. Guy looked up at me, oblivious to the screen, caring about me.

"I found my mother," I said.

My son was staring at me, utterly incredulous. Finally he asked, "Your *real* mother?"

Usually I take exception to the word "real," as natural parents and adoptive parents are *all* "real." But I knew what Guy meant. I nodded. "Yes, my real mother."

"Is she coming here to see us before we leave?" he asked expectantly.

"Yes." How marvelous a question; it was the only logical assumption. "As a matter of fact, either late tonight or tomorrow afternoon."

"If she comes tonight, then I'll get to see her in the morning at breakfast. That'll be nice." He was still staring at me in wonder. His gaze carried more than happiness, I realized; there was awe as well, that childhood conviction of parental omnipotence. I wanted to explain away this false magic, but no words came.

"I have to call my friends," I told him sheepishly.

As the other children returned home I told each of them the news of my mother and of her imminent arrival. I asked both Ian and Sarah, who had had plans to go out for the evening, if they would please stay home this one night. I still feared my joy could be instantly shattered by disaster. The children seemed to understand and unhesitatingly agreed to stay home. Emily took out her sketch pad to make posters of welcome.

There were more people to call: Murray, who drove the children's school bus and had become a friend to all the family; Sylvia, the family friend who had been a sympathetic ear throughout my searchings. The telephoning continued until dinner. Then finally 6:45 came and went without a call from Mexico City. My mother was on her way.

I was still afraid. What if the airplane crashed? The good cannot last, loving is dangerous. I had challenged Fate's tricks, I had taken action. If Fate chose to punish me, not only would I suffer the hurt, but I also would bear the guilt, for I was the one who had dared.

We were planning to leave for the airport at ten. At nine, I was in the bath, trying to collect myself, alone and quiet.

The telephone rang.

"Mrs. Katrina Maxtone-Graham?"

"Yes?" I recognized the voice of the man who had answered Ruth Ketiladze Jason's telephone. Had she missed her flight?

"This is your new brother." He had a wonderfully warm voice.

"Hello, brother!" I exclaimed. "Just don't tell me she's not on that plane!"

"Well," he spoke slowly, "she is on a plane—but it's not exactly *that* one . . . "

"She's still coming?"

"Oh, she's coming all right. Only thing is, she's coming to Philadelphia. Arriving 12:30 this morning. She missed the 4:45 by one minute."

"What will she do then? Spend the night?"

"Well, I don't think she knows what she's going to do," he answered casually.

"But I can't get there in time to meet her flight! It's too late for a train. Oh, dear. Does she have friends she can stay with?"

"Not in Philadelphia."

"Then where . . . ? What do you think she'll do?"

He laughed easily. "Knowing her, she'll get herself to New York somehow!"

"Well, don't worry, I'll think of something."

"Oh, I don't worry," he declared, "I never worry."

How extraordinary, I thought, how delightful his confi-

239

dence was—though it did serve to stifle further discussion of her plans.

"It'll work out," I proferred. There was nothing left now but our presence on the telephone.

"What's your name, brother?"

"Andrew."

"Hi, Andrew," I said.

"Hi, Katrina," he said.

Suddenly there was the delicious sense of just him and me alone together—and our mother was far away from this moment. My brother and I were free to speak in utter honesty.

"Well, Andrew," I posed the all-important question, "what do you think of it all?"

"Oh, I think it's just great!" he exclaimed. "Another one of us—all the more fun!"

What a response! I could never have invented it.

Andrew began to tell me about himself. He was the middle brother, the twenty-three-year-old, and he was in electronics.

"Oh," I commented enthusiastically, "just like your father."

"Well, he was an electrical engineer."

"What about the others?" This was the next most important question, and I was trusting Andrew for the truth. "What will they think?"

"They'll think the same as me," he replied.

"Really?"

"They'll be thrilled."

"I hope so." I was feeling very comfortable with this wonderful new brother.

"You shouldn't worry about it, Katrina."

"Yet I do. I mean, I want them to like me."

"They'll like you, I know." He paused; then he added thoughtfully, albeit lightly, "Maybe you should be worrying about whether you will like us!"

How preposterous! Of course I would like *them!*
Andrew said he was glad that my name was Russian
"just like the rest of us." Then, echoing my mother, he said,
"Thank you for finding us!"

Now the rush was on. John and I could drive to Philadelphia, but the timing was such that my mother might land and
head north before John and I could get to the Philadelphia
airport. I telephoned Nanny and arranged that she would
meet the plane, carrying a sign saying "Katrina's friend,"
while John and I would drive to her house to wait there. Seymour would come over to Nanny's to let us in. Next, I telephoned Florence, asking her to obtain Cyril Means's advice
about the morning's hearing. Were there any tactics I could
use tomorrow that would benefit other adoptees?

How tremendously fitting, I thought, that the practical
dénouement of this part of my search was depending on the
ALMA network. Phone calls, favors asked, help given, promises made—always dependence and dependability. Now joy
was being shared as misery once had been. Perhaps, later,
Nanny, Audrey, and Lorraine would cry a few tears because
they had not yet had Katrina's luck; but none of them would
begrudge me this day.

John was already out getting the car as I hurriedly
dressed. I grabbed a pair of red and white striped pants from
the front of the closet and then a navy and red striped shirt
which, surprisingly, did not clash with the pants. So this was
what-I-would-wear-to-meet-my-mother.

Then we drove off to Philadelphia. Downtown and
through the tunnel. The grey trucks were so long, the truck-
ers' cabs so high. "This is too fast, John." I put a recording of
the Emperor Concerto on the tape recorder. Beethoven was
grand, triumphant, sublime. "You're too close to that truck."
*I am driving to meet my mother! Had I known as a child on
car rides that one day I would be riding in a car toward a real
person* . . . "We've got to get there, drive slower!"

241

The concerto ended, John wanted to listen to the news. Thirty seconds of radio talk, and I was thinking my body would itch out of my skin. I put on the concerto a second time.

Nanny's house was large and rambling. A wooden porch stretched across the entire façade, with wide wooden steps descending to the cement path off the sidewalk. Seymour let us in. Nanny had just telephoned from the airport; the plane was due to land any moment. John went to an upstairs bedroom to catch some rest before the drive home and, I suspected, to ensure his absence so that I might greet my mother in privacy.

The phone rang; it was Florence, breathless. Cyril was thrilled to hear the news, his message was, "She can tell the whole story, tell Donohue, bring her mother, do whatever she wants. It won't make any difference to anyone else." Cyril as well as Florence would be coming to the hearing tomorrow.

I lay down thankfully on the living room sofa, just wanting to close my eyes and rest. I breathed in the early morning silence. Tomorrow was promising to be quite a day. And before the day even came, there would be the two-and-a-half-hour car ride with my mother. Now, I was in a delicious limbo between the reunion that had taken place and the relationship that lay ahead.

A car pulled up in front of the house. Then Nanny called, and I knew from her voice that my mother was safely with her. Seymour hurried outside.

"Katrina, we're here," Nanny called a second time, urging me to meet them.

Suddenly I was wishing that Seymour and Nanny would disappear. I wanted to greet my mother on my own, without any intermediary or audience. Perhaps if I stayed in the living room the others would remain outdoors while my mother came into the house alone.

But, no, they were still calling me, commanding my appearance outside.

I moved onto the porch. My mother was halfway up the steps. Short and dumpy, I thought, my mother was not tall and thin at all.

Then we were all in the living room, Seymour and Nanny were talking about coffee, my mother and I were hugging each other; and, with the hand that was behind my mother's shoulder, I was making flapping motions to the others to leave us. I felt ashamed that, after having wanted companionship through the waiting, I was now wishing for privacy. Seymour and Nanny lingered, then finally went into the kitchen.

Alone together, my mother and I sat side by side on the sofa. My mother did not look like anyone I had ever seen.

"Well, what do we say?" she asked.

"It doesn't matter," I responded.

Whatever happened would be just fine, I was thinking. This was only one moment, one small portion of time—infinitesimal beside all the remainder of our lives, and of no consequence to the whole. We talked for a while about nothing in particular. Then, mutually, comfortably, we decided it was time to join the others in the kitchen.

Over coffee and cookies with Seymour and Nanny, the four of us got acquainted. The presence of my friends became, once again, an asset. They were charming, and John joined us at just the right moment. It was relaxed, pleasant, comfortable. Nanny had a copy of my book, which she showed to my mother. I pointed out the pages where I had inserted the name Judith Williams as my message into the wild unknown. As we left to return to New York, everyone was kissing each other good-bye, and my mother was wishing Nanny a fervent good-luck on her own search.

On the ride home the real time of getting to know one another was beginning. Immediately we were talking, sharing. My mother told me about herself and her family, where she grew up, about her brother and her sisters. Her brother, Howard, had been wounded in World War II, she told me, and had died in the 1960's of complications from those wounds. I could not help but think of the letter Lyn and I had talked of

243

sending to all those male Williamses in the phone directories—none of whom would have been the right "brother of three Williams sisters."

Much of what my mother told me was already familiar to me, but I was careful not to unsettle her, at this first meeting, with the extent of my research. Remembering the adoption establishment's righteousness about "invasion of privacy," I was struck now with the conviction that the *real* invasion of privacy was not in our *meeting* our mothers, but rather in our knowing so much about a person whom we had *not* met.

Only when my mother began talking about her father was I tempted to relinquish my caution. "He died when I was very young," she was saying, "it must have been about . . . let me think . . . "

The opportunity was too good to resist. "January 17, 1924, actually."

"How on earth do you know that?" My mother looked at me admiringly.

"That's how I found you! Plus a lot of other things."

"Well, I'm so glad you did. So glad. So glad. I never dreamed . . . " Her voice trailed off in contentment.

I gazed at the dark out the window. How calm the night seemed, how gentle the passage of time.

"And a nice old lady called Esther in Queens," I added in fond memory.

"Esther. Yes, I remember Esther. She lived across the street. I sent her a plate from Mexico after I moved. How *is* Esther?"

"She's wonderful. And I'd like to see that plate some day!"

Quite early in the ride home my mother confessed, "I'm sorry, dear, but I've been racking my brain—and I still can't remember your father's name. It will come to me. But I've blocked so much."

"That's all right," I assured her. I was astonished that she should be referring to my father already. So many adoptees had found that it took several months for their mothers to be willing to talk about their fathers.

"Maybe Jim. Or Frank. One of those." She was silent, still struggling to recollect.

"His last name," I ventured delicately, "He, uh, he didn't happen to, uh, mention . . . "

"Of course he told me his last name!" She looked at me indignantly, then her gaze softened. "Didn't anyone tell you? Kelley. Kelley, with an E-Y. How terrible that you didn't know your own father's name!"

"Kelley, that sure *is* 'Irish-sounding'!" I exclaimed. And E-Y would be easier to research than Y.

"Southern," my mother corrected me. "He was very Southern. Very literate. He loved books, he loved music. Frank? No, I don't think so. That was one of the first things Andrew—your brother Andrew—asked me. 'Did she find her father, too?' I was going to ask you. But of course you *couldn't* have, if you didn't know his name."

I liked her manner. She was understanding, she was bright, she was direct.

"So he never knew about me," I commented.

"Not about you exactly. He knew I was pregnant."

"He did?"

"He certainly did!" She gave a half-laugh. "I can remember the day I told him, as clear as can be. I ran into him, by chance, on a train, coming home from work. I must have been four or five months pregnant. I had stopped seeing him, months before. I stopped seeing him before I realized that I was pregnant." She laughed again. "Of course, it took me a ridiculous amount of time to figure out that I was pregnant! But I knew by then, the day I saw him. And I told him, there, on the train."

"How did he react?"

"Not very well, I'm sorry to say. I can still hear that Southern drawl. He drew himself up, very straight, very superior. '*Now* I suppose you are going to say that I have to marry you!' And that got me mad. 'Most *certainly* not!' I replied."

She *was* spunky, I thought. "That took courage . . . "

"Not at *all!* I wouldn't have *dreamed* of it!" she exploded. "*And*, what he said *next!*"

"What did he say?"

"Well, I'm sorry to have to tell you, dear, because it wasn't very nice." She looked at me apologetically. "He said"—now she was arching her back, pursing her lips, and applying a slow Southern accent with gusto— " '*Besides*,' he said, '*besides*, how do I know that I am the father?' "

"Oh!"

"I was furious—oh! I was furious! So I pulled back my foot and I kicked him. I kicked him good and hard in the shin with the toe of my shoe."

"What happened then?" I asked.

"I got up and marched off. The train stopped just then, it was my stop. I never saw him again. But that was quite a smack I gave him!"

How much more real was this first-hand account than Mrs. Meinhauser's interpretation of an old record.

It occurred to me that if Mrs. Meinhauser had been wrong about my father's knowledge of the pregnancy she might also have been wrong about the report of his death in the 1940's. I asked my mother, "Do you think he could still be alive?"

"Can't think why not. He was older than I, he'd have to be about sixty-eight by now. Well, that's young enough, but I would have no way of knowing. I've never heard anything of him since."

When I told her what Mrs. Meinhauser had said, she grinned. "I may have blocked a lot of things, but if I knew he had died, I'm sure I would have remembered *that*."

We talked and lit up cigarettes incessantly. Sometimes my mother would turn to me and say nothing, just smile. She was the first person I had ever met who smoked as heavily as I did.

"Do you celebrate your birthday in March?" she asked abruptly.

"Yes," I was startled. "March 9th, actually."

"Really? I would have thought it was later, more toward the middle. Maybe the 15th, or the 17th."

"Well, uh, I could be wrong." I remembered having wanted to be a famous actress so that I would be described in theatre programs—"Born on March 9, 1935"—and my mother would find me.

"No, you're right, I'm sure. It's just me, I've blocked so much. Please forgive me. It's only beginning to come back. What's interesting is that George's birthday was the 8th. of March. Funny, don't you think?"

"Yes." Yes, indeed.

"Funny," she repeated.

"The time of day"—here it was at last—"would you remember the time, the hour I was born?"

"Oh, my goodness, dear, I wouldn't know *that*. They knocked us out in those days, and they never told me. Only with the last two was I able to get natural childbirth. Even then, I had to chase all over the city to find the one hospital where I could get it."

"New York Hospital?"

"How did you know?"

Because I too had made the same choice for the same reason.

Other coincidences began to crop up as the conversation flowed. She had a wonderful nephew—my cousin—almost exactly my age, and his name was Douglas Anderson; my friends, the Andersons, had a son named Douglas, too. My mother, like me, had considered advertising in the *New York Times* but had discarded the idea, thinking as I had, "Maybe she doesn't read it." Her actual religion was my preferred one, Quaker. We had both raised four children to bilingualism. We both kept notebooks.

"When you called me by name, did you use Judith or Judy?"

"Judith," she answered quickly. "Never Judy."

I smiled. "And in the foster homes, do you know?"

247

"Judith. Always Judith."

"I'm glad," I said. "Thank you."

She described her late husband, George. He seemed a wonderful man, both to my view and to my mother's.

"He taught me everything I know of art, of literature, of music. He was a wise, good man, he loved life; and he was always teaching, always sharing."

George Ketiladze had been born in the Soviet state of Georgia, as Sylvia had guessed. And, as Ed Goldfader had suggested, he had found the name Ketiladze impractical professionally and had taken the name of Jason, the mythical Greek hero who had found the Golden Fleece in Georgia. There would have been no change-of-name papers in the Queens courthouse, however, for the Ketiladzes had never made the change legally. As my mother told the story, I realized that I had heard the name Jason before: "Jason" was one of the string of tenants who had lived in the Ketiladzes' apartment. When the Ketiladzes had "moved out" in 1954, the Jasons had been the first to "move in." They had stayed on until 1958, and thus it had been possible for Esther, whatever the year of the purchase of her house, to have known "Ruth and George" but not "the Ketiladzes."

George had been trained as a concert pianist, his parents imagining him as a new Rachmaninoff. But the young George had left Georgia for Germany, where he had played the piano in bars to support himself. Later, he had immigrated to Canada. George had indeed been both an engineer and a teacher. He had even, in Canada, been a wrestling champion. But George's profession had not been any of these. George Jason had made his livelihood exactly as Esther had intimated—as a magician.

"Thank you for finding me." My mother said it again and again, beaming.

We had been driving for quite some time when I tentatively broached the subject of my court case. My mother had been reiterating her admiration for my perseverance and success in finding her.

248

"I sure worked hard," I introduced the topic gently. "As a matter of fact, I even took a case to court. I brought this." I handed her Mathilda Stern's first affidavit.

" 'Mathilda Stern, being duly sworn, deposes and says,' " my mother read aloud, " 'I have a Masters Degree in social work and have been a professional social worker for twenty-five years . . . ' Twenty-five years?" my mother snorted, "That's *far* too long!"

This mother of mine was pretty terrific. "As a matter of fact," I continued, "there's a hearing in court tomorrow morning at—"

"I'm going with you!" interrupted my mother.

"Will you really? I don't want to push you."

"You couldn't stop me if you tried." She looked at me determinedly. "Your mother is a very strong woman."

When we crept into the house, it was 4:30 in the morning. Tiptoeing up the stairs toward a few hours' sleep, we were faced suddenly with the tall loping frame of Ian. Eyes bleary and face hugely grinning, he strode past his father and me and went straight to his grandmother.

"My dear grandson," cried his grandmother as the two embraced.

Then we all collapsed, exhausted, into our beds.

The next sound I heard was the doorbell. Racing downstairs, I looked at my watch; it was exactly 8:00 A.M. Still half-asleep, I pulled open the door. There in the doorway stood a radiant Florence Fisher, blonde hair aglow in the sunlight; and beside her, his bow tie even wider than his smile, was Cyril Means.

Florence spoke first. "Mathilda Stern," she proclaimed with fervor, "is *not* your *mother*."

There were voices, lots of voices. Florence and Cyril, and my mother, the children . . . I had never seen so many people, all these people eating breakfast in our garden. "Grandmum, look at this! Grandmum . . . " The doorbell kept ringing. Izzie, Sylvia, Lorraine. I took a sip of tea from someone's cup. My mother was hugging people. Here was Murray, who would drive us to the courthouse; everyone was saying hello, and then it was time to go. Past the kitchen table, onto the sidewalk; then we were crowding into Murray's school van and just minutes later we were standing in the lobby of the courthouse.

We hurried to the elevator, Mum, me, Cyril. The whole group was in the same elevator. Cathy Browning was there. Everyone was whispering. Audrey, you got here, I'm so glad. Someone tried the courtroom door, but it was locked. We were on the wrong floor. This way, Cyril directed us.

Joe Donohue appeared from nowhere.

John was on my left, my mother on my right. Donohue was looking straight at me. He was so glum, and I was the cat that swallowed the canary.

"The agency is taking a new tack." Donohue pointed at some law papers in his hand. "They are now claiming . . . " He was obviously trying to prepare me to hear something unpleasant.

"Joe!" I was impatient for him to pause so that I could speak. I pushed Mum forward. "Joe . . . "

"The agency claims that you have hostile feelings toward your natural mother."

"Joe, I would like you to meet . . . " Now I had his full attention; I hung on to each word, enunciating each one distinctly, " . . . to meet Ruth Williams Ketiladze-Jason, my mother."

Joe looked at Mum and glanced quickly at me. Then, grinning, he looked back at her. "How do you do," said Joe Donohue, putting out his hand.

The others moved in closer, whispered louder. I began explaining to Donohue about Mexico and 1:30 in the morning and the drive to Philadelphia while Joe, still grinning at my mother, was saying something about papers to me, and she was describing to him how happy she was—

"That's our number," interrupted Joe. "It's time to go in."

The plain doors were opened, and we entered the courtroom and quickly took seats.

"Matter of Maxtone-Graham!"

It was Carpentieri, someone whispered, not Sylvane. Back to the very beginning; I wondered if Carpentieri remembered this case.

Donohue began speaking, very calmly, very coolly, as though he had rehearsed his lines a thousand times. "Your Honor, sir, it has just recently come to my attention, only a few moments ago, Your Honor, that my client, the petitioner, has located her natural mother."

Poor Donohue, I thought. Even poor Silver. They were pawns, too.

"Her mother is with us. My client only just located her, Your Honor, and I was informed just now in the corridor. My client met her mother very late last night."

"Does the petitioner's mother wish to make a statement?" asked the judge.

"Thank you, Your Honor," replied Donohue.

"Would the petitioner's mother please come forward?"

There was a flurry of activity. My mother was standing and beginning to move.

"Stand with her," whispered Sylvia, "go ahead."

Grateful for the suggestion, I maneuvered past knees and wishes of luck and love, then strode through the thicket of lawyers to stand at my mother's side. We were close to the judge, on our right, but considerably beneath him. Seated high above us at his table, he seemed foolishly tiny. I put my arm around my mother's shoulder. Someone asked my mother her name. She gave it.

I gazed straight ahead, beyond the immediate scene, and discovered the faces of Audrey, Florence, and Cyril. Cyril was leaning forward intently, Florence was crying, and Audrey was looking directly at me, nodding encouragement.

The courtroom was silent now.

"Your address, please."

My mother's voice was strong. "Care of my daughter."

I read the transcript of the hearing a few weeks later. The lifetimes which had led up to this occasion—my mother's and mine, and the lifetimes of all those who cared for us— were reduced to a brief series of questions and answers.

MR. DONOHUE: Are you acquainted with the application that your daughter has made to obtain her adoption records?

MRS. KETILADZE-JASON: I just saw her this morning.

MR. DONOHUE: You are aware that your daughter seeks these records?

MRS. KETILADZE-JASON: Yes, I am.

MR. DONOHUE: And are you aware that up until this point, the position of the agency has been that they have sought to protect you, and since they couldn't find you they objected to the relief requested?

MRS. KETILADZE-JASON: Why didn't they ask me? All these years that I—

THE SURROGATE: Just answer the question.

MRS. KETILADZE-JASON: I am sorry, sir.

THE SURROGATE: The reason why they didn't want to give this information is because they had to get your permission, and they couldn't find you. Now you are here.

MRS. KETILADZE-JASON: Yes, sir.

THE SURROGATE: And the lawyer wants to know whether you consent and give the agency the authority to release this information.

MRS. KETILADZE-JASON: Everything, yes, sir.

MR. DONOHUE: All adoption records pertaining to your daughter, Katrina Maxtone-Graham?

MRS. KETILADZE-JASON: Everything. Everything.

THE SURROGATE: All right.

MR. SILVER: Your Honor, that still doesn't help us with the foster parents.

THE SURROGATE: Yes, she can't waive the rights of others, if they have any rights.

252

MR. SILVER: We have provided, we will provide, everything that the petitioner's mother gave to us. That of course is waived now. We will provide all that, most of which we have already provided. With regard to the foster parents, this really doesn't change the situation with regard to them.

THE SURROGATE: How about the dead ones?

MR. SILVER: Those are the adoptive parents.

THE SURROGATE: You are not interested in that?

MR. SILVER: That information has already been made available.

THE SURROGATE: Now you are talking about the foster parents?

MR. SILVER: Yes.

THE SURROGATE: Are they here?

MR. SILVER: We have never been requested to look for them. The thrust of the petition up until now has been to locate the petitioner's natural mother.

THE SURROGATE: All right, we will call it again.

MRS. MAXTONE-GRAHAM: May I please speak?

THE SURROGATE: No.

MRS. MAXTONE-GRAHAM: Oh, please!

THE SURROGATE: We will call it again.

It was over, and our group was talking all at once in the center of the courtroom. We were hugging and crying. My mother was beaming. Donohue and Silver were talking. Donohue was saying, "I guess that takes care of the 'confidentiality,' doesn't it?" and Silver was agreeing. My God, my freedom of speech! Someone told us to be quiet, but we had too much to say. My mother had been brilliant, Donohue had been brilliant, all of us were brilliant . . .

The gavel sounded. I was startled as voices told us to be quiet or get out. Then I realized that the court was intending to go on with other business!

Somehow we managed to contain ourselves until all of our party were outside the courtroom and the doors were closing. Again everyone was congratulating, hugging, crying.

253

There was no hiding any more, no disguising that we were here, no pretending that we did not all belong together. Cyril congratulated Donohue on both his courtroom performances. Florence gave everyone in sight a pep talk on ALMA principles. While Joe was guessing that the agency would "just forget about their detective's fee," someone reported to him that Curry, Pell had telephoned the Children's Aid Society, and the Children's Aid Society had confirmed, "Yes, Mrs. Ketiladze-Jason is her mother." The ALMA crowd hooted at this "information," then we all told Cathy Browning what she ought to print in her article and whom else she ought to interview. In the camaraderie of the moment, I accepted the congratulations of Michael Silver and shook his hand.

"Reprieved, reprieved—Macheath has been reprieved," I hummed the conclusion of *The Threepenny Opera*. "The glorious messenger a-riding comes, a-riding comes."—Were those the words? How did it go exactly? "The glorious messenger, victorious messenger . . . "

We could celebrate the victory right here in the hall of the courthouse. Victory over secrecy. Victory over the court order. Victory over the courts. Victory over groveling. Victory over "good cause." Over fantasy. Over the adoption mythology. Victory over death and separation. Victory over all the enemies. Victory over Mathilda Stern. Victory, victory shared with my friends, with Florence, with Melia, and with Lyn and Audrey, with the receptionists who were kind on the phone, with my lawyers, and with my family. Victory shared with any and all who cared for me. All of us were victorious. It was a bloodless decimation of the enemy. No one maimed or killed. All the good guys won, all the bad guys lost. But the bad guys were flattened, and the good guys had conquered the mountain; the flag of truth would wave for all to see. Victory. Victory. Victory.

chapter nineteen

MUM'S STORY

For a long time afterwards, none of us knew what Audrey did when she left the courthouse that day.

Inspired, uplifted, Audrey marched straight off to the Bureau of Vital Records. She was sensing more deeply than ever her right to her certificate of birth; today she was going to *demand* it. She would state her facts, put down the fee, and not budge until the certificate was in her hands. No one could tell her this time that her birth certificate was not hers. The Commissioner himself would have to melt before her certainty. Once and for always, Audrey was going to vanquish failure.

Sitting on a bench in the park outside the building, Audrey had gone over her plan of action, recited her rights. Her resolve had been firm; yet her avoidance of reality's pain had been total. After two hours of sitting there, she had not been able to bring herself to the experience of rejection by a clerk. When she finally had left the park, she quite untypically had treated herself to a taxi for the trip back to her apartment.

Mum, John, and I ate a light lunch in the living room and tried to unwind. Mum pulled out a big red book she had brought from Mexico: "Williams-Enoch Genealogy with Allied Families."

A boring family genealogy, I marveled, just like other people's! Quickly I scanned the section about my mother. Included was her competitive acceptance at Hunter College

High School—"a severe test in which Ruth won the highest rating"—and her graduation "from high school on her 16th birthday." This early graduation, by changing the timing, explained a part of the story that had never made sense. And how opposite to Mrs. Meinhauser's determined non-admiration was this family history's proud bragging.

Mum began talking of my father. At the time she knew him, she said, he had been living with his married sister in Mount Vernon. Mum did not know what sort of work he had done; she remembered only his love for music, for literature and poetry. Especially, he had loved poetry. He and my mother used to have dinner in a nearby restaurant, walk back to his sister's house, and stay up late reading poetry together.

"But *really*"—my mother grimaced in self-mockery—"to think that I was seduced by *Swinburne*."

"I like Swinburne," I protested.

"Oh no, dear, Milton is so much better."

But I was thinking of some lines from Swinburne, hearing them with a new ear:

> In his eyes foreknowledge of death;
> He weaves, and is clothed with derision;
> Sows, and he shall not reap;
> His life is a watch or a vision
> Between a sleep and a sleep.

We talked a while longer; and then, for the first time in twenty-four hours, our thoughts returned to our everyday activities. John and I both had chores to do; Mum, who had not slept at all the night before, was going to rest. John was closing the shutters to darken the room. My mother was fumbling in her purse.

"I think I left my heart pills!" she exclaimed. "I've had three heart attacks, and in the rush yesterday, I must have forgotten them."

Oh, my God, she's going to die of a heart attack, I panicked. How stupid of me—not to have known, not to have guessed, not to have prepared for this. If my mother were to die today, I surely would be blamed and the adoption movement set back.

Dr. Thomas called to ask about the hearing and I told him about the three heart attacks and no heart pills.

"Don't worry, Mrs. Maxtone-Graham," he said, almost laughing. "People do not *die* from happiness."

I telephoned Melia about my family history. For her sake, I was glad my mother had brought the red book. Next I told Ed Goldfader about the name Kelley and about Mount Vernon, and he promised to do some research over the summer. I called McKinley and Hart; neither Charlie nor Donohue could come to our going-away party, but Donohue, wishing us all the best of everything, added that he had been in touch with the agency lawyers: "They tell me the agency's going berserk."

Later, Mum tried to telephone her other children. She was unable to reach either my sister, Rucy, or youngest brother, Nicholas, but she did get through to Alexander, whose reception of the news was as enthusiastic as Andrew's had been. "Boy, I'd like to shake the hand of that detective!" he exclaimed. He, too, thanked me for finding them, and for working so hard and keeping on, for being so persistent. "Thank you for *not giving up*."

That night, at the family supper, there was the usual talking, joking, questioning, narrating—as though nothing were unique about this event. And my mother was sitting there, glowing with pride and pleasure. A normal family life, and the happy grandmother was part of it.

For the remainder of the evening, my mother and I sat together on the living room sofa and talked.

"You've turned out just as I would have wanted you to," my mother said with admiration. How good it felt to be someone's "just right."

Mum brought out photographs she had grabbed off her mirror yesterday in her rush to catch the airplane, pictures of my sister and brothers, of George, of herself. As we looked at them, talking the whole time, I was again struck by her honesty and directness.

Why had she named me Judith Virginia? The Judith, Mum explained, had been after the actress Judith Anderson. We both laughed. I especially liked this recurring coincidence of the name Anderson. How wild and sentimental it all seemed. Judith Anderson had been her idol, said my mother, confiding that it had been her own ambition to be an actress. At the time of my birth, she had been a bank clerk; but she was, at last, an actress now, having been a publishing assistant, a radio commentator, and, for several years, a teacher of high school English.

"And Virginia?" I asked.

My mother's face clouded. Virginia had been *her* mother's idea, she explained. Mum had been planning to call me Judith Alicia, Alicia after her mother, and because it was a family tradition that the first daughter carry the name Alicia. Mum's older sister was Alicia, her mother was Alicia. But when Mum had told her mother that the baby was to be named Judith Alicia, the elder Alicia had objected. "She looks like a Virginia to me."

So I was named for my natural grandmother after all, I mused, even though not in any of the ways I had ever guessed when I was searching.

As the story of what had happened thirty-nine years before spilled out, I was struck both at the similarities to and the dissimilarities from Mrs. Meinhauser's account. The same events, without the overlay of prejudice, were ringing true for the first time. Here was a bright and rebellious girl who had been unequipped, at the age of seventeen, to carry through her revolt against a rigid but adored mother.

My mother had indeed been, as Mrs. Meinhauser had said, the third of four children, fatherless, living in a crowded house with her mother, her younger sister, her older sister, and the older sister's husband and two sons, my first cousins. Her father—my grandfather—had been an engineer, but he had never gone to sea. He had, however, worked as an engineer for Con Edison on the conversion of the great liner, *Leviathan*.

It was my grandmother who had introduced my mother and father. The section of the Bronx where the Williams family had lived bordered on Mount Vernon. They had gone out together for several months, my mother explained, but she had been uncomfortable with the somewhat older man's sexual demands and finally had stopped seeing him. When the pregnancy had been discovered, my mother had been confined to her room and permitted no visitors. And as I had guessed, Clare Engelhardt of Mount Vernon, her younger sister, had not been told. The only people who had known of my mother's pregnancy besides her mother and Kelley were her older sister and her brother-in-law, and one girlfriend. To this day, she said, there was no one else who knew.

For the final months of her pregnancy, my mother had been sent to the Salvation Army Home in Manhattan. The plan had been for her to have the baby and then give it up for adoption. But when she saw her child, she had wanted to keep the baby.

In order to be near her child, she had offered to work in the Salvation Army nursery. So, for the next three months she had been able to feed and care for her baby. Then she had had to place the infant in a foster home. She had still been hoping to find a way of keeping her child. Her mother, however, would not allow an illegitimate baby in the house; and for two years her child had remained a terrible secret, visited by the young mother on her days off but never spoken of by the family.

Only one person, the girlfriend who had known about the pregnancy, did mention the child. About six months after giving birth, my mother had been alone with her friend. "I was so sorry," the friend had gently confided, "to hear that your little boy was born dead."

A boy born dead. This, then, was the report my grandmother had created. Stunned, my mother had been unable to reply. Neither the dead boy, nor the little girl living in a foster home, was ever referred to again.

My mother was not unmarked by her experience. Several times she had sought the aid of psychiatrists and had talked to them of her gnawing depression, but she never had told any of them about the child she had lost. So a diet theory had evolved in explanation—the background, I realized, of the "insufficiency to absorb calcium through normal channels." The haunting yearning emptiness had remained. Late at night, alone with her thoughts, she had remembered and wondered.

She had never told her husband, George. Not because George would have disapproved, she explained, but because he would not have understood the impossibility of the situation. "So you have a little girl? Well, let's go get her!" he would have insisted.

In 1945, the first of their four children had been born. Their child's middle name, in the family tradition for the first daughter, had been Alicia. In 1958, the six Ketiladze-Jasons had left Queens and had moved to Mexico. One year later, in 1959, George had died unexpectedly, of a heart attack, in Saginaw, Michigan.

Saginaw was familiar to me; that was where my adoptive father had been born and raised and had even, for a time in his youth, played first violin in the symphony orchestra.

At the mention of my adoptive father, my mother began talking about some lost photographs. She spoke disjointedly, and at first it was not clear to me that she must be referring to that "picture left for me" at the agency. It turned out that there had been not one, but rather a number of pictures; and that my adoptive father had in fact requested to see them. Thus my mother had lent the pictures, her entire collection, to the agency. Several months later, the agency had informed her that the pictures had been "inadvertently destroyed by the adoptive father."

Mum talked, too, of visiting the foster homes. One Saturday after work she had gone to the home and discovered her child had been moved, and that no one knew where. She had been instructed to wait until the agency's business hours the following week, and then to "put in a request for the change of address."

There was one particular summer afternoon, in another home, a good home, which she had never forgotten. Mother, child, and foster mother had been together in the garden. Mum could remember the scene very clearly. I had called my foster mother "Mama," and the foster mother had corrected me: "No, I'm not your Mama, *that's* your Mama." Bewildered, I had looked from grown-up to grown-up; and the young mother had thought, "This cannot go on."

So this was "the good foster mother" of my imaginings, and the garden was, unquestionably, the garden in the photo of the blonde-haired girl in a sunsuit. How vividly I now had answers to last fall's questions about "my mother's visits and my reactions to same, also her reactions."

The foster homes had been in Queens, Mum remembered, but she could recall no names. Nor could she recollect which agency had been in charge of the foster care. But she certainly remembered the one person who, throughout her struggle to keep me, had been kind to her—Winifred Hewitt, a social worker with the foster-care service. In the summer of 1937, not long after that distressing scene in the garden, the foster-care service had decided to remove me from this foster home "because the family was getting too attached." Winifred Hewitt, breaking the rules, had confided to my mother the threat of this further change, and it was then that my mother had decided she ought to surrender me. She had known it would be years, and possibly several more foster homes, before she could financially support a child. So she had signed the papers in August, 1937, in order that I might have a permanent home as soon as possible. And once the papers had been signed, there could be no more visits to her daughter.

Had my mother been helped from the beginning, she would not have had to give in to her mother's will. But there had been no sustaining help, so my grandmother—"Lulu" to

261

the adoring grandchildren who knew her—had won. In 1940, when my mother had married George Ketiladze, Lulu had given her a "facts-of-life" talk on the eve of the wedding, as though her grandchild's death-disappearance had restored her daughter's virginity. Lulu herself—who had not been "sickly" after all—had made a successful second marriage and had lived on, twenty-seven years past my birth, to a hearty eighty.

Although my mother had never seen me again, she had kept up her relationship with Winifred Hewitt. They had never spoken of "the child," but had remained friends. Now the social worker was in her eighties and living in a nursing home in upstate New York. Her last letter to my mother had been written last February but, as sometimes happens with mail to Mexico, the letter had gone astray and had not reached my mother until just one week ago. So when the call had come from New York, my mother had thought it might be her old friend who had known her little girl.

Having learned, at last, what had happened back in the late 1930's, I realized how little all this story had had to do with me. Rather, it had had to do with my mother, and her mother, and the family circumstances. Although I had intellectually known that my being given away had had nothing to do with my qualities as a human being, not until I sat beside my mother and heard the story of my early childhood directly from her could I fully believe that the rejection of me had not been the fruit of my own inadequacy.

Finally we said good-night. It was just before midnight. My mother selected a book with which she hoped to read herself to sleep, and I went upstairs to pack my suitcases for our trip.

When I had finished, I peeked in at my mother. She was asleep, the book open on her chest, the light on, her reading glasses dripping from her nose. I tiptoed to her side, removed the book and glasses and turned off the light. Walking up through the calm, resting house, I snuggled into bed. All was well with the world. Now, at last, I could glance over the documents Joe Donohue had handed me in the morning. On top of the legal papers was my mother's unmailed letter to ALMA, which she had slipped into my bag sometime during the celebratory scene outside the courtroom. Now I ripped open the envelope and read the message.

> My daughter Judith Virginia Williams (or Kelley, her father's name) was born at the Salvation Army Home for Unmarried Mothers on East 13th or 15th Street in New York City in March, 1935, when I was 17.
> Although it had previously been arranged that she be adopted at birth, I just *couldn't bear* to sign adoption papers and give her up for adoption, for almost three years. Meanwhile, she'd been boarded out; I used to visit her on Saturdays—but the "homes" kept changing.
> Finally, although it tore my soul then and has forever since, I thought it better for her to be adopted into a permanent home. (Through something called State Charities Aid.)
> Until I read the article in the June issue of *Cosmopolitan*, I'd thought all the pain was on my side.
> Perhaps my baby, now 39, will never look for me—
> But please tell other adoptees that sometimes they are relinquished from love—*not* from rejection at all.
> Thank you for being.

Fortified yet again, I went on to the legal documents from Donohue, the papers that would have been presented before the judge this morning had my mother's extraordinary appearance not altered the scene. From my present perch on top of the world, I surely ought not to have been vulnerable to the Children's Aid Society tongue, and yet I was. I was hurt by Michael Silver's statement of my lesser status, "Her natural mother and the other persons whose identities are contained in the agency's records have equal, if not superior, rights in connection with this proceeding." And I was actually trembling at the vindictive words of Mathilda Stern's latest affidavit: "Based on my experience as a social worker, it ap-

263

pears to me that petitioner has a strong anger toward her mother. . . . [T]he petitioner is searching for her mother in order to vent her hostility toward her. . . ." If my mother had not been in court today and spoken for herself, the judge would have had to pay heed to this expert witness's professional opinion: "If the records are turned over to this woman, there is no way the court can safeguard any of the individuals who are named in them."

I knew it was laughable—Michael Silver trotting out the old arguments about "detrimental effects on the natural mother and her family," Mathilda Stern attesting to "the natural mother who wanted to cut off all ties to her daughter" on the very day my mother had told me, "Thank you for finding me." Nevertheless, their words stung, and I was crying as I finally fell asleep.

chapter twenty

MOVING ONWARD

The following morning I was so busy completing last-minute preparations for our family's trip that the affidavits of Silver and Stern were pushed to the back of my mind. My mother meanwhile was arranging to stay a few days in New York with Sylvia and then go on to visit Rucy in Miami.

A bottle of champagne arrived from Joe Donohue. Someday I should send one to him, too. But when I did I'd make it three bottles, one for each of my missing families.

Before going to the ship, my mother telephoned Winifred Hewitt. "This is Ruth Williams. I've found my little girl!" Then my mother called me to the phone.

"Judith," cried Winifred, "Oh, Judith, *tell* them! *Tell* them!" Her voice tore through my flesh.

I felt foolish not to be understanding her. "Tell . . . tell who?"

"The social workers! Tell the other social workers not to separate mothers and children!"

The bags were already loaded into the car. When we walked outside, Ian took a few quick pictures of my mother and me together, and then we were off.

The shipboard going-away party was an orgy of triumph. Mum, Lorraine, Audrey, Sylvia, Florence, Cathy Browning. Ed Goldfader greeted my mother with a huge hug: "I always get to find them, but I never get to *see* them!" As I introduced my mother I realized that I was proud to be identified with her. It was the same feeling as I had seen glowing from the faces of my girlhood friends when we were all nine or ten, or thirteen or fourteen; I had seen the expression sometimes on my own children's faces. But I had never experienced the sensation myself. As a child, I had been ashamed of introducing my adoptive parents. Then I had thought my shame was because they seemed pretentious and haughty and old. But those had not been the real reasons. Rather, my shame had been because something unacknowledged inside me had sensed that when I introduced those two loved-hated enigmas as "my parents," I was telling a lie.

People took turns reading aloud from Mum's letter to ALMA and from the affidavits of Mathilda Stern and Michael Silver. Then Audrey found a further affidavit, one I had not even noticed the night before. It was a statement from Friedman about the agency's search.

Audrey read for all to hear, "Court records in the above cities, which were legally available, were searched and no criminal record was revealed for either name." Squeals and guffaws rose from the group. "There was no evidence of any suits, judgments or bankruptcies in either name."

Hoots and cheers. We drank the champagne sent by Joe Donohue, and the ship's photographer took a photo that I could only call a "group victory picture." We were certainly high, high on happiness. Mum gave a copy of her ALMA letter to Cathy Browning and discussed Cathy's newspaper story. I was as careful as possible not to pressure Mum, but she had as much conviction as I of the importance of spreading our message. She was eager for the whole story to appear, and adamant that her identity be openly given. I asked only that the article not be released until I had had time to write the news to my adoptive brothers.

Hark, Hark, Hark—Victoria's messenger riding comes,
Riding comes, riding comes . . .
Macheath has been reprieved
And I am happy.

The guests left; the ship sailed; the entire crossing was one continuous celebration. Meeting new friends and retelling the story, I noticed that the beginning of the narration was not greeted, as before, with concerned expressions of, "Just think what you might find!" Now no one questioned, no one worried, whether the person I had found would turn out to be "undesirable." The assumption, once a mother became real, was that she must be just like every other mother.

How different it all would have been had the agency not opposed me. I would have received my records, located my mother, been reunited. The ordeal of yearning for nearly forty years would have been no less, the joy of knowledge no greater. But because the agency had chosen to fight, the original need to know my origins had been equaled by the further need to defeat my irrational attacker, the Children's Aid Society. To become human, and to overcome inhumanity, had evolved into two separate crusades, and I, who was once life's failure, was now a double victor.

The sense of victory continued into the summer. I was participating fully in our family vacation, accepting the wait until the fall to have my records, my history, the good foster mother, the long-ago brother. At least the court case was over and won; having found my mother, I had finished with the Children's Aid Society. Now I had my own family to concentrate upon, to *enjoy*.

As we wended our way through Europe on Eurailpasses, stopping spontaneously here and there, I considered how I, the dead leaf in the wind, had been at last an instrument of my own fate. I had not been alone; others had supported and aided me. But the greatest event of my life had been accomplished by me. No others—owners, betters, intermediaries, professionals—had executed my own salvation. No one else had dialed that telephone. No one had spoken my words for me. In my moment of truth it was I who had had the power of action. And thus it was that I had become a real human being.

In the Hamburg railway station, there was an old, poor

woman picking up trash. For an instant I stared at her, wondering; and then I remembered. In Copenhagen in the Tivoli Gardens, a smiling middle-aged couple from the Midwest made space on their bench for me to sit; and again the habitual question framed itself, then subsided. No, I did not have to keep wondering anymore. The world was not my mother. The searching, the fearing, the apologizing could all end. I, Katrina, had the right to be alive.

More than that. I did not have to fault myself for my continuing ignorance. I did not have to confront, each minute, the possibility that I was right then missing the one chance of a lifetime, not recognizing my mother in the crowd, not guessing that the house just passed was hers. Just as I was no longer responsible for my having been born, neither was I still guilty for my having failed to find life.

"I am real." I kept hearing myself repeat the phrase, aloud or in my head, "I am *real*." It should have seemed silly, a thirty-nine-year-old mother of four walking around declaring, "I'm a real person," yet how startling it was to conceive of oneself as real—how marvelous, how joyful. I had not quite realized the extent of my prior convictions of sub-humanity until I acquired this new belief in my humanness.

Something else was changing that summer, quietly, subtly, yet definitely. Now and then, unconsciously, casually, I found myself narrating anecdotes from my adoptive childhood. "When I was little, my father used to . . . " "I remember how the three of us kids would . . . " I was beginning to recollect moments of joy or fun or pleasure. Hearing myself recounting long-forgotten remembrances of happiness, I could only surmise that I had spent years—up until July 9, 1974—internally, unintentionally, declaring to my adoptive parents, "Since you took away and repressed all memory of what I brought of me, of my family, of my own history—so will I, then, repress all memory of what it was that you have given."

Joyous letters found me in new places. D'Arcy sent a flowered pink card, "Congratulations on your new daughter" with the word "daughter" crossed out and replaced with "mother." Melia, enclosing a bill for her year's expenses—$23—wrote a warm letter and concluded, "Hope you do find that foster mother, know it truly matters to you." Cyril forwarded a copy of a letter he had written on behalf of ALMA in which he described that breakfast in my garden, my mother "greeting her newly found grandchildren for the first time." He went on, "I cannot remember a more touching scene. Later that morning, I witnessed the two of them, both radiantly happy, make a declaration in the Surrogate's Court. In thirty-three years at the Bar, I have never witnessed a more moving scene in a courtroom."

Early in August, a cable came from Miami: "I am so happy and excited to have a sister. I cannot wait to meet you. Plan to be in New York in early September. Hope I will have time to write long letter before then. Welcome to our family. Love, Your sister, Rucy."

That night—at three o'clock the following morning, actually—a Swedish radio program was interrupted by the unmistakable voice of Richard Nixon. It took until his second paragraph before we could be certain that he was, finally and truly, resigning the presidency of the United States. The times were indeed changing.

chapter twenty-one

IN PURSUIT
OF COMPLETION

My quest was not over. There were more facts to uncover, other people to trace, the lost three and a hàlf years to find. When Mrs. Meinhauser had asked me what I wanted to know, I had told her, "Everything, everything." Now I was home, and anxious for that speedy conclusion. Once this records issue was resolved, I would be free to think ahead, to contemplate that newfound jewel, a future.

I telephoned my mother on our first evening in New York. She, too, had had a summer of emotion and change. There had been periods of such tremendous elation, she said, that the world had seemed unreal. She had one time considered throwing herself from a tenth-floor window—to confirm to herself that what had happened had really happened. Whose suffering was greater, I asked myself, the abandoned child's or the relinquishing mother's? Ours or theirs? It was a question without an answer; the pain of amputation from history, in either direction, cannot be measured.

Suddenly my mother asked excitedly, "When are you coming to visit?"

"I've only just arrived home," I replied, startled. "I don't know."

"All my friends are dying to meet you."

Of course I would have to visit her in Mexico. But how could I take an airplane? How could I leave my children? These were demands for internal rearrangements such as I had never anticipated. And how were they to be effected? Was I capable?

Also that night, I telephoned my adoptive brothers. One of them did not acknowledge my letter until asked, then he changed the subject to questions about our trip. My other brother, however, was thrilled with my news and began reminiscing about "how cute" I had been when I had arrived; he said he wanted to find his natural family too.

I quickly learned that my records were *not* awaiting me. On the contrary, over the summer another legal war had begun: Silver had given stunned protest against my receiving my foster-care file as though it were the first time he had heard this request, Donohue had neatly and clearly refuted his arguments, and the judge had requested a further affidavit from the doctor. The surrogate had also "intimated," as Joe put it, "that at this stage the Court might not be willing to give you the records in the first instance and that for tactical purposes I should request Dr. Thomas to ask for the right to review all of the records."

The "tactical purposes" were obviously to save the agency's face. Let the agency try to save its face on its own, I thought, and not make us be helpmates. But Dr. Thomas's affidavit, while accepting the review, had not compromised our stand in the least: "I reconfirm the opinion I expressed in my prior affidavit and my testimony in court. . . . There is no information contained in the agency's files which is unimportant and, therefore, I re-emphasize the importance of total and complete disclosure."

Just another week, I told myself once again.

But again the weeks passed, and again I was waiting for lawyers to get in touch with lawyers, for other people to determine the course of my actions, for fellow adults to arrange the release of the beginning of my life. Autumn progressed, and I was feeling as frustrated as ever by these obstacles, as angry as I had felt last year, to be the agency's possession.

Rucy and Andrew came North to meet me. Exclaiming, embracing, we marveled at our relationship and attempted to find correspondences in our physical entities. Andrew was large, broad, bearded, and completely unlike me in appearance. Rucy, too, considerably shorter than I, seemed dissimilar in frame; but we did see a resemblance in our faces—long foreheads, high cheekbones, deep smile lines. Although her hair was dark like her father's, Rucy wore it as I did, long and center-parted. They spoke of "our mother," smiling with pleasure at the phrase, and of "our family," Alexander, Nicholas, Aunt Clare, Aunt Licia, the cousins.

When I had first learned that I was not my mother's only child I had felt—after an initial pang of jealousy—great relief: My mother would surely be easier to get along with if she already had grown-up offspring. The fact of having three brothers and a sister, therefore, had seemed an advantage since the beginning. But I had not guessed until this September day—nor imagined, nor dreamed—that siblings represented a great bonus in themselves.

After three or four hours of talking, Rucy, Andrew, and I went to the Museum of Natural History. We were already halfway there when the realization struck: *I am riding on the crosstown bus with my brother and my sister.* I looked at them again—Andrew so broad, Rucy so short—and I knew for sure that they both would have evoked a "no" in all my searches of fellow passengers.

That evening, with the same spontaneity and sense of adventure as on last July's visit, John and I drove Andrew and Rucy to the Ketiladzes' old neighborhood in Queens.

"Four people ringing my bell?" came Esther's unforgettable voice from inside her dark house. The door opened and there she stood in a pink quilted housecoat and fuzzy blue slippers with huge wool pom-poms. "They tell you, 'It's not safe, don't open your door.' " She was motioning for us to enter, although she clearly had no idea who her visitors were. "But I say, they're not going to send *four* people to come and kill me. It only takes *one!*"

In the center of Esther's coffee table was the dish my mother had sent from Mexico. It was plain and ordinary, yet I knew that it would have meant the world to me not long ago. While Esther talked on, of that departure with the car and all the belongings, of her girlhood in Poland, of the son who never came to visit, my imagination played with that magical aura which would have once surrounded the dish. How beautiful, how precious, how radiant it would have been, then, wrapped in its mist of meaning. How hazed the air used to be, how obscured the simple realities.

When we left, Esther presented us with a large brown paper bag full of cookies she had made for the neighborhood children. She padded after us into the street in her fuzzy slippers with the pom-poms, calling more good-byes.

Andrew and I tried to lead her back to her steps. As we both kissed her gently on the cheek, Esther reached out and grasped our elbows.

"Maybe what you give to your own," she said as she looked up into our faces, "you get back from other people's."

Several days later, Rucy left for Florida to begin her final semester of college. When we parted, she said, "Thank you—for adopting us."

Andrew did not return to Florida, but decided to relocate in New York. He found himself a good job and an apartment on Long Island close to his office. Now, once or twice a week, "Uncle Andrew" would join us at the six o'clock family dinner table. Andrew or I, or both, telephoned our mother fairly often. We spoke also to Nick and Alexander, and finally to Aunt Clare. Aunt Clare, my mother had discovered when she had confessed her thirty-nine-year-old secret, had known it for the past twenty years. It was a story often heard at ALMA: One night, after a few drinks, the older sister's husband had spilled out the family secret.

My father's name, recollected Mum at last, was Sam. That was nice; I liked the name Sam. Sam Kelley. Both my sons had three-letter names, too.

"But I should warn you," apologized my mother, "he was a bit of a louse. He knew I was pregnant, but he never did anything. He never came around, never called."

"And, if he had called," I asked, "would your mother have told you?"

Mum was quiet for a moment. "Now that I think of it, it's true, he *might* have called! My mother would never have let him in the house, nor given me a message."

If Sam Kelley had called, what would he have been told? That Ruth had had "a little boy, born dead"?

Although both Ed Goldfader and I were working on my father's case, the name Sam brought no further leads. The only documented Kelley in Mount Vernon in 1934 had been Jack; and Jack had moved to nearby Port Chester in 1935, stayed a year, and then had disappeared altogether.

Not understanding how deep-rooted was the agency's desire not to release my records, I believed that as soon as the lawyers' dance was done my foster-care history would appear. I still called Donohue, not as often as last spring, but fairly frequently. As before, our relationship was uneven. There were times when he seemed to grasp all the issues; he would suggest that my story ought to be told—perhaps the two of us could go on TV together and wouldn't that be fun? Other times he sounded quite oblivious to my needs, declaring calmly that we would probably win the foster-care records but without the names and addresses.

The names and addresses were essential, I insisted to Donohue. But to myself I acknowledged my fear that Dr. Thomas would not be able to justify my demand for these specifics. Finally I asked him directly. His response was unequivocally in my favor: Anything could trigger a memory, he told me—a name, a place, a nickname—and therefore everything had to be regarded as potentially important. He could not "know" that something was "unimportant" to someone else. As a doctor, he would fight for every possible clue, which would include, without any question, all the addresses and names.

Meanwhile, Cathy Browning's article was appearing in newspapers across the country, and the ALMA office was being deluged with applications for membership. At October's meeting, the first of the new season, there was standing room only.

I was to be one of the speakers. Talking before me was Luther, who had driven six hours, accompanied by his recently found maternal aunt, to address the group. It seemed particularly fitting to be sharing my day in the sun with Luther, whom I had met at my first meeting. Although his story was not as golden as mine—his mother had died three years ago, after having spent most of her adult life in a mental institution—it was as shining with love. Luther's Aunt Rose had wanted to keep him from the start and had fought to gain custody of her sister's child. Although Rose had lost her battle first against foster care and then against adoption, she had not lost Luther forever. And Luther's sense of wholeness and contentment seemed no less than mine.

Then, with utter exultation, I told my story at last: The impossible *can* happen. And if it could happen even for me, a loser so soon ago, then yes, it really can happen for you.

One of the new adoptee members was Celia, a stunning woman who looked fiftyish but was in fact sixty-nine. Celia's agency was the Children's Aid Society, and she called me for advice before her first meeting with Mrs. Meinhauser. About thirty years ago—when Celia would have been my present age—she had hired a detective to research her adoption. The detective had come up with a name, Jenny Hoffman, but the name had been untraceable, and it had never been established whether it was Celia's, her mother's, or both. Celia still had no birth certificate under any name, and no further information other than the facts that she was born sometime in the spring of 1905 and had lived in a foster home until she was three years old.

Celia called again after her appointment. "Mrs. Meinhauser is very sweet," she told me quickly. "Why, she even telephoned a judge on my behalf! A Judge Silvan, it sounded like."

"Sylvane?" I asked.

"That's right! But there was nothing about me in the court, apparently."

Mrs. Meinhauser would actually telephone a judge direct? I tried to absorb, to accept, the concept. Celia went on:

Mrs. Meinhauser had not made any reference to the name Jenny Hoffman at the appointment, and Celia had not let on that she knew it. When Celia had asked to be told her mother's name, Mrs. Meinhauser had said that she was bound by the law not to reveal it.

"She said she was very sorry," continued Celia, "and then she volunteered the name of Catherine Connell, who was my foster mother until I was three."

"She told you your foster mother's name?"

"And gave me the address, too. Catherine Connell, someplace in the East Sixties. I've got it written down."

I could barely believe my ears. While the agency was battling in court to withhold from me the name of my foster mother, they were freely offering similar information to another adoptee!

"And it's true, too," Celia said, "because I recognized the name as one the detective gave me thirty years ago. I've checked the detective's papers, and even the address Mrs. Meinhauser told me was true." She paused, then went on tentatively, "You know, I'd sort of like to go to that address one day. Just to take a look. I wonder if it's safe."

"Safe? The East Sixties?"

"How do you get there? Is it a bad area? I wouldn't know how to get there."

Slowly, I understood what Celia was telling me. Although she had lived in New York for over twenty years, she had never been in the East Sixties. Celia never left her apartment unless she was escorted. She had been able to attend the ALMA meeting because she had found someone to take her. Celia was unable to do anything on her own. This charming, intelligent woman was, I realized, a fragile, helpless child. Afraid of taxis, of elevators, of subways, of buses, of stores, of the dark, of the light, of people. She was myself, thirty years worse.

"I only wish," Celia's voice was calm, devoid of bitterness, "it all hadn't had to be this way."

Celia thanked me profusely—too profusely—for listening. She told me that she was yearning to pursue her search, but she regarded her case as hopeless. And I did not know what to say. How does one suggest tramping the halls of the New York Public Library and making useless calls to irrelevant places, on an impossible search with no information, to a sixty-nine-year-old woman who cannot get out of her house?

Donohue seemed genuinely shocked when I told him about Celia, and I got excited, thinking he might report it to the court, compose a fiery affidavit, request a hearing. Maybe her experience would help me win my case. But he did not even write down Celia's telephone number.

Andrew, John, and I went to dinner at Aunt Clare's and Uncle Frank's. As we arrived, Aunt Clare was bringing out my mother's high school yearbook, and later she showed me the old family albums. I devoured them all. Pages and pages of brown and white photos of great-grandparents, grandparents, groups, scenes—unrecognizable people in old-fashioned clothes, striking stern or "natural" poses. I, too, had photographable relatives! I thought of all the times my in-laws had accosted me with theirs, all those predecessors on their side who had solely created our children's abilities, features, characters, goodnesses. Now my children's heritage as well as my own was being restored.

Only the first sight of Lulu, my grandmother, brought pain. For an instant I wanted to tear off that flat, smiling face and march into the brain behind. But Lulu's picture just kept on smiling, and I got used to the sight of it after a while. "Oh, that's Lulu, isn't it?" I could say pleasantly to Aunt Clare. Nothing further was upsetting except one series: The family group in the garden, Lulu, my mother, my aunts and uncles, and two little boys of one and four, who were the acknowledged grandchildren. This time the discomfort I was feeling was not for myself but for my mother. While this "family group with the grandchildren" was being photographed, there had been another grandchild a few miles away, waiting for a visit on the weekends. What had that pretty young woman standing at the side of her nephews felt as "the whole family" posed for its portrait?

I made the decision to go to Mexico. To fly, on my own,

and spend a week with my mother. I was going for my mother's sake, I believed, because she wanted to see me, because she wanted to show me off to her friends, and because she felt my visit would help her to comprehend the reality of this extraordinary experience. But as the trip came closer, I realized that I needed this visit for my own sake. The "reaction," which I had not had over the summer, was now beginning. As the world around me reversed—truths of my childhood emerging as lies, impossibles evolving into facts, mysteries being simple knowledge—I was starting into the ups and downs of the aftermath. I, too, needed to grasp reality, whatever that was.

When I arrived in Mexico Mum gave a huge party to introduce me to her friends. I was greeted with letters and gifts and cards, all thanking me, telling of their love and happiness for my mother and for me. "I wish *I* had a long-lost child," sighed a seventy-year-old woman, "to come back and find *me*." There was a flower for me from the man with the flower cart on the corner. The baker, with tears in his eyes, refused to let me pay for my roll.

In the quiet moments of that pleasant week, my mother and I talked. She with the endless coffee, me with the endless tea, both of us with the endless cigarettes, we sat across from one another at the kitchen table and talked away long mornings. If I made an allusion, or cracked a joke, or uttered an abbreviated opinion, I never had to wonder, "Will she get it?" As with people one has known all one's life, there was no need to make explanations. My mother and I had been related, all this time; but I had never imagined that "related to" could be as strong as "lived with." After so many years without genetic inheritance, I was still reluctant to believe in genetics. Now, however, the genetic relationship was forcing itself upon me, demanding acknowledgment. The strength of a genetic relationship is certainly one more reason why children and parents ought not to be separated.

The week in Mexico was a busy time, full of activities,

invitations, and new friendships. My reactions were comfortable and calm, without any inner turbulence. But then, on my
last night, I took out a pad and wrote feverishly:

> *I am unable to feel. All I can feel is an overwhelm-
> ing sense of tragedy in other people's lives. Others'
> sufferings, I absorb—but feelings I do not have.
> This is what I have learned: That I am an observer.
> That I am horrified by what I see. But I do not re-
> spond. The only human response I know is to fear. I
> can analyze intellectually that which I see. But I
> cannot respond to any personal feeling, as there are
> no personal feelings at my fingertips, except the
> feelings of fear. The other feelings, I only watch in
> other people. Hence the observer, hence the intellec-
> tual awareness of other feelings, hence the unending
> personal response to life: Fear.*
>
> *The question is, is "purpose" still important?
> Until now, purpose was all-important. For the first
> time I wonder: Maybe there is living in life.*

> *Et maintenant
> que vais-je faire
> de tout ce temps
> que sera ma vie?*

chapter twenty-two

AGENCY OPERATIONS: FIRST EXPOSURES

Awaiting me in New York was an envelope from Donohue. Inside was the one set of agency papers I had thought I
would never see, Mrs. Meinhauser's reports of my two visits
to her office. Together with an affidavit declaring that these
were indeed her reports, Mrs. Meinhauser set forth her assessment of me:

> 4/16/73 Mrs. Katrina Maxtone-Graham called for an inter-
> view in order to learn about her background. She was the
> former Judith Williams. . . . She was told there would be
> a little delay until we were able to obtain the material and
> we would be calling her. She nevertheless did call the fol-
> lowing day and reached me indicating great urgency and
> an inability to wait long for an appointment. There was
> actually no realistic reason for an immediate appointment
> except her own anxiety. I arranged to meet her down-
> stairs since she is phobic about riding alone in elevators.

> 4/26/73 Mrs. MG in office. She is a tall, thin woman with a
> prominent nose, deep blue eyes. She was very casually
> dressed, has long hair which she wears loose. She is very
> intense.

For nine single-spaced pages Mrs. Meinhauser continued. Her facts, though familiar, were ever strangely inaccu-
rate. The dates of my phone calls were incorrect, she had not
met me downstairs at the agency before our first meeting—
small differences, but crucial. I was startled by her opinion of

my carefully chosen, favorite clothes. My reaction to my father's "Irish-sounding name" was noted, but not my immediate clarification. The omissions and distortions were astounding. Yet there were accuracies too—precise details, exact quotations—whose presence was as startling as that of the inaccuracies.

The report of each meeting was dated, and I noticed that Mrs. Meinhauser had not written them within a week of each interview as she had boasted was her practice, but a full month later. Sometimes Mrs. Meinhauser stated she had provided information that she had in fact withheld. Other times she had indeed given the information, but she placed it in the wrong meeting. The more I read, the more I suspected that Mrs. Meinhauser had copied these write-ups out of the file itself. These were notes of what Mrs. Meinhauser thought she *ought* to have said.

And in all her nine pages, I realized by the third reading, Mrs. Meinhauser had been unable to attribute to me any positive qualities. She had observed, in four hours of talking together, no likeableness. Had my mother returned to the agency for news of me, she would have acquired a daughter without a single good trait.

I remembered Mrs. Meinhauser's warm smile of appreciation, her laughs at my jokes, her tone of compassion. She had seemed so attentive; and I had believed I was being useful, telling her of my childhood circumstances and of how "advantages" were not a substitute for a sense of belonging. But she had heard nothing. My attempts were twisted in her report into rude comments about my parents. Much as I had hated my upbringing, I would not have revealed one word of it to Mrs. Meinhauser had I suspected her interpretations. How distant were her conclusions here from my hopes, at the time, of benefiting some child of the future.

It enraged me to recognize the extent to which I had been duped in Mrs. Meinhauser's office. Naively, I had ascribed her "funny mannerisms" to an inexplicable superior knowledge and her "peculiar notions" to some failure on my

281

part. Now I knew that each evasion, each wave of the hand, each unfathomable attitude had not been a response to me, but rather a move in the game. She alone had held the rule book and all the cards; indeed, she alone had known that it was a game that we were playing.

"Your foster mother may not even know which one you were," Florence warned. "You've got to face that, Katrina. She may not remember you. 'The fat one, or the thin one?' "

"Yes, but still—"

"For all we know, she could have had a whole slew of foster children. It's garbage, Katrina, they're fighting for their *power*. They don't care about her, they don't care about you."

Peg Lawrence telephoned. She had found her mother, living in a small town in Connecticut, healthy and responsive—but stunned: Peg's mother had never agreed to any adoption. When Peg had been three days old, Peg's mother had been told her baby was dead.

Another of the recent ALMA members was Roger, an earnest young man in his mid-twenties with slash scars on his wrists. Roger called me after having applied for the first time for an appointment at his adoption agency, Spence-Chapin. "You won't believe what that social worker said to me," he exclaimed. "She tried to give me an appointment at the end of December." His voice was breaking. "That's two months away, and I said, no, it had to be sooner. I told her I was ready today, tomorrow, maybe even next week, but—"

Roger stopped. I remembered too well my own request for a first appointment.

"And she said," Roger began again, "her answer to me was, 'After—all—these—years?' "

Audrey, too, had been attempting to get an appointment at her agency. She had met with the usual delays, then had written a letter in which she had hinted at taking legal action. The agency had responded by return mail.

After her appointment, Audrey came straight to my

house. Her face was ashen, her manner disoriented. She sat on the arm of the sofa and for several minutes she did not speak.

The agency meeting, Audrey told me at last, had not gone as expected. Before Audrey had had the chance to even introduce her own questions, the social worker had announced, "We think you are ready to know, Mrs. Bondy: You were a foundling. There is no record of your family at all."

Audrey had asked the social worker, "Why didn't you tell me this before?" and had been told in reply, "We didn't feel you could handle it."

"Katrina, if they'd just told me," Audrey cried, "I've spent ten years. And all this time they could have told me!"

"Last year, you went to the agency, too," I said helplessly.

"And the year before! I've been there five or six times. But they felt I wasn't 'ready'! And now," she laughed feebly, "I guess I am."

After a while, Audrey began to draw on her powers of acceptance and resignation. "In a way, I'm almost relieved," she declared. "If it's hopeless, at least now I *know*. At least now it's over." She sighed and forced a smile. "Now, I suppose I start living with it."

But for Audrey it was not really over, because without seeing some documentation, she had no cause to believe the agency. This new information could be a lie to stop her search and to protect the agency from her threatened lawsuit. It could also, equally possibly, be true. Until Audrey had proof, she could not even work for the solace of acceptance and resignation but must keep on with her search. Before there could be rest for Audrey, the agency would have to go beyond claiming to tell her the truth; the agency would have to *give* her the truth.

On November 19—four months and nine days after it had been promised in court by Michael Silver—the mail brought "the records resulting from [meetings with] your natural mother." So this is what a file looks like, I thought as I pulled out the packet of papers.

Under the printed "Judith Williams" was the heading, "Family History." Here, in the first two lines, was everything I had once needed for search!

MOTHER

Ruth Williams, unmarried, born 6-1-17 in New York City; American, Protestant, white. Present address—4024 Dyre Avenue, Bronx, New York—12-17-37.

"4024 Dyre Avenue." Why had the agency's detective not found her, as we had, within a day of seeing that address?

Miss Williams is a tall, thin, willowy girl with blue eyes and fair complexion. She gives the impression of being genteel and refined. She makes a good appearance.

Coming up were paragraphs on "Health," "Education," "Intelligence," "Character," and "Occupation and Earning Capacity." A file was appallingly not like a person, I was thinking. There was no denying, however, that for someone who was searching it would be a marvelous resource. I jumped ahead.

Miss Williams has at least good average intelligence. She probably gives the impression of being brighter than she actually is, as she converses very well and is exceedingly well read.

There followed a section on "Relatives: Maternal" with full paragraphs each for "Grandfather," "Grandmother," "Aunt," "Uncle," "Aunt"—giving names, birthdates, school and work histories, places of employment, salaries. The specificness of the information was staggering. I was about to turn the page to see if there would be clues for my remaining searches when the name James Williams caught my eye. I stopped and looked back at the notes about my grandfather.

GRANDFATHER
James Williams, born in 1881 in New York City. He was
American, Protestant and white. He died in 1923 and the
cause of his death was acute indigestion.

But my grandfather was named Albert Tell Williams!
Last spring I had received the death certificate for a James
Williams. It had contained no usable information; James's res-
idency in New York City had been a mere four months, and he
had been untraceable. So if Mrs. Meinhauser *had* given me
my grandfather's name from the file, it would have been
wrong! Moreover, the year of death, 1923—which was also
given incorrectly in the file—was nonetheless the year told
me by Mrs. Meinhauser. On this Mrs. Meinhauser had *not* lied
to me but in fact had told me the truth as she knew it. Only
through her defeat were her moments of honesty coming to
light.

I found myself feeling glad about Mrs. Meinhauser.
Something in me wanted her not to be 100 percent bad; something in me wanted an excuse to like her just a little bit. I
wondered why. Was it the adoptees' nature to cling to the
master, forever grateful for any kind of notice taken?

The file went on, single-spaced, with the most incredible
minutiae, for over fifteen pages. Suddenly there was information on my father.

FATHER
Samuel Kelly, unmarried, born 10-15-05 in Virginia;
American, Protestant, white. Last known address, Mt.
Vernon, N.Y. care of Mr. Jack Kelly—1935.

Here, at last, were some facts to search with! But was
this new spelling of "Kelley" a mistake? And not a married
sister but a *brother*.

Jack Kelly was listed as well—"Paternal Uncle"—and
described as having "two sons, ages ten and thirteen." The
two sons were my cousins. Whatever the spelling, Kelley or

285

Kelly, I was now sure that I had an Uncle Jack and two cousins in their forties.

Finally, my foster homes were mentioned, though only briefly and without names or addresses; and there was a section on "Child's Attitude," which declared in its entirety:

> Judith has always had good care and has no unpleasant memories.

How little—how much—a file revealed.

The next several pages were repetitions, in variation, of the earlier pages. Then I saw the name Ketiladze. This would be the report of my mother's return to the agency. The year was 1943. In a hurry to read the file's version of the destroyed photographs, I did not recognize the significance of the exact date of my mother's visit. It was some years later when I realized that my own return to the agency, on April 26, 1973, had been on the thirtieth anniversary of my mother's return.

> 4-26-43 Note by T. Rees. Miss Williams called by appointment. She is now Mrs. George Ketiladze, 220 East 52nd Street, New York, N.Y., telephone ELdorado 5-6597.
>
> Agent remembers having had a talk with Miss Williams when the direct surrender was signed on June 30, 1938. Worker evidently did not dictate the interview at that time. The interview was held primarily to get some further personal impression of Miss Williams and worker remembers being very well impressed with her and thinking of her as a person of intelligence and character. At the time there evidently had been some discussion about the possibility of having some photographs on file of the mother in the event that the child should ever want to see them. The prospective foster family who were interested in the child wanted to know something of the physical type of the mother. When Miss Williams telephoned she recalled the request for photographs and said she had been meaning to bring them in but had not. She had them all together now.
>
> Miss Williams was married about three years ago to a

Russian who is an engineer. She met him while she was off with a party for a country week end. She is very happy with him and feels that life has turned out, on the whole, very favorably for her. She apparently has quite a longing for Judy at times, but still believes that she made the right decision when she surrendered her so that the child could be settled in a home. She said Judy would have been at least six or seven before she would have been in any position to provide properly for her and by that time her life would have been a confused one. Her husband thinks she was married before and knows there was a child. He thinks that the child died. Miss Williams said the father of Judy is dead now.

There was a mark in the margin beside the last three sentences. I might have discounted it had I not recognized these particular sentences as among the "facts" quoted by the agency in their legal documents. Alerted now, I noticed that, a little farther on, the margin was marked a second time. Skipping ahead, I quickly read that paragraph, which was checkmarked at its end:

Miss Williams left a large collection of pictures of herself so that the foster parents could see them if they wished to do so. She had no question about the rightness of that, having trust in the judgment of the foster parents. Miss Williams herself thinks it would probably be happiest for Judy if she could believe her own mother was dead, and as far as she is concerned she would like to have the foster parents let Judy believe her own mother was gone.

Again the marked section was one that had been used by the agency. I recognized it from an affidavit by Mathilda Stern. I felt frustration at the image of Mathilda Stern marking those margins, fascination with the use of the word "gone" to mean "dead," and—strongest of all—utter rage at being called Judy, not Judith.

Then I began to read the paragraph I had skipped, the paragraph in between the two marked passages.

Worker told Miss Williams something about the home to which Judy has gone and Miss Williams felt very content with that. She was particularly glad to know that there were other children in the family so that Judy would not be an only child. She wanted it understood that if Judy were ever in need and the Association know of it they would be sure to call on her for help.

I read it slowly through again, just to be sure.

She wanted it understood that if Judy were ever in need and the Association know of it they would be sure to call on her for help.

Somehow, I thought, the Children's Aid Society must be stopped.

The file concluded with copies of my mother's two surrenders for adoption. A surrender, I could now see, was not the proclamation of "protection" and "privilege" that the adoption establishment would have us imagine; on the contrary, it was a dry confession of helplessness and acquiescence: "That I am unable to provide for my child, Judith Williams," "I do hereby voluntarily absolutely and unconditionally surrender her." Here, in print, was absolute proof that our mothers had never been given their alleged "assurances" of "anonymity," had never retained any "rights of privacy."

I kept thinking about those two marked, selected, quoted passages, a mere sixteen lines apart; and between them, the unmarked, unquoted—intentionally withheld—paragraph that would have negated the agency's entire premise in court.

All along, I had been asking that the surrogate should know what was in these records. It hurt now to discover I was right. It was not pleasure, but stinging pain, to be able to declare, "I told you so."

chapter twenty-three

RECORDS
WITH DELETIONS

Despite the new information on my father, I could not make any progress in my search for him. Mum said she might have been mistaken about the married sister and she had no recollection of the two nephews, but she believed that she was remembering correctly the spelling of Sam Kelley's name. Most clearly, she remembered the restaurant where she and my father used to have dinner. If she could find that restaurant again, she was sure she would be able to retrace the five or six blocks' walk back from the restaurant to his family's house. The search for my father, I finally was obliged to recognize, would have to wait until my mother returned to New York. I put it into the back of my mind and focused my attention on the continuing battle for my file.

After three months' planning, an appointment was at last set up and confirmed for Dr. Thomas's "review" of my foster care record. The afternoon before, however, as final arrangements were being made, one of the lawyers casually remarked to the doctor, "Of course you do realize that you will not be able to divulge what you read to your patient." Dr. Thomas replied that he could not participate under those conditions. The appointment was canceled; we were back at square one.

To my surprise, I was not depressed, but utterly exultant. The doctor had refused to compromise himself. I felt decidedly not alone.

It was December again, and again I was waiting, waiting for lawyers to speak with lawyers, waiting for time to not have passed, waiting for Christmas never to come. There was much to do, but little I could concentrate upon. I should be working on Christmas preparations, I told myself; and I wondered—as I had wondered every December for years—whether my seasonal anxiety might come from some Christmas long ago, from a Christmas *before*. What were those Christmases like?

Another date, December 16, was set for Dr. Thomas's viewing of my records, but the good news was accompanied by a new snag. The court, while accepting, as Joe put it, "that Dr. Thomas can disclose to you the information he reviews relative to your foster care," nonetheless had a further requirement: "As far as the release of one portion of confidential material and the names of your foster parents, the Court has concluded that a good-cause hearing is required and has scheduled this hearing for February 3rd at 10:00 A.M." Once again, this ordeal was not going to be finished by Christmas.

Knowing I had to wait until the hearing in February before receiving any genuine information, I was not expecting true news from Dr. Thomas's reading. Nonetheless, a contact with my file was an event, so I was surprised when the afternoon of the 16th passed with no report from Dr. Thomas. It was almost six o'clock when he finally telephoned.

"I just got back," he said wearily. "It happened again. I was there for nearly three hours."

Dr. Thomas described the afternoon. Accompanied by a junior lawyer from McKinley and Hart, Dr. Thomas had gone to the offices of the agency's law firm. The file, in the hands of a junior Curry, Pell lawyer, had been ready for Dr. Thomas's reading. Then, just as he was presenting the papers, the Curry, Pell lawyer had said, "Oh, but of course, these portions marked off between brackets—you are not allowed to repeat to your patient." Dr. Thomas had refused to read; a scene had ensued. The junior lawyer from Curry, Pell had gone to confer with a senior colleague; the McKinley and Hart junior lawyer had telephoned her office to confer with Donohue. The higher echelon lawyers then had spoken to each other. Several phone calls and conferences later, a solution had finally been reached: The information presently marked between brackets would be deleted; whatever remained could be divulged by the doctor to his patient. Another delay had followed while a Curry, Pell lawyer sat in another room for three-quarters of an hour, scratching out the non-divulgeable passages with a black felt-tip marker.

At last Dr. Thomas had been able to see the file. The crossed-out portions represented only a part of the deletions; blank spaces appeared where my various families' names and addresses already had been removed. The file was quite long, he said, but contained nothing which he regarded as outstanding or unexpected. Curiously, there had been only one brief mention—with the name and address whited out—of the "good foster mother." A child called Billy had been with me in that foster home, he noted. Although the name meant nothing to me, my knees began to shake, just hearing, just knowing, that there *was* a Billy. The bulk of the material, continued the doctor, had been about the adoptive family which had returned me, and it included a lengthy report of a meeting between a psychologist and that adoptive mother. Dr. Thomas's impression of this family was very much the impression we had had already, and he felt that the blacked-out passages were probably inconsequential.

All this was really non-information, but at least the "review" had been accomplished; the agency could not use that as an excuse for delay next February.

On December 19 the mail brought a thick envelope from McKinley and Hart. As I was expecting nothing from Donohue, I assumed this was from Charlie on some other matter. I set the envelope, unopened, on the edge of my desk. I had to go out and do Christmas chores, but first I wanted to telephone Roger, who was trying to develop a good cause with which to petition the court.

Roger had nothing new to report. As we chatted on, I idly picked up the manila envelope, opened it with one hand, and withdrew the papers. There seemed to be about a hundred sheets, interminable paragraphs of single-spaced typing with gaps of whited-out blanks and obscuring black wavy lines. My eyes picked out a sentence at random.

> Judith protests against being given any endearing names such as "Judy" and she insists upon holding _____ at a distance by calling her "Mother."

"Roger, can you hang on one second?" I flipped the pages over to the front. The plain first sheet said, very simply:

JUDITH WILLIAMS
CHRONOLOGICAL LIST OF BOARDING HOMES

12-7-37 _____

12-18-37 Removed from board & placed in free home _____

5-27-38 _____

6-30-38 Visiting home _____

The first date, December 7, 1937, was my official beginning at the State Charities Aid Association. The last one, June 30, 1938, was my beginning with the Kanzlers. Unannounced, unexpected, unpromised, here in my hands was my file!

> Judith was sitting in the swing and there were two other children—a little boy Larry of whom she thinks a good deal, and a little girl.

Names were whited out, and the black felt-tip marker covered up many portions, but the rest was there for me to see. Why? How? Why now? Why at all? No "Pursuant to the Application of," no "At a hearing in the County of," no "It is

Ordered that," no pale blue cover, no pleading calls, no promises nor postponements.

> . . . whereupon Judith began to scream and yell. . . . She was on the gate. XXXXX went over to comfort her and wanted to get on the gate, too.

The name was sloppily crossed out. I could see it was "Larry," whose name had not been removed a few lines above.

> She wouldn't let him and after fighting a little while he got tired and let her have it alone. This just shows the tenacity she has.

"Tenacity." Maybe something of the former Judith Williams had remained, after all. Maybe the Children's Aid Society ought to have studied their own records!

I returned my attention to Roger, somehow reluctant to let go of his companionship. With a desperate energy I kept our conversation going, only half-looking at my hands grasping and turning pages: Discharge slips from the Bureau of Child Welfare, another copy of Mrs. Meinhauser's reports, some extra tall sheets, sticking out, which were my order of adoption, a letter from Booth Memorial Hospital declaring that I had been full term and weighed eight pounds, four ounces, but not including an hour of birth.

Suddenly I came upon a letter addressed to one of the social workers at the agency from my adoptive father. My father's familiar script was rising in Xerox from the page as though his own voice were speaking to me:

> Something awful has happened! I have *destroyed* the pictures you sent me. I had no thought at the time that you wanted them back. I looked them over with the greatest interest—But having done so and having satisfied myself as to the many fears and doubts and uncertainties that I

293

had entertained, all of which resolved themselves very favorably as a result of the pictures, I then talked it over with Mrs. K. and advised her not to look at them—on the theory that it just reopened a series of impressions which now have completely closed themselves. With this thought in mind we wanted the pictures destroyed and so I tore them up and then burned them.

Burned. And I had said, "I'll bet they burned it."
Still I kept on talking with Roger.
The social worker had replied to my father:

You will be relieved to know that I had a talk with Ruth and that she was very understanding and forgiving.

"Roger! I've just found out: My adoptive parents knew my mother's name. Ruth. All along, they knew it." The name I had needed. But "confidentiality" was broken for them, not for me.

She was really very fine about it all, and as far as this chapter is concerned we can consider the whole matter closed. . . .

"I think I have to get off the phone, Roger, sorry."
Now I turned my full attention to the papers. I went back to the opening pages and skimmed the dates, from December, 1937, through June, 1938. Well, if I was already two and three-quarter years old when this file began, then the first entry was going to be the day I left the "good foster mother." Yes, here she was described:

12-7-37 _____, N.Y.C.F.H.S. boarding mother, brought Judith to the office on this day. Agent talked to her briefly about Judith's characteristics. _____ stated that Judith is a very determined child. She definitely has a mind of her own and knows what she wants to do. When she first came to her she was ex-

tremely fussy but _____ feels that she is much less so
now. She has no eating fads, is toilet-trained, and
_____ does not feel that she is a problem in any way.
_____ did not seem to make the parting with Judith
as easy as she might have. She kissed her and mumbled
some words in Judith's ear.

Here, so quickly passed, was the file's only reference to
the woman whose farewell kiss I must once have treasured.
One mere paragraph, and my foster mother was already lost
to me. I felt cheated as I slowly realized that this file was not
my "foster-care record" at all! This file began on the day the
real foster-care file would have *ended*. Was it possible that
the agency had been fighting to keep from me records which
they did not even possess? And if the agency did not have
them, where were they?

I was both furious and intrigued. I read on. The next
home should be the adoptive home with the brother. But it
was not. Starting on that same December 7, for eleven days
there had been another whited-out address, another whited-
out name. As of this moment, I had acquired a whole new
foster home I had not been told of. Although no explanation
was offered for this extra stop, its purpose was clear: This
further home had been a transit camp, an eleven-day brain-
wash to flush out the yearning for the remembered, and to
sterilize the remaining emotions, so that the heart would be
ready to receive, in purity and in gratitude, the next impressions.

12-16-37 Visit by K. Stover. Judith was shy but friendly
with Worker. _____ has had considerable trouble
with Judith's eating. At first she ate practically nothing
and slept all of the time. On the third day _____
started urging her to eat, which she kept up for two days.
Judith ate but was sick at her stomach after each meal and
lost most of what she had eaten.

This might be the origin of the pattern I have been following unconsciously all my adult years, when I am struck by depression: I sleep and do not eat. Why could this insight not have been mine before? *Why was it mine now?*

I kept on reading. Finally came the section about the family that had intended to adopt me. Here was the home of the once-upon-a-time brother.

12-18-37 Removed from Board and placed in a free home.

12-18-37 Placement by G. L. Hubbard. Judith was placed in the home of _____ on this date. _____ came to the office to see Judith. They had heard of Judith already through _____ of the D.W. who had sent them a picture of her but had told them nothing about her history. XXXX XXXXXXXXXXXXXXXXXXXXXXXXXXXXXXXXXXXXXXXX XXXXXXXXXXXXXXXXXXXXXXXXXXXXXXXX . . . [T]hey both decided that Judith appealed to them and that they were really very much drawn to her. Judith's history was given them verbally and rather briefly. When they saw Judith the second time in the play room after they had decided to take her she seemed to feel well acquainted with them and quite willingly allowed them to help her on with her outside things. By the time she left the office she had accepted them as Mother and Daddy and was calling them by these names. While they were in the office Miss Ougheltree talked with them also and discussed in general the importance of not having anyone know Judith's history and advised that they ask _____ to be particularly careful in regard to the records in her office and in regard to telling anyone there that they have taken this particular child. They planned to take Judith to lunch before going home and later in the afternoon Agent happened to see them leaving the restaurant. _____ was carrying Judith, who seemed perfectly content. They did not see Agent.

What was all this mystery about "Judith's history," I wondered.

1938 Letter from _____ asking for a complete history of Judith's temper tantrums, behavior, etc.

2-2-38 Visit, dict. by L. Graff. Directions to home_____

_____

Agent called by appointment and was very cordially received. XXXXXXXXXXXXXXXXXXXXXXXXXXXXXXX _____ and the _____ home is very attractive.

Then came page upon page of description—the social worker's analysis of "Home Conditions," "Child Health," "Family," and a section about "School."

_____ had not intended sending Judith to Nursery School but Judith was very much attached to their first maid, _____, and _____ thought that she would miss her so especially as she disliked the present maid.

The paragraphs were all long, tedious to read through, but the boredom was laced with fascination. Increasingly I felt the accumulating insult of the gaps of white and black.

She is rather independent, likes to do things for herself. . . . She is at a very negativistic stage. . . . M_____ thinks that she could not have had any toys or been used to very much celebration at Christmas. Agent said that usually the boarding mothers made a great deal of Christmas. _____ said that they gave her a toy a day just before Christmas so that she would not be too overcome with so many on Christmas Day. However, when she saw the tree she seemed completely overwhelmed. She just stood there and then for a long time she didn't look at it at all. . . .

Christmas—was this the clue? Had the sight of that Christmas tree evoked a memory then? And though there now were no memories left, somewhere might there be feelings?

I glanced ahead. This same paragraph went on relentlessly for another page and a half. I wondered if I could actually sit still long enough to take in each following word.

> She would have two tantrums a day, sometimes would cry and scream, sometimes for over two hours. . . . It is making home rather unpleasant to have this screaming going on so much. _____ has been very good about it, usually just gets up and leaves the room.

That short blank, I realized, was my brother's first name. Seeing that more of these brief white holes were coming up, I forced myself to keep plodding on.

> [Judith] is devoted to _____ and he is very patient and calm with her. Just today he had just taken great pains to mend her doll's ironing board for her. . . . Agent told _____ that her home was such a different one from any that Judith had been in that she might feel strange and insecure in it. That her tantrums was a way of testing them out unconsciously. _____ said that Judith was devoted to their maid, _____. She described _____ as being a very warm hearted woman but who did not use much judgment with Judith and when Judith would get into a tantrum she would go to her and say, "Oh well now Honey don't cry," etc. Their present maid has much more sense and doesn't do this but Judith doesn't like her at all.

There followed descriptions of a doctor's visit, then "Relationship to Family" with several references to being "very fond of" both the father and the brother, and then more summation:

> The _____ feel they have a child of superior caliber. She has a good mind and imagination but the tantrums have been somewhat disturbing. . . . Agent suggested that if Mrs. Harris wanted to she could talk directly with Dr. Luehrs but she felt at present it was not necessary.

Agent told her that she would see if she could get any further information about Judith.

I stopped and reread those three sentences. Surely this Mrs. Harris was one of the social workers, another "Agent." I read the sentences again. Was it possible? I tried to reread the entire paragraph, but I was so shaken that I could not take in its meaning. Finally I felt it could be true: "Harris" *might* be the family's name.

Count letters—M-r-s-dot-space-H-a-r-r-i-s-space. Fill in the blank: M-r-s-dot-space-H-a-r-r-i-s-space. Yes! I looked at the words above and below those gaping blanks and counted the letters again. M-r-s-dot-space . . . It was fitting! In each case, the "Mrs. Harris," "Mr. Harris," "Harrises," fit neatly in the appropriate space. It might be, I told myself, it just might be.

Now I read in earnest. The file moved on to May of 1938. What followed, for three pages, was obviously the report of the mother's visit with the psychologist, nearly one-third of it blacked out. What interested me more, however, was that the very first deletion of a name had left an "s" exposed:

> _____s had come in to get help in managing her foster daughter, Judith. . . . Judith has been resistant in almost every way and has shown very clearly that she does not trust nor accept her foster mother. There had been difficulty about eating, about toilet habits, and about sleep.

Was the name Harris?

> In view of the fact that _____ is acting as registrar in the progressive school where her 11 year old son is a pupil, she has been under some necessity to arrange the household in an orderly fashion. . . . Actually the household has been in such turmoil that far from getting any satisfaction _____ has been driven to distraction. XXXXXXXXXXXXXXXXXXXXXXXXXXXXXXXXX . . .

Finally the psychologist's report concluded with a reference to "the plan to give up this child and a willingness to wait for a suitable substitute."

I was too distracted to read on in the file. Instead, I began flipping through the pages at the back. Again I came to the letters section. Here was the request for information from the adoptive mother—the signature and address removed— asking "(1) How many homes [Judith] has been in to date. (2) Did she have tantrums? (3) How old was she when they began?" I was interested that an adoptive mother, like an adoptee, had been deprived of her child's history. Poor woman, it had not been made easy for her, either.

Next came the agency's letter in reply: "I have been able to get a little more definite information about Judith." I skimmed through quickly, feeling relief in the familiarity of the narrative and pleased to find a reference to Billy:

> Her second home was with a large motherly woman of German extraction, very calm, a person in whom the visitor had a good deal of confidence. Her home was an unusually nice one. Billy, whom you said Judith speaks of, was in this home. He was her own age and according to the visitor a very delightful child, very calm. Although they quarrelled some, they were devoted to each other. . . .

A few pages later, in a letter from the adoptive mother reporting an improvement, Billy was mentioned again:

> She no longer starts an argument just for the sake of flying off the handle. I think she has almost forgotten about the last foster home as she has not mentioned Billy for several weeks.

How sad that our lost pasts are so frightening to our adoptive parents, I thought; and how wrong that our repressions should be the measures of their successes.

I came upon a letter addressed to the agency from the Department of Public Welfare, which had two instances of whiting out—one sentence in the bulk of the letter and, surprisingly, the signature. The letter, "Re: CB-17046 Williams," was recommending that I be placed with a specific family for adoption. The first cut would have been a reference to the adoptive family, but there seemed no explanation for the removal of the letter-writer's signature. Why was the agency protecting, so many years later, someone who had worked at the Department of Public Welfare? Then I noticed that the dictating author's initials had not been removed from the left-hand corner: "EIH:AQ." H for *Harris*. A Harris of the Department of Public Welfare had recommended placing "CB-17046 Williams" with her relatives, the Harrises! I had no further doubt; the family's name had to be Harris.

Then I was counting letters furiously above and below the white scars, rereading, checking over, counting out. H-a-r-r-i-s. Harris worked every time. I was ecstatic, I had won the name. The stupid agency had flubbed, and I had outsmarted them. I had beaten the agency, the lawyers, the assistant lawyers; everyone else had missed that one "Mrs. Harris," but I had not.

Hurriedly, I turned to the section on the good foster mother. Yes, it could be done here, too. Here the blanks took up nine spaces. Now subtract five for M-r-s-dot-space. Four letters, my foster mother's last name was *four letters* long.

Suddenly, from elation over the agency's error I descended to the base realization of my own degradation. Counting out letters was no brilliant victory; counting out letters was grubbing. A common name, Harris, six letters long, and an unknown name of four letters, were not people. They were not even leads to people; they were mere numbers.

I was feeling as bad, right now, as during the worst periods of last spring. I had not imagined that that pain ever could be matched; I had not known that I could once again feel so small, so vulnerable, such a worm to the agency's overwhelming boot. It seemed then that parts of me were about to burst.

My body could no longer contain my soul, my self, my sanity.
I was physically losing grip of my being. I held on tight to the
pages in my hand. Then slowly I began to turn them one at a
time. It was working, I was hanging on. Another page. Yes, I
could focus again. A line from one of Mrs. Harris's letters now
caught my eye:

> She is devoted to _____ and calls him "my _____-boy." He
> in turn is very fond of her and boasts of her bright re-
> marks.

I have to find that brother, I was thinking, I *have* to find
him.

There was a further communication from Mrs. Harris,
requesting the appointment with Dr. Luehrs. It was written
on a letterhead! At the top of the page I read "Manhasset Bay
School, Inc."—the school where Mrs. Harris worked as regis-
trar! The address was crossed through, but some of the letters were still visible: "39 something Avenue, something,
N.Y." I called Long Island Information and asked for the
Manhasset Bay School in Manhasset. There was no listing.
All the while I was peering at the imperfectly blacked out
address, and suddenly I saw it: "Port Washington, N.Y."

Port Washington was certainly a familiar name—that
was where Andrew had taken an apartment!

Like a pigeon flying home, I dialed Tracers. "Quick,
please, I need a Harris in Port Washington in 1938."

"Hold on." Half a minute later the answer came. "Yes,
I've got R. D. Harris at 44 Sugar Cove Lane, Port Washington, in 1939. It's the only Harris in the book."

"Fantastic!"

Within three minutes Tracers established that R. D.
Harris had stayed on in Port Washington until 1945, then
moved and disappeared. Although there were now three Harrises in Port Washington, he said, they were of no apparent
connection: Natalie, Joseph, and Roy.

Roy. R. Three letters. The son's name in the file was a blank three, maybe four, letters long. Possibly three.

Roy resided at Camelot Terrace, but his phone was unlisted.

I telephoned Andrew at work. "Andrew, do me a favor? I may have found my long-lost adoptive brother. Roy Harris. He lives in Port Washington, 68 Camelot Terrace, with an unlisted phone."

"Shall I drive by there on my way to your house for dinner?"

"Terrific."

Then there was nothing more to do. It would be so easy, if Roy were outside his house just as Andrew was passing, and Andrew could see he was just the right age . . .

The afternoon was moving on, and I was sitting here, powerless, knowing that I had a Harris family who disappeared in 1945 and that somewhere in this country was that Harris boy who had been my brother. There must be a way of finding him, and yet it might take years. From "female Williams in 1935" to "male Harris in 1945"—Harris was no easier than Williams. Though possessor of a name and address, I was ever impotent. Resolution was just out of reach, and I was unable to move. Distance, silence—these were the weapons of bureaucracy. Without touching the body, they defoliated the spirit.

Finally, mechanically, I went back to the file and continued reading the section about the Harris family.

5-27-38 Removal, dict. by L. Graff. On this date Judith was removed from the free home of _____

_____

came in promptly with Judith. They had packed her clothes unknown to her and had not prepared Judith for any change so Agent suggested that they go in to the playroom with her for a little while and then slip out. Agent talked to them both after they had left Judith. _____ actually broke down. _____ was very nice with her but did not seem to feel particularly badly himself. She hastened to assure Agent that when she came to the office she had no idea of giving Judith up, but that Dr. Luehrs had thought it best. Agent said she felt it was surely the best too, that Judith was not the first baby to be returned, that sometimes even babies do not fit. XXXXXXXXXXXXXXXXXXXXXXXXXXXXXXXXXXXXX XXXXXXXXXXXXXXXXXXXXXXXXXXXXXXXXXXXXX XXXXXXXXXXXXXX She was glad that _____ was not there as he would feel badly at having to say goodbye to Judith. He had at several times said that he hoped she would get a home where people would be kind to her.

Oh, dear one-time brother.

_____ said that Judith had been so sweet coming down in the car that the separation was doubly hard. She said that Judith had asked her coming down if she would find her mother for her.

"Find her mother"—already, even then? So this quest had been going on for *longer* than memory!

5-27-38 Transfer, dict. by L. Graff. On this date Judith was placed in the boarding home of_____ _____ Judith went off with the boarding mother without any trouble.

Downstairs, the doorbell was ringing, and I could hear the guffaws and squeals of teenagers. Sarah had invited her friend Holly for supper; and Ian's friend Timmy—the boy to whom I had spent a spring weekend not speaking—was arriving, too. They were slamming icebox and cupboard doors in search of pre-dinner snacks.

I forced myself to keep on reading the file, but I was hardly comprehending what I read; the Harris family was everything. I had to find that brother. The file notes dealt with the new foster family, the fact that the foster mother did not consider me "a difficult child," and a lengthy description of my "playing about the house with _____, the other boarding child," whom I referred to as "my sister." There was reference to a visit at the end of June by new prospective adoptive parents— "before the visit was terminated, they were completely sold"—but the blank for their name was too short to be Kanzler.

Nonetheless, only two days later, on June 30, 1938, I became the Kanzlers' daughter and was taken to stay with a psychologist for testing. These events were noted simply as "Removed from Board and transferred to visiting home," without mention of the Kanzlers by name.

The next entry was in mid-September.

> 9-14-38 Note by M. Brainerd. While at the D.W. reading records _____ questioned Agent about Judith. She wanted to know whether she had been placed in an adoption home as yet. Agent told her she did not know. _____ said that h_____ continued to talk about Judith. She felt that Judith's removal had been very hard on the family. . . .

I stopped and counted letters. M-i-s-s-space-H-a-r-r-i-s-space. Yes. Second reference, faster now, yes again. Now for the next blank, where the "h" at the beginning still appeared. Her. H-e-r-space-s-i-s-t-e-r-dash-i-n-dash-l-a-w-space. It fit. Or cousin-in-law, or mother-in-law. Oh, God, it is so clear, I am going crazy.

Now the implications of this September exchange between Miss Harris of the Department of Welfare and the "Agent" of State Charities Aid began to sink in: Although by this time I had been living with the Kanzlers for two and a half months, the "Agent" had withheld the fact of my placement from the very woman who had referred "CB-17046 Williams" to State Charities Aid in the first place. What was going on?

Finally, six months after my placement, my adoptive parents were mentioned.

Mr. Kanzler saw Judith at the office sometime during
June 1938 and was very much interested in her and subse-
quently it was arranged for Mr. and Mrs. Kanzler to see
Judith in her boarding home.

The report of that visit, however, had not been included.
Then came the summary of the adoption's results:

Subsequently, frequent reports were received from either
Mr. or Mrs. Kanzler as to the child's progress. They were
at all times favorable. . . . She was somewhat tempestu-
ous at first but responded to training amazingly quickly. . . . Mrs. Kanzler has expressed more than the ordinary amount of enthusiasm and the child is being called
Katrina.

There were discussions of the legal formalities—"the
adoption was completed on May 12, 1939"—and a final observation by "Agent":

Katrina looks very well. Her eyes seemed bluer than ever, probably partly because of her very suitable clothes.

I stared out the window, yearning for my Harris brother.

Then my children were calling me downstairs. Andrew
had still not arrived. At dinner, the children all chatted excitedly about the day's activities and their plans for the evening.
I felt on the verge of exploding, but I managed to contain
myself and even to participate in the conversation. I told
them about the unexpected papers and how the agency had
once missed removing a name.

After dinner, there was a great deal of hubbub in the
kitchen, the scraping and stacking of plates, and eight different voices seeking to be noticed. Andrew came in and reported that he had not been able to see anyone at Camelot Terrace. Ian and his friend Timmy, almost out the door, were
inviting Andrew to go to the movies with them. In the midst

of asking the boys what time they would be home, I heard Andrew say something to me about Port Washington.

Timmy King turned abruptly in the doorway. "Mrs. Maxtone-Graham," he interrupted, regarding me directly, "my mother grew up in Port Washington."

I knew Timmy had an older sister, and therefore the chances of Timmy's mother being, like the Harris boy, in her mid to late forties were very good. Timmy and I were both thinking the same thing: Timmy's mother and my long-lost brother could have been childhood friends!

"Timmy, where's your mother? Can you call her?"

"She's not home," said Timmy. "She's gone to a school play to see my little sister."

"Then your grandma."

"Okay! She's in town, at my uncle's."

Timmy went to the telephone. "Hi, Grumma, this is Timmy. I'm here at Ian's house . . . "

So as not to hover over the boy, I went into the next room.

"And it turns out that one of Mrs. Maxtone-Graham's childhood homes was with a family in Port Washington, and their name was Harris . . . R. D. Harris, that's all she knows . . . I see . . . Yes . . . Yes . . . "

Timmy's grandmother at least had not yet rejected the possibility.

"Maybe Robert? or Raymond . . . Yes . . . No, Mrs. Maxtone-Graham doesn't know about that . . . Yes . . . And there would have been a son about Mom's age . . . "

"Tell her Sugar Cove Lane," I called out.

"Yes . . . Mrs. Maxtone-Graham says Sugar Cove Lane . . . Lizzie and Robert, or Lizzie and Raymond . . . and their son was John—"

"Yes!" I shouted, racing back into the kitchen. "That's it!" John—*Cowboy John.* The Cowboy John who had been the imaginary playmate of my early years as Katrina Kanzler had once been a real person. "John! Four letters!" I realized that I had known all along that the boy's name was four, not three, letters. "John Harris is the one!"

"Timmy," I reached for the phone, "I think I'd better speak with your grandma myself."

Timmy's grandmother told me there had been a Raymond and Lizzie Harris—Lizzie died about five years ago, and Raymond was now living in Vineland, New Jersey. The Harrises' son, John, had gone to school with her daughter Lorna—Timmy's mother—at a small progressive school, the Manhasset Bay School, now defunct. When John Harris and Lorna were children, the two families had known each other well.

I asked Timmy's grandmother if she might have any recollection of the Harrises having a little girl who then had disappeared.

"Yes, you know, I do remember about that. There had been a daughter, and then one day I went to the house and the child was gone. But I had seen her there, a little girl of about three, and I remembered her sitting on a blanket on the lawn. A blonde daughter, sitting outside."

"Mrs. Fisher, *you knew me.*"

I had broken the barrier. I had entered the forbidden territory of my life before three and a half. And I had been led there by a fifteen-year-old's grandmother, whose name happened to be the same as that of the founder of ALMA, Florence Fisher.

Raymond Harris's telephone number was listed.

"Mr. Harris, I'm a friend of Lorna Fisher King, and . . . " How much easier it was, having a name to drop!

Raymond Harris was very cordial. Yes, he remembered me. We talked agreeably for several minutes. Then suddenly the conversation took a strange turn.

"And you came with your sister," said Mr. Harris.

"No, sir, I didn't have a sister."

"Yes, I remember, she was your natural sister. You came with your natural sister."

"I don't believe so, sir."

It was all perfectly friendly, but we both clung to our opposing stories. Wild ideas were flashing through my mind: Could my mother have had another daughter then? Did I have the wrong Raymond Harris?

I changed the subject, asking casually, "And how's John?"

"Just fine. He's up in Boston." Mr. Harris began talking again about my natural sister.

It was a stalemate. Mr. Harris was an elderly man, and I did not feel I should persist. I asked him to take my name and address "in case either of us should obtain some more information."

Immediately, before any discouragement could sink in, I called Boston Information. There were three John Harrises. The first did not answer; the second was a doctor's answering service. At the final John Harris number, a woman answered.

"John is out and won't be back until late. This is Anne Harris, his wife." Her voice, not unpleasant, was very direct and strong. "What do you want John for?"

Although I had hoped to speak with John first, there seemed no way to hang up. I spoke as blandly as possible, but the more I tried to say nothing, the more Anne Harris seemed to be learning. Finally, when both our stories spilled out, they meshed well.

Judith Williams had not been the Harris family's last experience with adoption. Not long after my departure the Harrises had tried again, with two girls. Jenny and Pam were about five and seven then, and they were natural sisters, the ones Raymond Harris had remembered. Pam had "not worked out" either, and after a year or two Pam had "moved on." Jenny had stayed and been brought up as a member of the family. At seventeen she had run away. Since then, Jenny Harris had had only occasional contacts, maybe once every

309

six or seven years, with the family, and John Harris had become once again an only child.

Then Anne announced that she recognized my present name. She had seen my book the day before at a friend's house. Moreover, this friend was very close to one of the women I had interviewed. We talked about my book, and about the role of coincidence.

"Are you going to write a new book now about your experiences?" Anne asked.

"No," I answered quickly. I had been determined from the start that I would never write about this. "But sometimes I wonder"—the words were coming out in spite òf myself—"what the agencies are doing is wrong."

At the end of our conversation, Anne said she would tell John about my call, and I could phone again tomorrow evening.

I told my family, I called Dr. Thomas. Finally I got through to Florence, ALMA's Florence Fisher.

"They'll never believe there's two of us," she exclaimed, laughing.

It was 8:30 in the evening on December 19, and the search for John Harris was over. Oh, I was so wildly high.

Ever since that first meeting with Mrs. Meinhauser, there had been three special people whom I really had sought. Now I had two of the three. I had found my mother. I had found the adoptive family that gave me back. There was only the good foster mother left. In the back of my mind was the thought that if I could get that third, then—no, one cannot wish for *too* much. Two out of three was a larger portion of success then most people gain. Perhaps it was not complete, but it was pretty damned good. Sky high blessed good.

chapter twenty-four

REUNIONS ACHIEVED

In a quiet, warm voice, John Harris articulated the very feelings I had imagined for him in Mrs. Meinhauser's office: Relief at my well-being and at the resolution for him of years of wondering, and gratitude for the truth. His descriptions of his family, my screaming tantrums, his mother's rigidity, were confirmation of everything I had already learned. He told me, too, that there had indeed been a relative on his father's side, a Miss Harris, who had worked in the adoption field.

I felt completely content. John Harris and I had spoken together, a relationship was begun. After Christmas, I would write the Harrises a letter and send them a copy of my book. I was fully satisfied; I had carried through my pledge to find that one-time brother and offer him my reassurance.

"I was pretty surprised myself," acknowledged Donohue when we talked about the agency's sending of my papers. "I don't know why—I really don't." He sighed. "Maybe they're just sick of this case."

Meanwhile, in the twenty-four hours since I had located the Harrises I had come to realize that the organization that had handled my foster care was in fact named in those papers. The initials N.Y.C.F.H.S., which appeared several times, stood for the New York Child's Foster Home Service. This was the agency, not the Children's Aid Society, from whom I should have originally sought help. And I would certainly have appealed to this other agency, but for one simple and ridiculous reason: Mrs. Meinhauser had refused to tell me the name of my foster-care service.

It was not hard to discover that the New York Child's Foster Home Service, like the State Charities Aid Association, had been swallowed up by another organization, in this instance the Trafalgar League Family Services. Wiser than before, I did not this time assume that an organization's history, upon a change of hands, was annihilated like a child's. I persisted with my questions until it was acknowledged that yes, old records existed.

"But no one can *see* them," continued the Trafalgar League worker pleasantly, matter-of-factly. "Except ourselves. Absolutely. Of course, if you were *fifteen* . . . "

There was no sense arguing; but I knew, even if she did not, that if I were fifteen, I would be the wrong age then, too.

The worker wanted to be helpful. Maybe a letter from a professional person, she suggested—a counselor, perhaps, or a doctor?

What she was suggesting was, of course, my original petition all over again. To be sure, this time it could work: It was actually possible that a letter could be drafted, approved, received, conferred upon, delayed over, and in a matter of six or eight weeks I might in fact receive the information I had been asking for all this while. On the other hand, it was also possible that I might have the same results with the Trafalgar League as I had had with the Children's Aid Society. I might even end up in court with *two* social agencies against me.

In any event, no begging letter was acceptable to me now. I telephoned Athenia Microfilm in Worcester, Massachusetts. Yes, the New York Child's Foster Home Service records were there! The repository was due to close in two hours for the Christmas holiday, however; so I hurriedly telephoned my ALMA friend Vivian Raminer, who lived in the area. Vivian agreed to make the forty-mile drive from her home.

Two hours later, Vivian called back. She had been able to

find the correct drawer for "N.Y.C.F.H.S.," but the R to Z reels were not there. Vivian had arranged with Athenia to return for a more careful search as soon as the warehouse reopened after the New Year.

Anxiously I waited for the holidays to pass. On January 2, at six in the evening, Vivian telephoned. She had located the reel with Judith Williams.

"Hill, Amelia and Herbert," I wrote as Vivian dictated. Hill—four letters long! This would have to be it. "Transfer to Mrs. Amelia Hill, June 1936; discharged December 7, 1937, to S.C.A.A. Mrs. Hill about age 39. Son, Herbert Junior, aged 12. Address: 67-54 83rd Place, Forest Hills, Long Island."

Before Mrs. Hill, from June '35 to June '36, I had been with Rowena Koerner—another K in my life—in Ozone Park, Long Island. Vivian had made note as well of the one person who had shown a serious desire to help my mother keep me—a Miss Ivins from the Salvation Army. Even then, it was the independent-thinking Sallies who helped, I thought, the funny old Sallies. Vivian's most infuriating discovery was the fact that despite a "permanent discharge," my name had remained on the welfare rolls. Checking through the annual financial statements, Vivian had verified that for twelve years after my adoption—while I, as Katrina Kanzler, was "enjoying advantages" in Michigan—New York City had been still supporting CB-17406 Williams with the payment of funds to a private agency.

Amelia Hill, by now in her late seventies, could still be alive.

There were four A. Hills in New York City. None was right. Next I tried Long Island. No Amelia Hill; but Herbert Hill, Jr., her son, was listed.

"Mr. Herbert Hill, Junior?"

"Nope, this is Bert. His son. Dad and Mom are out."

"Oh, I'm trying to locate a Mrs. Amelia Hill."

"That's my grandmother."

Amelia Hill was still living.

His grandmother had her own apartment in nearby Huntington, Bert told me. With youth's absence of paranoia, he promptly gave me her telephone number.

I was so elated that I forgot to think out my words in advance.

"Is this Mrs. Amelia Hill?"

"Yes," replied a small anxious voice.

"My name is Judith Williams, I used to be a foster child with you," I began. "Of course, that was a long time ago, in the late thirties."

"That was a very long time ago," echoed Mrs. Hill.

"A very long time, you're right. So many years have—"

Mrs. Hill interrupted, "I remember you, Judith."

"You do?" I breathed.

"You were such a good child. But I never dreamed I would . . ." Her voice trailed off. When she spoke again, it was as though from a faraway place. "I remember the day I took you to the agency to get adopted."

_____, *N.Y.C.F.H.S. boarding mother, brought Judith to the office on this day . . .*

"You did get adopted, didn't you?" Mrs. Hill asked anxiously.

"Oh yes," I answered cheerily to reassure her.

She kissed her and mumbled some words in Judith's ear.

"I remember it," Mrs. Hill's voice was full of emotion, "as though it were today."

This was a dream beyond even dreaming.

"What was it like?" I heard myself ask in a whisper. I wanted to hang there forever.

"Very heartbreaking," answered Mrs. Hill quickly.

Neither of us spoke for a moment.

"And your mother used to come and visit you," Mrs. Hill went on.

"Yes, she's told me."

"I hope she is keeping well?"

"Very well, thank you. She sends you her best."

"You were always a lovely little girl, Judith."

Mrs. Hill told me more about herself. Her husband had died fifteen years ago; she shared an apartment with her brother. Her son lived nearby with his family and they visited every Sunday. Then she talked again of the old days and how "good" I had been; she spoke of my foster brother, Billy, too, and a girl called Louise.

"I've often thought of you, Judith. I hoped you were well," Mrs. Hill said. "All these years, but I never dreamed . . . I never thought I'd hear—" She stopped herself. "But why did you call?" she asked uneasily.

"To say hello, to wish you well."

Although Mrs. Hill relaxed, she was not completely comfortable. That I might care as she cared was still too impossible for her to grasp. Judith was not "hers," neither by blood nor by judicial decree. Despite Mr. Silver's claims of rights "equal, if not superior," the foster mother really lacked even the most simple right to express affection, or to ask news of her foster child's welfare.

Mrs. Hill gave me her address, but when I casually suggested "maybe one day stopping by," she became nervous once more. We agreed, very tentatively, that "perhaps I would telephone again."

In a few days, I would make that phone call. I would telephone, write a chatty letter, enclose snapshots of my family. There was much that I could do to reassure her. As with John Harris, the relationship was not established, but it held potential. Ultimately, I would probably convince Mrs. Hill that it was safe to dare trust.

All three were found. I could rest now. It was over.

But why me? I asked myself. Who am I to deserve such happiness? Is there a reason for such good fortune? Is there a purpose which I am intended to fulfill? Three times saved. It could have been someone else, someone yet more needing, more deserving. Why, instead, this specific individual called me?

The next day I telephoned Cyril Means and quickly summarized my news: The Harrises, the second Florence Fisher, Mrs. Hill. Then I asked Cyril if there was some way, at my good-cause hearing for my foster-care records, to make my case more useful to others. Considering these recent developments, I was now free to risk a change of tactics.

No, Cyril told me, there was no way my case could establish a beneficial precedent.

"There's only ALMA's case, then, which will do any good." I sighed. "And that's far away."

"But your story, Katrina, it's like a *novel*."

I knew what he was suggesting. "Yes, but I don't want to think of that."

Cyril's voice was serious. "Maybe you should."

"Sometimes," I confided, "especially lately. But it's too much pain."

"If you want to help others, Katrina . . . you know, a book can mean more than a thousand judicial decisions."

I was startled. "Really?"

"Oh, yes."

"Are you telling me—you of all people, Professor Means—are you telling me that the pen is mightier than the gavel?"

Cyril laughed, then stated soberly, "Yes, Katrina, I am."

I wanted to refute him, but no words came.

"Damn," I said at last. "I wish it weren't true."

That day, the 3rd of January, 1975, I acknowledged my obligation and decided to write a book.

chapter twenty-five

UNRAVELINGS

Mrs. Hill and her brother, James Stroud, had me to lunch in their apartment on the Saturday of the next monthly ALMA meeting. Mrs. Hill, tiny and old, and Mr. Stroud, younger, broad, and smiling, fluttered around me, cooing. Mrs. Hill, walking excruciatingly slowly because of arthritis, brought out a photo album and proudly set it on my lap. Little white slips of paper, sticking out from between certain pages, informed me that the album had already been gone through carefully.

The first picture was the one Mrs. Meinhauser had given me. In the sunsuit in the garden. There were more pictures of me in the garden, some at a playground, a few sitting on the beach. Mrs. Hill and Mr. Stroud exclaimed with admiration over each. "Isn't she lovely?" "She was so good . . . " "That's Judith under the umbrella." "Always a lovely girl . . . " Mrs. Hill told me about the various things the children used to do, the places we had gone together.

"And here's Tom. Tom was the baby." "That's Louise and Tom." "And here you are, Judith."

"Oh, look, there's Billy!" exclaimed Mrs. Hill.

I looked at Billy's photograph. He was wearing the same sunsuit I had worn. Mrs. Hill turned the pages. More pictures, Billy, Tom . . .

"Are you hungry, Judith?" "Judith must be hungry from her trip."

Mrs. Hill and her brother began to set out lunch. First a

317

plate of bread, next a plate of ham slices, then a plate of sliced cheese. "Judith's place doesn't have a spoon, Judith needs a spoon." They insisted I stay seated, the album on my lap, loose pictures in my hands. "No, Jim, give Judith the *blue* glass."

They nodded at me to take my seat at the dinette table. Now Mrs. Hill was attempting, despite her arthritic grasp, to cut up a pickle. The operation was endless, but Mrs. Hill would not accept help.

"How do you take your coffee, Judith?"

I never drank coffee. "With sugar, please."

Finally Mrs. Hill and Mr. Stroud sat. They began to prepare their sandwiches, a single layer of ham, a single layer of cheese. They passed the plates to me, and I made my sandwich the same way.

"How did we children call you, Mrs. Hill?"

"Mama," she answered promptly.

"And what did we call you, sir?"

"Jim." Mr. Stroud beamed.

"Uncle Jim," Mrs. Hill gently corrected.

They were a sweet couple together, comfortable and accepting, considerate, polite. If one had to grow old, this was a nice way to do it.

"You did get adopted, didn't you?" asked Mrs. Hill uneasily as before.

"Oh yes," I again answered reassuringly.

The plate with the pickle was passed around. The pickle was now sliced lengthwise into four slender quarters.

"Have another slice of pickle, Judith."

After lunch, I took a snapshot of Mrs. Hill and her brother together in the window, then the three of us returned to the photo album. Mrs. Hill had more loose photographs, in an envelope. There were also some little booklets with perforated stubs. I saw my name on the stubs, "Judith Williams CB 17406," my birthdate, and the date of a "worker's" visit. Mrs. Hill thought they were "not very interesting" and set them on the opposite side of the table. But I could see that there were dozens of them, dozens of "Judith Williams CB 17406." I really had existed in this dear woman's home! It was true!

Did I want to keep any of the pictures? Which ones did I want? I could take any of the loose pictures. I could take pictures out of the album, too, if I wanted.

We moved on in the album, into the period after I had left the Hills. The clothes kept reappearing; now Tom was in the white smock that Louise had worn earlier. There was Billy in a dress suit like the ones my adoptive brothers had had to wear for photographs. There was a picture taken the summer after I had left—at about the time I would have returned from the Harrises and been in that next home and soon to go to the Kanzlers—of Mrs. Hill and her three remaining foster children, Billy, Louise, and Tom. They were seated in a row on the garden wall. This was the first picture I had seen of Mrs. Hill. She looked tall, handsome, strong. I stared to see if there was anything familiar about the person in the photograph, but there was nothing. Nor did there seem to be any resemblance to the tiny frail woman beside me. Maybe something around the mouth, vaguely. She would have been, in the photograph, the age I was now. I wondered if that were all that would one day be recognizable of me—something vague around the mouth.

There were several spare copies of this foster-children portrait. "May I have one?" I asked. "Because it's of you, and all the others."

Mrs. Hill had still more pictures to show me. She led me to her bedroom and took her wallet from the top of her bureau. Here was her grandson in his graduation portrait, in color. Her granddaughter's first communion, an I.D. card, a snapshot of her son and his wife and some friends, a color portrait of her granddaughter at age sixteen. Then came the picture of herself with her foster children.

This copy of the picture was brown with age, as was the plastic photo slot that held it. And there was another difference about this picture in her wallet: It had been cut, a long

time ago, between Billy and Louise, and an additional photo—of the foster child who had left—inserted between them.
Held together by the cracking plastic were Mrs. Hill and all
four of her foster children, right to left: Mrs. Hill, Tom,
Louise, Judith, Billy.

So while I had been floating for so long without a history,
a woman in Queens had been carrying my picture in her wallet. To shopping centers, and on buses, out with friends, and
into her home to rest at night on the bureau. I, who had not
existed, was finding my own self in the snapshot section of an
old lady's wallet.

When the time came to say good-bye, Mrs. Hill and Mr.
Stroud stretched out their arms to me. Mr. Stroud glowed as
lovingly as his sister; we kissed each other and muttered our
farewells.

"Good-bye, Mama Hill; good-bye, Uncle Jim."

I returned to Manhattan and went straight to the ALMA
meeting. I was very late, and there was no one in the lobby.
The elevator was open at the ground floor. I walked in,
pushed the button, and rode up the five floors alone.

After the meeting, I showed Vivian my pictures, and
then Lyn came over to join us. There had been an article, Lyn
told us, in her local paper. Someone had exposed Sister Chris-
topher. There would be no more leaks of information from the
New York Foundling Hospital.

A few days later, I heard from John Harris.

Dear Katrina,

I want to thank you for your thoughtfulness in sending *Pregnant By Mistake*. As it happens, I was already
half way through a borrowed copy, and finding it very
interesting going. . . .

A couple of recollections of our brief and unlikely life
together: You were called Judith, not Judy, as I remember. I also remember with great clarity a conversation between my mother and myself when it had been decided
that the adoption was a failure: My mother said, "It isn't
any different than if Sally Lee Sloan (a friend's child) had

been visiting us for a few months and then went home, is it?" I remember very clearly the sensation of lying: Saying "no, it isn't," but knowing all the while that it was. Other than that all I can recall is an aura of tension, screaming tantrums, and general unhappiness.

I had also been wondering, before you ever called us, how old I had been when all this happened. I was born in March, 1927, and you say you were with us in the spring and summer of 1938 (correct?), so I was 10 or 11. I know I was 11 when Jenny and her sister arrived, so things apparently happened pretty fast. I am also left with the bizarre thought that you missed the 1938 hurricane in Port Washington. That was quite a scene, and one which my memory system was better prepared to deal with and retain than the more painful things that happened about the same time.

Give my best to Lorna Fisher King, and tell her she was always one of my favorite people.

Yours,
JOHN

Donohue and I were fighting over my desire to attend my approaching hearing. This would be the day I had been waiting for—the argument, at last, of Domestic Relations Law §114, "access and inspection . . . on good cause shown"—and he was letting me know I was not welcome.

"But they might cross-examine you."

"So what if I'm cross-examined?"

"I'd rather not."

The conversation was repeated over and over, and I could never ascertain whether his fear was that I would appear too sane or that I would appear too crazy. Donohue seemed a little uncomfortable, too, with my knowing so much of the information my petition sought. "Joe, it is legitimate, don't worry," I would argue. "There are still other names, other people and homes, more places I might remember." And I would repeat Dr. Thomas's assertion that any name, any place, could be a clue.

321

Accompanied by Vivian, I went to Worcester and read my N.Y.C.F.H.S. foster-care record. The first page I turned to opened with a description of the final agency visit made before I left Mama Hill.

10-7-37 Visited: Children were having an early lunch as they were tired and F.M. planned to have them nap. Judith was seated at the table in a high chair eating her bread and butter while F.M. served the food. Child had mashed potatoes, green beans and lamb mixed together. This was to prevent her fishing out the pieces of meat. Child is so fond of meat that F.M. believes she would eat it three times a day with nothing else. She would almost prefer meat for dessert. . . . F.M. asked about Judith's mother. . . . She said that she hoped that some plan would be made for mother and Judith. Visitor said that possibly adoption would be considered. F.M. was surprised although this idea was not new to her. She said she would be broken-hearted, however, if Judith left before Christmas as she is planning to buy her a doll and carriage, a table and chairs, and some other things. Visitor suggested that she put off making purchases until sometime in November as by then we might know something about what would be happening. F.M. praised Judith extravagantly, saying she was the best and most well-behaved child in the world.

11-19-37 Following receipt of letter from D.P.W. stating that child had been referred for adoption, visitor sent letter to F.M. explaining this and suggesting that she put off purchases and any plans indefinitely. Visitor stated rather definitely that Judith will probably not be in the home at Christmas time.

12-3-37 Following call from S.C.A.A. asking for child's discharge on 12-7-, visitor wrote F.M. about this. . . . Visitor reminded F.M. that adoption is imminent.

12-4-37 F.M. telephoned to acknowledge receipt of letter. She was very much upset that child would be leaving her so soon and asked for another baby as soon as possible to take the place of Judith.

12-7-37 Judith discharged to S.C.A.A.

12-9-37 Letter from F.M. stating she had taken child to S.C.A.A. and how much she missed her.

There, in one entry—"12-7-37 Judith discharged to S.C.A.A."—was that farewell moment at the agency, the scene Mama Hill remembered "as though it were today."

The file contained a note of another Christmas, a year earlier. This time the visitor had come on Christmas Eve:

12-24-36 Visited: F.M. has an X-mas tree in basement for children and has purchased a number of toys for them. Among them a doll carriage. Visitor brought a xylophone. Judith continues to improve and is very happy in foster home.

Yes, I certainly possessed a childhood. And with names: Foster parents' names, foster siblings' names, social workers' names, secretaries' names. Here was I, the child without a history, possessing more details about her early childhood than did surely 99 percent of the regular population!

Reading quickly through "Family History Sheets" about my relatives—again detailed, giving birth years and school and work histories, and again my grandfather named as James, not Albert, and dying in the wrong year—I came upon a letter addressed to "Miss Eudora Harris, Asst. Dir., Department of Public Welfare." The name leapt out, flashing the excitement of forbidden fruit. It was as though that name were always written with a blank, and to have it appear in actual print were an archaeological event.

Details from my mother's story appeared as well—notations that she "would be allowed to visit [in the foster home] twice a month," that she was having "to support her mother and younger sister" on her salary of $24 a week, that the

D.P.W. worker had gone to her home and called her at work "asking her to contribute to Judith's care." The notes gave a glimpse of what it must have been like to be young, poor, and an unmarried mother: "Mo wished she could earn sufficient to pay some board to care for Judith and then there would be no question of adoption." My mother's ultimate acquiescence to adoption and its mythology was described by the record keeper: "From Judith's point of view it seems best to permit her to be adopted so that she will be given plenty of opportunity to develop her potentialities" and "[Mo] realizes that the only way to carry through the plan would be to continually keep in mind that it was for the child's best interest."

When I had finished reading, I began to photocopy the most important pages. I did not ask permission, I simply put the coins in the machine and printed. Later, in the car, Vivian asked whether I had made a copy of the once-crucial list of foster-home names and addresses. I had totally forgotten it, concentrating instead on the descriptive passages. How quickly a need, once filled, can be obsolete. At last, I thought, I was able to forsake the minutiae of searching and to seek instead what had been, from the beginning, searching's goal: Understanding.

chapter twenty-six

THE GOOD-CAUSE
HEARING

Finally February 3 came, the day of my good-cause hearing. As I had not been able to prevail on Donohue, I did not attend. Instead, I went with John to 44 Sugar Cove Lane in Port Washington. As the court would be deciding whether I could be allowed to know the Harrises' name and address, I would be taking pictures of their house.

It was a charming place, but thoroughly unfamiliar. To the side of the house was an undeveloped lot—a wooded slope—and in the back a lawn, several flower beds, a bit of woods, and a little path. There was no field anywhere, no hint of tall grasses. The present owner, a smiling round-faced middle-aged woman, to whom I had said simply that "my name used to be Harris," not only invited us to tour her garden and house, but also made tea for us. As we left, she extended gifts of pachysandra cuttings and artificial flowers she had made from orange peels and of cookies originally intended for—of course—"the neighborhood children."

I did not win my good-cause hearing. The judge allowed the blacked-out material, which now appeared simply between brackets, but not the names and addresses of my former families. The judge found that I "had shown good cause," explained Donohue, "but this had been outweighed by the importance of confidentiality in social work."

It was not even the villainous Domestic Relations Law §114 that defeated me, the transcript revealed. As Silver de-

325

clared, "Our privilege argument really stems from §372, subdivisions 1, 2 and 3 of the Social Services Law." The moral was obvious: You cannot unseal adoption records through Domestic Relations Law §114; and even if you could, social worker privilege will still defeat you in the end.

Neither Donohue's repeated efforts nor Dr. Thomas's had made a difference. Surrogate Sylvane's stance was perfectly clear:

> What I am saying is that even if in some extraordinary fashion a name can trigger some memory, which is unlikely enough, even if that be true, the countervailing equities are for keeping some privacy for the fostèr parents, at least in view of the Social Services Law . . . to keep their lives from being interrupted thirty-odd years later by a lot of questionings. . . . I don't see any real purpose in giving [the doctor] names on the off chance that they might do some good, knowing that those disclosures would harm the relationship of the agency to foster parents in general.

The judge had seemed a totally different man, Dr. Thomas told me, from the one who had been in court last spring. Moreover, the judge had seemed unprepared; toward the end of the hearing, he had had to be reminded that we had been asking for the foster-care record since the beginning of these proceedings. There had been a momentary flare-up then as Donohue and Thomas had made one more effort. It seemed to me that at this juncture there could have been a quite different conclusion. But there was not:

> THE SURROGATE: She is a very persistent person. She didn't ask for this information in the first place. She thought all her problems would disappear when she found her mother. As I predicted, they did not. Now she thinks all her problems will disappear when she finds names, and I predict they will not. . . .
> MR. DONOHUE: The original petition here was to obtain all of the records relating to her adoption.

THE SURROGATE: To find her mother. That is all I heard about in court.

MR. DONOHUE: No, that was just at the first hearing. You suggested that. You said, "Look, in the first instance the mother has a privilege, and the only way you can get these records is if the mother waives the privilege."

THE SURROGATE: You mean you were asking for all of this in the first instance?

MR. DONOHUE: Yes. Right from the very beginning she has asked for all her records.

MR. SILVER: Your Honor, they asked for the adoptive records. We have had a disagreement, ever since the beginning, as to what were adoptive records and what weren't. Certainly the thrust of this from the beginning, as I understood it, was the natural mother and the sealed adoption records.

DR. THOMAS: Not according to the petition that I initiated.

THE SURROGATE: Were you there in the first instance, Doctor?

DR. THOMAS: Everything. From the very beginning. It is stated in the petition.

THE SURROGATE: I don't remember that that was brought to my attention too well. Of course my memory can be faulty. In any event, enough is enough. I think an order ought to be drawn up in accordance with how I feel. I think it gives the doctor nine-tenths of what he wants or maybe ninety-nine hundredths of what he wants. I don't think anything more is going to be helpful to him anyway. I mean, what's in a name?

The hearing drew to a close as the judge handed a copy of my file "without simply names of foster parents" to Dr. Thomas "as petitioner's property."

The same afternoon, without having looked at it, Dr. Thomas turned the file over to me. I was eager to read the material that used to be blacked out, to discover what the agency had tried to keep hidden. And despite the judge's ruling I

327

could still hope: Maybe in *this* version, the agency had again made a usable slip.

I started at the beginning. Following the Harrises' still censored address, I found the now-readable-between-brackets statement: "This is one of the best residential sections in _____." Mrs. Harris, I was now allowed to learn, "had been having some trouble with maids." I was not surprised that the agency had preferred to hide their additional observation that "they were colored maids."

The most extensively blacked-out sections, concerning Mrs. Harris's difficulties with me and the ultimate decision to return me, I now saw were mostly repetition of what had not been blacked out. In December I had read, "Agent was quite surprised to see how very nervous and upset _____ had become"; now I had the right to read, "She was at the end of her rope."

In the section relating to my final foster home, I came upon another of today's hard-won pieces of "confidential information." The social worker, observing the other foster child in that home—whose first name was still a blank—had written, "_____ is a very ordinary peasant type of child while Judith is of the aristocratic type."

What silly sentences! This victory of the blacked-out material was merely documented evidence that a social worker could be condescending. Surely I had not needed to go to court to learn that.

The "Boarding Record" section—the most crucial section—contained no new slips, no clues to any of those other foster homes. Moreover, this new copy did not have all the first names of people other than foster parents, which the judge had in fact granted me. The name of the Harrises' earlier, kindly maid—"Oh well now Honey don't cry"—was, still, a four-letter blank. Similarly, there were some other blanks that I knew I was allowed. The battle was not over.

I kept on with the file. Nearly at the end was a letter from the Salvation Army Home and Hospital addressed to the State Charities Aid Association. I assumed it was, like everything else, another copy of something I had seen already, last December. But I was wrong; this was a letter that had not been included before.

> In response to your recent letter of inquiry regarding Judith Williams, child of Ruth, we are glad to supply the following information:
> Judith was born at William Booth Memorial Hospital at 12:25 P.M. on March 9th 1935.

At last, the exact time I was born. For the price of a good-cause hearing, I had learned about "colored maids" and "ordinary peasant types" of children and that I was born at 12:25 in the afternoon. This was what I had won. I was glad to know the hour of my birth. But I still did not have the legal right to know where and with whom I had lived for the first three and a half years of my life.

Although Donohue did not tell me so, I knew I could appeal. There were still those few names I did not know; and I wanted the *right* to know those names I did know. I wanted to be free, 100 percent, from the Children's Aid Society. But what if I appealed and lost? Would I end up with still less than I had now? At least I had been acknowledged as the owner of my papers. "Petitioner's property," the surrogate had said: I ought not to risk that ownership. Besides, even if I won, the agency could appeal to a yet higher court. The case could drag on for another year or more. No; although I liked to defend a principle, this was a principle of limited benefit. If I was going to wear out my life in battles, I would rather do it for ALMA's constitutional case.

My film came back from Kodak. The picture of Mama Hill and Uncle Jim was separated from the rest by a blurb suggesting I might want enlargements. Even the salespitch folks at Kodak realized that these two people might have a special meaning.

Over the weekend, we went again to Mohonk. There was

329

snow and I went cross-country skiing. It was President's Weekend again, exactly one year since I had first faced the prospect of "mutual consent." I was at the peak of the ski trail, turning to make ready for a long, sweet descent. I was alone, at the top of the mountain, overlooking glorious trees, and trails, and sun-caressed snow. The skis seemed to be a part of me, and my feet felt attached to the world around me and below me. I looked at that glorious world, and I heard myself say, "I am Judith Williams."

Then, intentionally this time, I spoke again: "Hello mountains, hello sky, I am Judith Williams."

It really was true, and it really was complete. I, Katrina, was Judith Williams.

Judith Williams, the child born to Ruth Williams and Sam Kelley, Judith Williams who was happy with Mama Hill, who was "the best and most well-behaved child in the world"; Judith Williams who loved meat; Judith Williams who was Judith Harris and went to a nursery school and was attached to a maid whose name was four letters long; the lonely sulky child I was when growing up; myself now, myself last year. Judith Williams had been a part of each.

It was a long way to have come, from the Salvation Army, to Queens, to Port Washington, to Michigan, to New York, to Mohonk and up the trail to a mountaintop. But Judith Williams had done it; and I was that Judith Williams.

The formal judgment on my case came down a few weeks later. The final paragraph of the judge's decision began,

> To permit discovery of the names and addresses of the foster parents, after all these years, will serve no purpose with regard to the petitioner. . . .

"After all these years"—again.

chapter twenty-seven

CHANGES

Two years had passed since I had returned to the agency. The needless ordeal set in motion that day—an ordeal such as no adoptive parents nor natural parents could possibly have intended for their child—was coming to completion for me. But similar ordeals were continuing, around the country, for other adoptees at other agencies. I was one of the lucky ones, with happy endings and with changes.

The changes were still taking place. In the spring of 1975, I was experiencing internal readjustments that were as intense, or perhaps more intense, as those of last summer. Now I was really beginning to grasp what it meant to be the same as, equal to, everyone else. I stared at the people in the check-out line at the supermarket and exclaimed to myself, "They are biologically related to the human race, I am biologically related . . . " How beautiful we all seemed. I wanted to burst with joy. I had ancestors, I was descended from the ape. I found it glorious to be a participant, at last, in Darwin's principle. Each day the emotions seemed stronger. Each day the world was new. I sat in a movie theater and watched the lights dim for the beginning of the film and was overwhelmed with an ecstasy of realizing, "This is the first time I have watched the lights dim and *known who I am*." There were so many of these firsts, and I reveled in them all.

I was active for ALMA, working as one of the volunteers who answered the telephone. For four or five hours a day, I talked to adoptees or parents who called in for help. The majority of the calls were from adoptees, and I was shocked by the number of horror stories I was hearing: Deceptions, disownings, physical or verbal sexual advances. I became familiar with the continuing cycle of adoptees who themselves had given up a child for adoption. And I found myself thinking that I had been lucky, landing where I had. That irrational Fate whom I had so despised had been kinder to me than to many others. I did not have to hate my adoptive home anymore, now that I was free. As I learned about other people's adoptions, I was grateful about mine. Grateful to have been adopted—no. Not then; not ever. But comparing myself with my own kind, with those who were also adopted—yes, I was grateful for my home. I was astonished to realize that I had actually breathed such words: "I am grateful for my home." I would never have dreamed it possible.

Changed, too, were my relationships with my adoptive brothers. They were being more brotherly than they had been since childhood, and I was being more sisterly. This development was particularly evident in my response to learning that my elder brother's daughter—my niece whom I had met only three or four times—was to be married on an island in Maine. I was aware that a year ago, or two years or three, I would not have considered taking the two-airplane trip to go to the wedding. But now it was not only I, but also the four children and John, who went.

Changes were evident, too, in the status of the adoption movement. Lorraine's article for the Op-Ed page of the *New York Times*—on which I had placed so many hopes in January and February of 1974—had finally been published on a Saturday in March of 1975. The resulting publicity was tremendous. Network television, magazines, newspapers, radio— five hundred simple words on a Saturday morning, and our movement commanded national attention. Lyn Cobb and her mothers Theresa and Natalie appeared as a threesome on television with Barbara Walters. *Newsweek* magazine ran an article carrying a photograph of me and my mother, and my mother was quoted: "I felt like someone put LSD in my

Sanka," she said of my phone call. "For years I had pretended her birthday was March 17 rather than March 9 so St. Patrick could take some of the sharpness out of the day." That comment sounded like my mother, all right; and it also shed light on her uncertainty about my birthdate.

The head prune of the Louise Wise agency was also quoted in the *Newsweek* article: "The person who gave up the child would also have the right to seek the child then. It could open a Pandora's box." The "Pandora's box" that used to be our "prostitute" mothers was now *us*. When would the prunes realize that it was their own files which were the "Pandora's box"—and that the nasties inside were simply their prejudices? Besides, they were omitting the conclusion of the story: After the nasties flew off, what remained in Pandora's box was Hope.

Also that spring the New York Foundling Hospital invited ALMA to send speakers to address their social workers! Although the highest positioned workers at Foundling were still clinging to their power by proclaiming a "mother's right to privacy," the hospital was at least re-evaluating its policy. Indeed, the Foundling Hospital was starting to conduct searches—the allotted time was one hour, and they were usually successful—and forwarding adoptees' letters. Not long after that conference, a mother who had received such a letter from her twenty-six-year-old daughter was referred by Foundling to me. The mother wanted advice about whether to respond: A warm, thoughtful woman, she was nonetheless afraid to admit her willingness to meet with her daughter, fearful that any assertion of her caring would necessarily *hurt* either her child or the adoptive parents. Only a few years ago, she might have had no support against society's automatic warning, "Stay away"; but now there was a network of information and people to encourage her to trust her love. Although Foundling was practicing only "mutual consent," it was the first of the mighty New York agencies at least to stop and think. And all these changes at Foundling could be traced back, I was quite certain, to a seventy-year-old nun who had

333

once taken it upon herself to sneak helpful information to the needy.

Becky and Nanny were both reunited with their families in early 1975. Nanny's mother, it turned out, was a member of the very family Nanny had once recommended for *me* to research, because she had believed I resembled them. Soon after, Sister Barbara, who had finally contacted the Children's Aid Society, was given an appointment with Mrs. Meinhauser within one week, and her worst fear was immediately assuaged: Her elder sister had *not* been her mother. Sister Barbara received, as well, confirmation of a surname—but as her mother's name, not her father's as she had thought. Curiously, Mrs. Meinhauser had even provided her mother's first name. That evening Sister Barbara looked in a Westchester directory and there—fifty years later—was the name! Sister Barbara's reunion was followed, a week later, by April's.

This was most of us, now, from those first days. In our immediate group of friends, Audrey stood out from the rest. True, Barry was still being refused a meeting by his mother although she "might write him a letter in a month or so," and April's mother was passing April off as her "niece." But Audrey had found no one.

And our success made a separation between us. We were different, those of us who had found a relative. No matter what our memories and our empathies, we were no longer the same as we once had been. We had climbed over the wall, and now the wall was dividing us from those on the other side. And we had new bonds too, to each other, based on our new and different framework of shared experience. We tried to deny our separation, working all the harder to help the others; but we were no longer really, wholly, exactly, one of them.

My mother's trip to New York, originally planned for early summer, was postponed until the fall. But I had a visit over the Fourth of July weekend from Nick, the youngest of my new brothers. Again I felt an immediate sense of family; and the eighteen-year difference between our ages, like the fact that we had never before met, seemed irrelevant. A new neighbor, who knew nothing of our story, came over the second day of Nick's visit, and afterwards she confided her admiration for the ease and companionability of our brother-sister relationship: "You two must have worked hard to accomplish it."

My appearance in Nick's and Andrew's lives awakened their own curiosity about their family background. They talked of trying to find our cousin Mac, Uncle Howard's son, who had been their childhood playmate. And they wondered if they had cousins in Russia, in Georgia, where their father's family might still be. Andrew talked of going to Georgia for his vacation.

That summer, I met John Harris. I did not recognize him. Nor did we resemble each other, which both startled and angered me. It was not fair; we had once been brother and sister, I wanted to be brother and sister now.

My dream-remembered field, John Harris quickly told me, would be the wooded lot next door. Though it was all grown over now, it had once been a grassy hill. And there was a view from the top; it was one of the highest points in Port Washington. I asked John if he might have some old photographs or photo albums, but he said there were none. I asked, too, about the kindly maid whose name was four letters long. Yes, John had always especially liked her—Lucy.

Lucy. How simple it had been, to ask and be answered.

Anne Harris talked about my original telephone call; John had been very upset, she said.

"Upset," John repeated thoughtfully. "Actually, much more than upset." There was a long pause as John struggled to find the word. Finally he mumbled, "Reorganized."

"Reorganized?"

"Yes. Completely reorganized." Pause. "It was very moving." He sighed. "Very touching, really."

We talked a long time, about our children, about our lives, like old friends who have been separated for less ex-

335

traordinary reasons. John began drawing on a paper napkin, while Anne and I continued our conversation.

"Here," John Harris suddenly spoke up. "I will give you your field."

He showed me the map he had been making of the house, the field, the crest of the hill.

"On a clear day, from the top of the hill," John said, "On a clear day you can see—" He stopped.

Anne and I looked at each other, smiled, and said the obvious: "Forever."

"New York City," completed John Harris.

chapter twenty-eight

THE SEARCH
FOR MY FATHER

My mother came to visit me in September of 1975, and together with my husband and our friend Sylvia, with whom Mum had stayed the year before, we drove to Mount Vernon.

I felt that my father would not still be alive. I wondered if this conviction was a self-protective device, or if I held it because Mrs. Meinhauser had killed him off so quickly, just moments after her first mention of him.

As the others commented on the signs and sights out the window, I stared at the index card on which was written the only possible clue I possessed, the address of that untraceable Jack Kelley who had been in Mount Vernon in 1934, Port Chester in 1935, and nowhere to be found ever since. I was neither concentrating nor contributing. I was simply longing for this day to be finished and the answer revealed: Could my mother locate the restaurant and from there the house where Sam Kelley had stayed in 1934? Or could she not?

We had been driving around for an hour and were getting nowhere. Everyone was discouraged except Sylvia, who continued to speak calmly and patiently. Maybe we should try the Jack Kelley address, I suggested, and even as I spoke I spotted the street, Amsterdam Place, on our right. It was a one-way street the wrong way, so John drove a block farther to make a right turn. On the left was Gobbo's, a diner.

"That's it!" suddenly exclaimed my mother. "That's the restaurant." But there was traffic behind us, so John had to complete the turn off Columbus.

"From here," continued my mother, pointing back down Columbus Avenue, "we would have walked, about six blocks."

I did not want to retrace the six blocks; I wanted to get to Amsterdam Place and hear a yes or a no. John was driving slowly, looking for a turn that would take us back parallel to Columbus.

"What about these houses, Ruth?" Sylvia asked. "Does anything seem familiar?"

We stared at the tall shutters here, the extra chimneys there, the roofs, the lawns. It was the right sort of area, my mother said, but nothing was familiar. Then we were on Amsterdam Place; we found a parking space across from number 20. The house was only a half-block from Columbus Avenue, a mere block and a half from Gobbo's.

"I don't think so." My mother shook her head.

What was there to do now, I wondered.

"Let's get out and walk around," said Sylvia cheerfully, opening the car door. "Let's get a feel of the place."

The other three got out of the car; resignedly, I followed. The neighborhood was pleasant and residential, small, neat houses on separate small neat lots. There were only occasional pedestrians, all of them black.

Sylvia and my mother strolled up and down the sidewalk, chatting naturally. I was overwhelmed with discomfort—the outsider again, a white in black people's land. And what was I to say? "My uncle hasn't lived here since 1935 and do you know him?"

"We don't belong here," I said anxiously, "they don't want us here."

"Oh, pooh!" exclaimed Sylvia, turning with my mother to cross the street and approach the house.

I stayed back on the other side. I could hear my mother repeating that this house was not large enough, she remembered that it had been big, impressive. Sylvia was telling her to come look at the building from the avenue side because, from that angle, the house seemed quite large. It was good that the others were stronger than I, I thought; they could keep me from acknowledging defeat.

Sylvia went up close to the windows. "Oh, Ruth," she called. "Come here and take a look inside." Sylvia put her face right up to the glass.

"I don't think you should," I called feebly from across the street.

But neither of them took any notice of me. Mum was joining Sylvia. This was useless, and I felt embarrassed. I turned away and went to stand by the car door. Finally I could hear my mother and Sylvia coming back from the window and crossing the lawn. I barely listened to their talk, only relieved that they were no longer snooping.

"Your mother recognized the stairs," Sylvia said, giving my mother an admiring, congratulatory pat on the back.

"I remember that dark, wood staircase, from having gone up the stairs to use the bathroom."

Jack Kelley—Kelley, E-Y. So my father had been staying with a married brother, not a married sister. My father, Sam Kelley, and good-bye to all you Kellys without the E.

Although to date Jack Kelley had been impossible to trace, impossible searches are easier to take on for a certain target than for a mere hunch.

Two weeks had passed, however, since our Mount Vernon expedition, and we still had no leads. It was ridiculous that we should be doing so poorly, I said to Ed Goldfader. Jack had had two sons, my first cousins. Where were they?

We agreed that Ed should concentrate less on Jack and try to trace through the children.

Within the week, Ed telephoned. "Your cousin's name—" he began.

How typical of him that he had not said "Jack's son" or "the person I've found."

"—is Anderson Kelley."

"*Anderson* Kelley!" Not Mike Kelley, or Paul Kelley, or John Kelley, or Charles or Fred or David. Anderson Kelley was a traceable name.

"Son of Jack L. and Doris A. A, no doubt, for Anderson," Ed went on. "And he's the only child I find; there only seems to be one, not two. Born March, 1925, would be fifty now."

Anderson Kelley, my neighbors the Andersons, my aunt and cousins Anderson, my namesake Judith Anderson . . .

"I've done a bit of work. Got a pencil? Anderson G. Kelley, 964 Champlain, Beauchamp, Michigan—886-4971."

Mr. Anderson G. Kelley was very cordial, but he was not my cousin.

Later that night, as I stared at the scraps of notes on my desk, I realized that I was not finished with Anderson G. Kelley. Our conversation would have to be written up in my search diary. Although there could not be many Anderson Kelleys, it would be essential to remember which one was which. My search diary was still on the shelf to my left. As I opened it and inserted a fresh page of paper, I realized that I was back where I had been two years before, making careful notes of useless conversations with unrelated strangers. I had to force myself to complete the account. One more nice stranger, one more blind alley. It was only a single page, but it was the reverberation of all those other pages, the echo of years of pathetic endeavors. Now I knew why some people who found their mothers did not go on to find other members of their family. Each new search was really an accumulation of all previous searches, and there came a point where one could stand no more.

Two days later, Ed Goldfader telephoned; he had located another Anderson Kelley. This one had been living outside Chicago since 1966. I felt certain that today's Anderson Kelley was right.

I dialed the Illinois phone number. An elderly woman answered. She might be Jack's wife, Doris A. Kelley.

Trying to sound like a long distance operator, I asked for Mr. Anderson Kelley.

"This is Mr. Kelley's mother," she replied. "He's not here."

"Do you know where he might be reached?" I asked. To

my relief, she immediately gave me Anderson's number at work.

Anderson Kelley answered his phone in a pleasant, relaxed voice. I began a recital about my mother visiting from out of town, old friends of the family, Sam and Jack, especially Sam.

"Sam's been dead for a long time," Anderson Kelley replied calmly.

"Oh? When did he die?" I was not really thinking about my father's death, only of getting through this phone call.

"In the early '40's."

"Are there any survivors? His widow? My mother might want to write a note."

"Ellen died in childbirth in 1933, when Joey was born, Sam Joseph."

"I see. Well, maybe my mother would want to contact Joey."

"He lived in Savannah, Georgia, for a long time, but I believe he's moved. I have the address at home, but not in the office."

"And Joey is the only one left?"

"Sam remarried, but his wife died seven or eight years ago. Their daughter, Kelda, is somewhere in California. If you want to call tomorrow, I'll get Joey's address and give it to you."

"That would be most kind."

So my father had died in the 1940's, just as the agency had said. Damn, I thought, I did not like the agency's being right about anything.

Twenty-four hours to wait. In that short time the situation could change. Anderson's mother, who might know of my existence, could have realized who had called her son. Immediate relatives, assuming the role of "protectors," were often the people most opposed to reunions. My aunt might persuade Anderson to withhold the address, or even prejudice Joey against me.

But when I called Anderson the next day he was still

pleasant, open. Asking no questions, he provided Joey's address, now in Houston, and apologized for not having his phone number as well and for having no information on Kelda.

Though unperturbed and civil, Joey was not particularly interested. His reaction was startling at first, but not uncomfortable. Joey had no idea where Kelda was; they had not been in communication for over four years.

"What I don't get," said Joey suddenly, "is why are you bothering to tell me all this?"

"Because I thought you might like to know," I replied firmly. "If *I* know that you are my brother, then I feel it's only fair that *you* should know it, too."

This idea seemed to impress Joey, but he still did not display any real curiosity. We talked a few minutes longer, then thanked one another for our time, and said good-bye.

Well, I thought, if success were defined as a glorious reunion, this phone call could not be deemed successful. But success did not lie in the quality of the reception; I had known that all along. Success lay in the completion of the search. Having located and contacted my father's family, I had succeeded. The job was finished. Moreover, I had fulfilled my obligation: I was not holding information over another person. And further, having spoken first with my father's son, I was now free to talk openly to his nephew.

Anderson Kelley was delighted, really delighted, to learn who I was.

My father, Sam Kelley, had died of tuberculosis in a New York State sanitarium; he had not died in the early 1940's, Anderson corrected himself, but in 1953. By not dying in the 1940's, my father had proved the agency wrong. Just as my mother had. Just as I had.

Anderson's own father, Jack—who had been my one link for searching—had died of pneumonia in February of 1935, one month before I was born. Anderson had been ten then, and Joey had been living with his family; the two boys of the file were not my two cousins, but rather one cousin and one brother. When Jack died, his wife, Doris, left the house on Amsterdam Place and moved into an apartment in Port Chester with the two boys. They stayed there only a few months, and then they moved to Massachusetts. A few years later, when Sam remarried, Sam came and took Joey back to live with him in New York City.

Sam and Jack had been the last of seven children, six brothers and one sister, who grew up in Anniston, Alabama. Their parents, Anderson's and my grandparents, died in the late 1950's, said Anderson. He guessed that the cause of their deaths was probably—what a lovely affliction to be presented with as one's inheritance—old age.

Anderson continued to pour out information. My father had been "a loner," Anderson said, "he loved music, books." He was "vague, romantic, an idealist." Sam had left the South when he was about sixteen and had come to Chicago, where his brother Jack was then living. Sam had stayed with Jack and Doris, going to high school until one day one of his teachers had had some good words to say about Zane Grey; this had so incensed Sam that he had left school and had gone off to sea.

Sam had never gone to college, but had spent a number of years traveling the world as a merchant seaman. He married Joey's mother, Ellen, in 1931, but went to sea again after she died. When he remarried, he settled in New York. Kelda was born in 1938. Sam and Kelda's mother both worked for RKO. But what his Uncle Sam had most wanted to do, said Anderson, was to write. He had never really had the chance, but he was always "writing on the side." My father, a writer! There was in fact a children's book, Anderson said, which Sam Kelley had written and which had been published before he died, *The Adventures of Walter M. Duffle Duff*. Anderson had a copy of it and he would be glad to show it to me if I ever came out to Chicago.

Sam Kelley. Though I could sense gentle breezes of similarity between us, I never would know, really, who was this

343

man, my father. The reality which was mine instead was the openness of Anderson Kelley. It was the reality and humanity of Anderson Kelley that was giving me a belief in the reality and humanity of my father.

I remembered the words of Melia Portoverdi in her first phone call: "No one disappears without a trace." People go places, work, cross the paths of other people, they live a life. Yes, I thought, and so did Sam Kelley, whose path crossed Ruth Williams's path for about six months in 1934. And I crossed both of theirs, and backwards to the Kelleys of Alabama, the Williamses of Dyre Avenue in the Bronx, the Kanzlers of Michigan, the Harrises of Port Washington, the Ketiladzes of Russia. Spinoza's mosaic of history again—but this time it was not flat like Cimabue. It was multidimensional, a spiraling, meandering, fluid loop, a ribbon of interconnection, a finite thread woven into the infinite webbed tapestry of history.

Anderson followed his telephone welcome with a long letter. When I called to thank him, his mother answered.

"You're Andy's cousin," pronounced Doris Kelley as though to identify me.

"Yes, that's right." Tentatively I continued, "That means, then, that you're my aunt?"

"That's right, I'm your aunt," she responded lovingly, almost proudly.

"May I call you Aunt Doris?"

"I *want* you to. I was so happy when I heard!"

Aunt Doris told me that she had known Sam since he was sixteen; now she was nearly eighty. She talked about him freely: "He was not conventional . . . very idealistic . . . he was always thinking of what would help others." Then she said abruptly, "I loved your father—very much."

I was startled when she said, "Your father." I had been so busy thinking about her, her sweetness, Anderson's warmth, that I had forgotten that this moment had to do with my own father. I was startled also by the tone of Aunt Doris's voice, the admiration she was bestowing upon me simply because I was Sam's daughter. She who had known Sam Kelley so many years was complimenting me who had never met him. It should have been the other way around, I was thinking; still I accepted her compliment and took pleasure in the admiration. Irrational, of course—we can take no credit for our parents' accomplishments and qualities. But I saw that this was part of the privilege of being a daughter. I liked it; and I felt proud of my father—"idealist," "loner," "concerned for others."

I was proud, too, I realized, of my adoptive father. He was quite a marvelous man. I had known this as a child, but I had not then been able to feel the child's accompanying pride. I had not had the right to that pride, I had believed then; somehow the absence of an original father had made it impossible for me to accept the fatherhood of a substitute one. But now the gaps were filled in, and I could view the people of my past no longer as who they had *not* been, but as who they were. Now I was free to be the daughter of Sam Kelley and of Ernie Kanzler. I was; and I basked in my pride of both of them.

Andrew and Rucy begged for every possible detail about my father and his family. My mother telephoned from Mexico. "I was so happy, dear, to hear that your father wrote a book." She was happy not only for me, but also for herself. She could remember now that she had once thought of Sam Kelley as someone quite terrific. Over the years, she had come to fear that she had been mistaken. She was relieved to have her memories, and her judgment, confirmed.

It occurred to me that Sam Kelley might have suffered not only his first wife's dying in childbirth but also quite possibly the belief, from Grandmother Lulu's invention, that the next time he fathered, his child was born dead. From two conceptions, two deaths. What a burden for a man to carry—the conviction of his own power to kill.

Taking up both Aunt Doris's and Andy's suggestions that they "would love to meet" me, I arranged to go to Chicago for a weekend in mid-November.

Andy and his wife, Gloria—and their married children, who came for dinner on Saturday night—were warm, easy-going, and welcoming. But the outstanding feature of my trip was Aunt Doris. She had loved my father, and now she loved me. I had thought myself to be the lucky one, having this chance to meet my relatives and to learn more about my father; Aunt Doris, though, insisted that *she* was the beneficiary of our meeting.

Aunt Doris was happy to tell me about the Kelleys. Both Jack and Sam had left the South because they objected to the racism there. Sam, as a merchant seaman, had traveled a great deal, especially to Germany and France. Jack and Doris had met at the International House of the University of Chicago; they had worked together in a settlement house. "Sam was not orthodox—about anything," she said, "but that does not mean he was not lovable."

Aunt Doris, herself, had been—what else?—a social worker! Even now at nearly eighty she did volunteer work several days a week. Back in the 1930's she had worked for the Department of Child Welfare in Westchester. She had seen adopted children then. "All of them, every one," she told me fervently, "they all wanted to know who their real parents were."

Late in the afternoon of my first day, Andy showed me the copy of my father's book. The book was yellow, with a teddy bear on the cover, and about eighty pages long. *The Adventures of Walter M. Duffle Duff*, by Sam Kelley.

Andy pointed out the inscription to his children, "from your Great Uncle Sam." That's my father's handwriting, I was thinking. That's my father, in pen and ink. I opened the book to the first page.

Walter the Bear, sometimes called Walt for short, lived at the home of Mr. and Mrs. G. Atwater McRobinson at Number One North Campbell Drive.

Andy was about to go out. I set the book down and we

chatted for a few minutes before he left. Then I picked up the book again and casually flipped the pages as I walked toward my room.

Miss Williams.

I looked again. Yes, printed in the book were the words "Miss Williams." There, on page 56, I saw the name before me.

"Yes," Miss Williams said, "I will be glad to take Walter as a pupil."

I closed the book and mechanically continued to my room. I sat on the bed for several minutes, stunned and excited. "Miss Williams"—I had seen it, it was there.

Finally, slowly, I reopened the book. First, I skimmed the section in which the name "Miss Williams" had appeared. Chapter Four. Then I started at the beginning of the book and read it through. It was a nice story, about a bear who has a few adventures; in the end, he finds happiness in the arrival of a playmate, another bear, whose fur is not brown like Walter's, but black. It was a quiet suggestion for integration, made in 1952, by Sam Kelley.

Then I took out my notebook and, shaking, I began copying the portion of the story that referred to Miss Williams. Miss Williams was a prospective singing teacher for the then lonely Walter Bear.

"We must send away for a teacher," said Mr. McRobinson, "and it must be the best. We must send to some foreign city, say, to Vienna, Salzburg, or Paris. No, Paris wouldn't do. Vienna sounds better, and they have long and important names in Vienna. I am sure they would be the best teachers."

"But, George," said Mrs. McRobinson, "that would cost too much money, and we can't afford it. Besides, we have good teachers right here in this country. I know one who is only a few blocks away. . . . She is known as one of the best. Her name is Miss Williams."

Mr. McRobinson, who had been sitting in the big club chair near the window, got up quickly. "Did you say her name is Williams?" he asked. He walked around the room with his hands behind his back. "No, no, that won't do— Williams, Williams. That does not sound like Vienna or Salzburg. Can't you think of someone else, say, someone with a name like Von Fishtigkeit or Herr Doctor some-one?"

"I am so sorry, George, but I am sure Miss Williams is very good," said Mrs. McRobinson, "and I think you will like her. I understand she is very reasonable, and, George, haven't you always said, 'After all, what's in a name?' and 'It doesn't matter what a person's name is'?"

"I mean, what's in a name?" Surrogate Sylvane had declared at my good-cause hearing, his intent quite different.

"Yes, Mary, I have said that," Mr. McRobinson admitted, "and you are right, absolutely right. I am sure you know best about these things."

So Mrs. McRobinson phoned Miss Williams the next day. "Yes," Miss Williams said, "I will be glad to take Walter as a pupil."

What had Sam Kelley been thinking, I asked myself, when he put the name Miss Williams in his book? Could an author make so much fuss over a name that was just a coincidence? Or could Sam Kelley have thought that my mother might be married by now, might have young children, might be looking for a children's book? Recognizing his name she would read the book and find the "Miss Williams." It was a wild notion, that someone could dream of sending a message that way—but *I* had done it in my book. So why not my father?

When Andy said good-bye at the end of my visit, he told me that he had asked each of his children, separately and in private, if their shared copy of *The Adventures of Walter M. Duffle Duff* could be given to me, and each had said yes.

Heading for the airport to return to New York, I thought about my fear of flying. I might have to relinquish that, I realized. I was not a child any longer. I was a grown-up. It was time for me to give up some of the old identities to which I had clung because I believed there was nothing else for me. It was time, for instance, to give up the role of "terrified passenger"—which, irritatingly, had never impressed anyone anyway—and succumb to the fascination of the vitality, power, and ultimate accomplishment—getting places—of flying. Although I had no regrets about my new fledgling strength, I was still feeling the tug of the security blanket recalling me to those beloved, because familiar, companions of my life until now: Not Knowing, Differentness, Being a Freak, Terror.

Barely was I home when I received a visit from the last of my Ketiladze-Jason brothers, Alexander. He showed me photos of his log cabin home in the Midwest and asked what it was like to be adopted, remarking as had Rucy and Andrew over a year ago, "It's something I never thought about before." Like them, he glowed with pleasure at being an uncle. When he left he said, quite simply and naturally, "Thank you for enriching my life."

Over long distance telephone to Mexico, I read the pertinent pages of Sam Kelley's book to my mother and marveled to think that Sam's message had been read and passed on, twenty-three years later, by me, his daughter. Sam Kelley had found his reader, and his reader was me.

chapter twenty-nine

CONTINUATION

My good-cause hearing was not the final courtroom event in this story. There was yet another battle between the Children's Aid Society and me. This time the dispute was over payment for the agency's unsuccessful search. The issue had arisen soon after the good-cause hearing, when Donohue had forwarded the invoices—totaling $2,750—from the agency's detective for "services in attempting to locate your mother." I had written Donohue promptly in reply: "Inasmuch as there is the very serious possibility that the agency, Children's Aid Society, did not act in good faith in this matter, I certainly do not intend to pay the bill"; and for nine months I had heard nothing. Then the agency again had demanded payment, and again I had refused. Orders, counter-orders, affidavits, responding affidavits had been exchanged. A lawyer from McKinley and Hart had conferred with Ed Goldfader, who had agreed to testify. I had made clear my priorities: To retain my ownership of the file, to obtain those permitted-but-still-not-yet-delivered names, to avoid paying their detective's bill if possible. But, whether or not I would have to pay, I wanted to prove my instinctive hypothesis that the agency had not searched honestly.

Finally, in early March of 1976, Joe Donohue wrote that a hearing "into the reasonableness of the investigator's charges" was set for March 30. Before that, he would "try to work out with Michael Silver the complete record, save the names and addresses of the foster parents."

But the March 30 hearing did not take place, because of a

conflict in lawyers' schedules; and then it was April. Phil Ochs, the topical songwriter whose strength had sustained me when I was suicidal, had committed suicide. The day his death was reported, there was an ALMA meeting at which I talked with a young woman who had learned, after her infant son was circumcised, that he was a hemophiliac. She was adopted and had not known that she was a carrier. There had been much hardship for the boy and his young parents in the two years since then, but their experience was worse than any freak misfortune, for the hemophilia was no chance discovery. All along, both the young woman's adoptive parents and her agency had known she was a carrier and had never told her.

Also in April I received a letter from Ray Harris:

Dear Katrina,

John and Anne Harris were here briefly this week and they equipped me with the information I have needed to apologize for my impolite reception of your telephone call some time ago.

When you telephoned to me I was preoccupied and hurried; I made a note or two hastily; when I tried to read my notes I found I couldn't make anything out of them. Please excuse me.

I'm delighted, of course, that you met up with folks who could and did give you the things you wanted in life. Lizzie and I failed Judith Williams, as well as one or two others. Before you finish the book John says you are writing, include a chapter on would-be parents. In our case— and I'm sure we aren't alone—you and Jennifer and her sister suffered because of our ignorance or selfishness.

Even though I'll be 79 next month, I'm continuing the antique shop that Lizzie started twenty-five years ago right here in her family's large country home. When she died ten years ago friends moved in and, with their help, the household and shop continue.

With repeated apologies for my unseemly behavior, I am

Sincerely yours,
RAY HARRIS

351

Like son, like father—the Harris men wrote simple, beautiful letters. And their words did indeed make a difference. It had come full circle, I thought; it was over. If, as Ray Harris suggested, he had once failed Judith Williams, he had not failed her now. On the contrary, he had helped her attain a sense of completion.

But Lizzie Harris had gone to her grave, and Ray Harris had had to wait until he was seventy-nine to learn that the child they had abandoned had found a home within six weeks. This was a clear abuse by the agency of its files: To have knowingly inflicted these parents with a guilt they need not have borne.

On a morning early in May, I received a telephone call informing me that my next hearing was to take place—in five minutes. Not only was I not there, but neither was Ed Gold-fader nor even Joe Donohue. A junior lawyer named Murphy, who had never spoken with me before making that call from a pay phone outside the courtroom, was my sole champion against the agency's team of Silver and Friedman.

I did not win—Surrogate Sylvane decided that I must pay for the agency's detective—but I was not a complete loser. Murphy had caught on quickly. Although he had known for only five minutes of the Dyre Avenue address and its crucial role in locating my mother, he had nonetheless succeeded in establishing that it had not been given to the detective.

"Apparently they didn't give everything," Donohue reported to me that evening. "Not Dyre Avenue. Just some name—"

"Ketiladze?"

"That's the one."

"Only Ketiladze?"

"They said they gave all they thought was needed."

I was stunned. This was proof of all I had feared—that they would not try hard, that they would not provide the right information, that they would not act in good faith.

Murphy, too, called me. His account was the same,

though fuller. He told of the judge's impatience, his cracks—
"It is noon already," "Would you kindly not make a Federal
case out of this little matter"—and his apparent intention, as
Murphy put it, "to grant them the judgment, no matter
what." Murphy described the testimony of the agency's detective and the acknowledgment by the agency's lawyer of providing insufficient information.

"Then the attorney, Jerry Friedman, got up and he admitted that he had neglected to give all the information,"
Murphy continued. "Jerry Friedman accepted the responsibility, and afterwards, you know, we shook hands, and he
said, 'You made me look like a fool . . . '"

A few weeks later, Joe Donohue telephoned to say that
the agency was getting anxious about its money and was
threatening to send out a marshal to get it. But I was reluctant to pay, I explained, before I had received those names.

That would be no problem, asserted Donohue. McKinley
and Hart had a copy of my file; he would Xerox it, and then I
should mark that Xerox with my requests. Our conversation
ended on a relaxed note: I complimented Joe on his handling
of the case, he invited me to be his guest on his sailboat for
the Bicentennial celebration in New York Harbor.

"You know," he said, "it would really be *fun* if you would
be with us."

And I was thinking, it *would* be fun.

The Xerox of my file arrived and I began the job, circling
the whited-out blanks in different colors of felt-tip markers.
Orange was for "Yes, I *do* have a right to it"; black, for "No, I
do not have a right to it"; blue, for "I honestly can't tell
whether this is a 'permitted' or a 'forbidden' name"; and green
for "This is what I want. I do not, actually, *have* the right, but
I'm hoping they'll slip." To write out this key to my color-
coding was indescribably demeaning.

I had not completed my task when the transcript of the
hearing arrived and brought a few surprises. To be sure, it
was a confirmation of the earlier reports. But I was not pre-

pared for the stings of the precise language, as in Friedman's "Your Honor, my honorable opponent has the wisdom of hindsight"—this was from the very lawyer who had given refusal to foresight—nor in the surrogate's remarks about my search: "Well, nobody asked her to go looking by herself. . . . But I will tell you something else about her search. . . . This court couldn't restrain her from taking a page ad in the *New York Times* saying, 'I want my mother. My mother's name is Ketiladze, and I don't care this, that, and the other.' . . . So she was able to do things in what might even be called a highhanded way, which the court couldn't do, because the Children's Aid Society was frowning upon even as far as I went."

The transcript's language, however, was less distressing than its revelations. I noticed, first, that the agency had not complied with the surrogate's order that the investigator not be informed "as to the reason for such investigation." The investigator, when asked what information he had been given, had responded, "The Ketiladze woman's name, her last known address in New York, and that she had a child and her name was Mrs. Maxtone-Graham. . . ."

The most upsetting of the transcript's disclosures was the claim by the two Curry, Pell attorneys that I had known the Dyre Avenue address! And known it because, of all extraordinary suggestions, *I possessed my birth certificate.* Mr. Silver said it first:

> Mrs. Maxtone-Graham had her birth certificate, on which is listed her mother's address. She had all that. The Kanzlers had given her all those papers.

And then Friedman said it, too:

> Your Honor, I was the person who informed him [the investigator]. And I will go under oath: I did not tell him. I did not have the birth certificate. But I know from our records that Mrs. Maxtone-Graham had her birth certificate, it was given to her by her adoptive parents.

Murphy had not refuted them. He had been good on what he knew, but he had been over his head on so much. Why had Donohue not been there? Why had Ed not been asked to testify? Why had I been excluded?

Although I was bursting, as always, to set the record straight, composing angry letters and copies to all concerned, I realized I could not make any protests just yet; I still had to get those missing names.

So I returned to the job of marking up the Xerox of my file for my request of names. Finally I did compose a calm, brief note to Donohue, in which, asking for a prompt response, I simply quoted Silver's and Friedman's totally erroneous assertions about the birth certificate and then concluded, "The suggestion that the Kanzlers gave me my birth certificate is utterly preposterous. Moreover, it is perfectly obvious from the agency's records, and from my dealings with them, that they knew this had not happened."

This whole experience was ending as it had begun, with the absurdity of not possessing my birth certificate.

Three years later, in April, 1979, I read that final transcript again. Again I felt the rages and the pleasure, the gratitude and the fury. But all were calmer. Another three years having passed, I was able to read more comfortably. My attention was caught this time by a passage which I had barely noticed in 1976: The agency's detective, in direct examination, was testifying regarding the search material provided him by the agency's counsel.

Well, you furnished us with an address. The last address that the Ketiladzes lived at you furnished, Mr. Friedman, at that interview, which was 200 East 52nd Street in New York. You also furnished the telephone number of EL5-2597. . . . We reported back to Mr. Friedman that the address in question was now a parking lot, and that the EL-dorado-5 number had been reassigned.

My emotions cooler in 1979, I was struck by the reference to "a parking lot." Had not Ed Goldfader told me, back in 1974, that the Ketiladze's building was now a Chinese laundry? There was an easy way to find out. Within thirty seconds, I had withdrawn my mother's file and had found the page. I read the address. "220 East 52nd Street." The detective testified to "200 East 52nd." One digit wrong. I read the telephone number, "ELdorado 5-6597." The telephone number given to the detective, however, was "EL[dorado] 5-2597." One digit wrong.

In each instance, one digit was wrong. Out of a total of two pieces of information, there were two mistakes.

I had been so preoccupied, back in 1976, with proving the *withholding* of crucial information, that it had never occurred to me to also question the *veracity* of that minimal information which was proffered.

And I was stunned, all over again.

chapter thirty

CONCLUSION

I have never received replies, either to that last letter to Donohue about the birth certificate allegations, or to my multicolored request for the still-missing names. I still do not know the locations, therefore, of either the "transition home" where I stayed after leaving Mama Hill and first had symptoms of depression, or of the foster home between the Harrises' and the Kanzlers'. Nor do I yet possess, to be sure, my certificate of birth. And although independently I gained much information about my earliest years, I still do not have the *right* to know where and with whom I lived for the first three and a half years of my life.

Among the remaining strings which have not been tied up, I have never learned the significance of the mysterious number in the upper righthand corner of my amended birth certificate. Nor have I been able to ascertain why my grandfather's name was always listed as James rather than Albert. And I regret to include that I still have not sent Joe Donohue those three bottles of champagne.

I continued to search for my sister Kelda but could find no record of her anywhere. Then, in December, 1976, I received a Christmas letter from Andy and Gloria Kelley, to which Andy had added at the bottom, "We just had a note from Kelda Kelley," and went on to give her address.

Kelda's telephone was unlisted, so I wrote a quick, innocuous note of introduction—"You and I are relatives on the

357

Kelley side"—and asked for a collect telephone call. For a week or so, I hovered by the phone. Kelda did not call. After Christmas, she still did not call.

At the beginning of February, 1977, I did something totally new: I went on a vacation alone. Never in my life had I traveled and stayed by myself. For one week, this was the grand experiment: Could Katrina manage on her own? At forty-one, here was my first attempt at being a grown-up.

And, yes, I could function as an adult. I did it.

As I sat in the airplane for the trip home, I stared out at the disappearing lights of the runway below, and I heard myself say to myself, "I think I am ready to not be adopted anymore. I think my adoption is over."

Three days later, February 13, 1977, Kelda Kelley telephoned.

She was terrific. She was warm and friendly, very bright, extremely direct. She regarded herself as having no family at all—both her parents being dead and her brother rarely communicating—and she was delighted to have a sister.

She told of her happy memories of her father, whom she had adored. She told of a purple blouse he had once bought her for no reason except that he knew she wanted it. And especially she treasured the recollection of his taking her to Central Park to go sledding. They had lived about five blocks from where I live and had sledded on the same hill as I used to sled with my children.

"He was very loving, very considerate," said Kelda. She paused, then added fervently, "He would have treated you the same, I know."

Both her parents, said Kelda, had been "high-strung and temperamental." They had met at a poetry reading. Her mother had been a writer of serious novels "with tragic endings," but the only one of her books which was accepted for publication was the one she had regarded as frivolous, *The Cartoonist's Cookbook*. Her parents had divorced, a few years before her father's death, and her mother's relatives had not been favorably disposed toward the Kelley family. That was why Kelda had not answered my letter right away; a relative "on the Kelley side" had seemed an unappealing prospect.

We each talked about our childhoods. I explained my one-time ambition to become an actress so that I could be famous and thereby be found.

"Did you know," Kelda asked, "that your father was an off-Broadway actor?"

As a girl, Kelda herself had been sent to the Neighborhood Playhouse to study acting. She had studied ballet, too, just as Rucy had—and as I had longed to do, but had never been allowed. When I asked if she had stayed in the arts, Kelda replied adamantly, "No, I wanted a more peaceful life."

It was passing through my mind that I seemed more like Ruth and Sam than the children they had raised. And I wondered: Did the adoptee, who never had the opportunity to rebel against the natural parents' personalities, retain more of the parents' genetic influence than those offspring who remained with their parents? Were genetic similarities repressed by those who were able to observe their prototypes?

"I was surprised you were on the Kelley side, not my mother's side, which was German," Kelda declared, "because you have a German script—"

"I have?"

"—and a German name, Katrina."

How nice, I thought, that my German-descent sister regarded my name as German and my Russian-descent brothers and sister regarded my name as Russian.

I asked, of course, the question about height. To my surprise, Kelda was the same height as Rucy, five foot three inches. I was wondering where my own height came from.

"Well, how tall *are* you?" asked Kelda.

"Five feet, eight inches."

She laughed easily. "You do take after your father!" she exclaimed.

We promised to write each other; in June, we would be

meeting in person when Kelda drove east during her vacation. By the time we said good-bye, we had been talking for
an hour and a half.

It was done, over. Kelda was the last one, really; she was
all I had been waiting for. After the call, I just sat on the bed,
and I felt a tremendous sense of calm.

I was free of the past, arrived in the present—and about
to have a future. What did it mean to be a human being?

A human being was a little bit like me, I supposed. I
supposed that *I* was a part of the definition of what it meant
to be human.

Some two months after the call from Kelda, on April 26,
1977—the fourth anniversary of my return to the Children's
Aid Society—Florence Fisher and Cyril Means together telephoned me. They were asking me to prepare a supporting affidavit to be filed with ALMA's constitutional case. I
worked on the affidavit over the next several weeks; on May
18, at about seven o'clock in the evening, the final typed version was ready to be signed.

I picked up my pen, made the three strokes of the K and
got partially into the first A, and I found I could not form the
letters. I started to cry, and I kept on pushing the pen along
the line to approach the next upsweep of the A. Over, up,
back, stop, lift, cross the T. Now I was sobbing hysterically.
Push the pen up, across, down, over, up, retrace. The letters
were getting larger and rounder. Three minutes had passed
already.

By the time I got to the R in Graham, so huge, so deliber-
ate, and the next painstaking big, round A, I was recognizing
these letters: It was the penmanship with which I had identified my schoolbooks in third grade.

At last I executed the final M, running it off the page. I
glanced above at the phrase, "as an individual plaintiff in this
lawsuit," and I cried some more. Here I was—finally, at
last—*after all these years.*

"It's over," I sobbed, and I recognized the phrase. It's

over, I've done it. I had made the same proclamation at every step along the way. But now these words themselves were over. There were new words. "It's beginning."

POSTSCRIPT

ALMA's case was filed that May. We were expecting to give our testimony as witnesses the following fall, but we were denied a hearing. The case was dismissed. In June, 1979, the U.S. Court of Appeals upheld the dismissal. ALMA then requested review by the U.S. Supreme Court. When, at the end of 1979, the Supreme Court refused to review the decision, our particular class action was finished. In 1981 ALMA filed a new suit, with a different set of adoptee co-plaintiffs, in California. As of the end of 1982, this second ALMA case is still pending.

I have made visits to both Mama Hill and Ray Harris and we continue to exchange letters and phone calls. John Harris and I see each other occasionally and talk on the telephone during the week we share birthdays. Andy Kelley and I write Christmas letters; we have open invitations to stay with each other when we travel. Aunt Clare invites me to dinner in Mount Vernon from time to time, and we chat on the telephone. Kelda has visited me in New York, and I visited her recently in California; Rucy has come to New York for a couple of extended stays with me; and both my sisters are terrific correspondents. Nick has spent a Christmas, Alexander stays in touch by telephone, and Andrew is with me a month or more each year. Aunt Doris kept up a warm correspondence until her death in the spring of 1976, less than six months after our meeting.

I have visited my mother in Mexico several times, as

have the children, and she has come up to New York several times, too. We talk on the telephone—not frequently, because of the distance—but always lengthily. We are, very much, mother and daughter. Like me, my mother is active in the movement to open records to adopted adults.

Thanksgiving of 1980 was the occasion of a family reunion in Mexico. Mum toasted, "The first time in history that all my children have been together." A family reunion at Rucy's house in Florida is planned for this Thanksgiving. Perhaps the greatest thrill of all was being Rucy's one honor attendant at her wedding in April of 1981.

My ALMA friendships have lasted and grown. Most of us keep regularly in touch; there are some who drop away for a season or two, or maybe even a few years, and then we are together again. Old-timers and new people too, we are still a special family to each other. Some of these relationships will always be adoption relationships, centered on the search, the remembering, the analyses of adoption's impact, while others have evolved into everyday-life relationships. But our shared past is always there.

All the changes in my life I regard as positive. Sometimes, of course, the process of their development has not been easy. John's and my decision, soon after the concluding events in this story, to end our marriage was certainly sad in part. Still it was—and remains—a happy decision for us both. Does finding one's past mean harming one's present? No—in fact quite the opposite. It brings strength, and this strength will then bring change to relationships in any number of possible directions.

In the years since my return to the agency, the general population has become considerably more aware of the complexities of adoption. So, too, have many individual social workers. This same growth has not taken place, however, in adoption agency policy, nor in judicial interpretation of good-cause laws. Adoptees returning to their agencies are receiving essentially the same treatment in 1982 as I received in 1973. Although the agency workers may in some cases use a

different rationale, their words still translate as "no." The issue of agency accountability is of great concern to adoptees,
natural parents, and adoptive parents, but it can not be pub-
licly raised by most of them, as they are still dependent upon
their agencies' good will. There are very few of us who are no
longer at an agency's mercy. On the legal front, only a handful
of the nation's judges, out of the several thousand who could,
are opening records to adult adoptees with any consistency.
And, still, there is virtually no cause "good enough" to unseal
an adoption record in New York State.

The indignities of American adoption are not the result of
immutable law. Rather, they are the result of assumptions
and policies of legal and social service institutions steeped in
myth, prejudice, and fallacy. The truths seem obvious: Children and parents should not be separated; human connections
should not be obliterated; lying benefits not the lied-to but
the liars; truth is preferable to mystery. There will always be
some children who are in need of care by non-family members, but this need should not be determined by selfishness or
bias, and this care should not be perverted by enforced anonymity. Adoption should be what it is meant to be, help for
the helpless; and adoptees should have the same liberty that
others have to know themselves.

I got free. I am having a chance at life. I wrote this book
in the hope that my experiences will serve a useful purpose
for others, in the hope that the powerful people will recognize
the human consequences of their so easily exercised power,
and in the hope that the powerless ones will take courage in
their everyday goodness as a force to move society.

KATRINA MAXTONE-GRAHAM
November 1982

The text type in this book is Century Expanded, and the display type is Aster Bold.

Text design was by Parallelogram/ Marsha Cohen. Production was supervised by Fred M. Kleeberg Associates. The type was set on a Mergenthaler Linotron 202N by David E. Seham Associates, Inc. Printing and binding were done by the Maple-Vail Book Manufacturing Group.